Legal Translation and Bilingual Law Drafting in Hong Kong

Legal Translation and Bilingual Law Drafting in Hong Kong presents a systematic account from a cross-disciplinary perspective of the activities of legal translation and bilingual law drafting in the bilingual international city of Hong Kong and its interaction with Mainland China and Taiwan in the use of legal terminology.

The study mainly examines the challenges posed to English-Chinese translation in the past three decades by elaborate drafting and terminological equivalence, and offers educational and research solutions. Its primary goals are to create legal Chinese that naturally accommodates common law concepts and statutes from the English legal system and to reconcile Chinese legal terms from the different legal systems adopted by Hong Kong, Mainland China and Taiwan. The new directions in legal translation and bilingual law drafting in Hong Kong will have implications for other Chinese regions and for the world.

The book is intended for scholars, researchers, teachers and students of legal translation and legal linguistics, legal translators, lawyers and legal practitioners who are engaged in translation, as well as all persons who are interested in legal language and legal translation.

Clara Ho-yan Chan is Associate Professor of the School of Humanities and Social Science, the Chinese University of Hong Kong, Shenzhen. Her research interests focus on language and law, especially legal translation, legal terminology and bilingual law drafting.

Routledge Studies in Chinese Translation
Series Editor: Chris Shei
Swansea University, UK

This series encompasses scholarly works on every possible translation activity and theory involving the use of Chinese language. Putting together an important knowledge base for Chinese and Westerner researchers on translation studies, the series draws on multiple disciplines for essential information and further research that is based on or relevant to Chinese translation.

A Discourse Analysis of News Translation in China
Liang Xia

Translating Chinese Art and Modern Literature
Edited by Yifeng Sun and Chris Song

An Overview of Chinese Translation Studies at the Beginning of the twenty-first century
Past, Present, Future
Weixiao Wei

Lao She's Teahouse and its Two English Translations
Exploring Chinese Drama Translation with Systemic Functional Linguistics
Bo Wang and Yuanyi Ma

Legal Translation and Bilingual Law Drafting in Hong Kong
Challenges and Interactions in Chinese Regions
Clara Ho-yan Chan

For more information about this series, please visit: www.routledge.com/languages/series/RSCT

Legal Translation and Bilingual Law Drafting in Hong Kong

Challenges and Interactions in Chinese Regions

Clara Ho-yan Chan

LONDON AND NEW YORK

First published 2020
by Routledge
2 Park Square, Milton Park, Abingdon, Oxon OX14 4RN

and by Routledge
52 Vanderbilt Avenue, New York, NY 10017

Routledge is an imprint of the Taylor & Francis Group, an informa business

© 2020 Clara Ho-yan Chan

The right of Clara Ho-yan Chan to be identified as author of this work has been asserted by her in accordance with sections 77 and 78 of the Copyright, Designs and Patents Act 1988.

All rights reserved. No part of this book may be reprinted or reproduced or utilised in any form or by any electronic, mechanical, or other means, now known or hereafter invented, including photocopying and recording, or in any information storage or retrieval system, without permission in writing from the publishers.

Trademark notice: Product or corporate names may be trademarks or registered trademarks, and are used only for identification and explanation without intent to infringe.

British Library Cataloguing-in-Publication Data
A catalogue record for this book is available from the British Library

Library of Congress Cataloging-in-Publication Data
A catalog record for this book has been requested

ISBN: 978-1-138-33590-5 (hbk)
ISBN: 978-1-138-33591-2 (pbk)
ISBN: 978-0-429-44346-6 (ebk)

Typeset in Times New Roman
by Apex CoVantage, LLC

To my parents and all those who have built the beautiful city of Hong Kong

Contents

List of tables and figures   xi
Preface   xii
Acknowledgments   xv

1 Introduction: about this book   1
   1.1 Background and purpose 1
      1.1.1 Legal translation in Modern China 1
      1.1.2 Legal translation in Hong Kong 2
   1.2 Review and framework 5
      1.2.1 Hong Kong: translation of English laws and bilingual law drafting for the 1997 change of sovereignty 5
      1.2.2 Mainland China and Taiwan: legal globalisation 7
   1.3 Terminology 10
      1.3.1 Legal Chinese 10
      1.3.2 Chinese legal terminology 11
      1.3.3 Legal translation 13
   1.4 Organisation and technicalities 15
      1.4.1 Structure and limitations 15
      1.4.2 Romanisation and convention 17

2 Challenges in legal translation: a language perspective   23
   2.1 Europeanisation of Chinese 24
      2.1.1 Lexical changes 24
      2.1.2 Morpho-syntactic changes 25
         2.1.2.1 Affixation 26
         2.1.2.2 Conjunctions 26
         2.1.2.3 Pronouns 27
         2.1.2.4 Pre-nominal modifiers and embedding levels 27

    2.1.2.5 *Passive voice* 28
    2.1.2.6 *Other types of syntactic change* 28
 2.2 *Europeanisation of legal Chinese* 29
  2.2.1 *Legislation* 29
   2.2.1.1 *Lexicon* 29
   2.2.1.2 *Syntax* 34
    (i) Huo (或) (or) . . . huo (或) (or) 34
    (ii) Prepositions and prepositional phrases 35
    (iii) Underpunctuation 35
    (iv) 'Empty verb' construction 36
    (v) Shi . . . de (是 . . . 的)/wei . . . de (為 . . . 的) construction 37
    (vi) Excessive use of nouns 37
  2.2.2 *Judgments* 39
  2.2.3 *Legal documents* 40
  2.2.4 *Legal translation textbook* 41
  2.2.5 *Responses from different sectors* 44

3 Challenges in legal translation: a legal perspective   51
 3.1 *'Equivalence' in Hong Kong bilingual legal terminology* 51
 3.2 *Equivalence in Chinese legal terminology in three Chinese regions* 53
  3.2.1 *Five translation categories in terms of equivalence* 54
   3.2.1.1 *Category 1 (near equivalents)—one or more similar foreign source term(s) with same renditions of same/similar meaning* 55
   3.2.1.2 *Category 2 (near equivalents)—one or more similar foreign source term(s) with different renditions of same/similar meaning* 55
   3.2.1.3 *Category 3 (partial or non-equivalents)—one or more similar foreign source terms with different renditions of different meanings* 57
   3.2.1.4 *Category 4 (partial or non-equivalents)—different foreign source terms with different renditions of different meanings (partial or non-equivalents)* 59
   3.2.1.5 *Category 5 (non-equivalents)—mistranslation* 60

3.3 Case study of terminology in international agreements: intellectual property rights in Mainland China, Taiwan and Hong Kong 63
    3.3.1 Introduction and methodology 63
    3.3.2 'Layout-design', its Chinese translations and the measurement of equivalence (waiguan sheji (外觀設計) vs dianlu buju (電路布局 (拓樸圖)) vs butu sheji (布圖設計 (拓撲圖)) 64
        3.3.2.1 Mainland China: waiguan sheji (外觀設計) 66
        3.3.2.2 Taiwan: dianlu buju (電路布局 (拓樸圖)) 67
        3.3.2.3 Hong Kong: butu sheji (布圖設計 (拓撲圖)) 68
    3.3.3 Summary and conclusion 70
3.4 Concluding remarks 71

4 Education in meeting challenges   74
    4.1 Education and training: theory and practice 74
    4.2 Broad and balanced approach: first lecture on legal translation 75
        4.2.1 A broad approach: legal systems, legal traditions and legal language 75
        4.2.2 A balanced approach: views on the Chinese legal system 77
    4.3 Interdisciplinary approach: language and law 79
        4.3.1 Case study: a legal knowledge-based translation course for Hong Kong translation students 79
            4.3.1.1 Background and aims 79
            4.3.1.2 Design and contents 80
            4.3.1.3 Feedback and reflections 84
        4.3.2 Case study: an English-Chinese glossary of terminology for Hong Kong law students 87
            4.3.2.1 Background and aims 87
            4.3.2.2 Design and contents 89
            4.3.2.3 Feedback and reflections 91
        4.3.3 Master's programmes on language and law in three regions 93
    4.4 Training for legal professionals and legal translators 95
        4.4.1 Government law drafters 96
        4.4.2 A mini-survey: use of Chinese by lawyers and legal translators 98
    4.5 Concluding remarks 100

5 Research in meeting challenges   104
    5.1 Major books and bilingual legal resources 104
        5.1.1 Research books 104
        5.1.2 Reference books 105
    5.2 Two potential research areas 107
        5.2.1 Enhancing language quality for bilingual legislation and judgments 108
            5.2.1.1 Co-drafting of bilingual legislation: plain language drafting 108
            5.2.1.2 Translation of judgments: Chinese proficiency and language style 113
        5.2.2 Comparative study of legal terminology and legal glossary compilation 118
            5.2.2.1 Relations with comparative law and existing works 118
            5.2.2.2 Framework for comparison 121

6 Conclusion: trends and prospects   132
    6.1 Training practitioners with language and law skills: status of legal translation 132
    6.2 Research work on terminology comparison: 'universal' translation methods 135
    6.3 Epilogue: a new era with new visions 137
        6.3.1 Past experience 137
        6.3.2 Development for the future 139

Index   146

Tables and figures

Tables

3.1	Measurement of equivalence between 'layout-design' and *waiguan sheji* (外觀設計) used in Mainland China	67
3.2	Measurement of equivalence between 'layout-design' and *dianlu butu* (電路布圖) used in Taiwan	69
3.3	Measurement of equivalence between 'layout-design' and *butu sheji* (布圖設計) used in Hong Kong	70
4.1	Glossary of 20 terms from 'Hong Kong Legal System' course and their Chinese equivalents	90
4.2	Glossary of ten terms from 'Contract Law' course and their Chinese equivalents from Hong Kong, Mainland China and Taiwan	91
5.1	One or more similar foreign source term(s) with same renditions of same/similar meaning in three Chinese regions	122
5.2	One or more similar foreign source term(s) with different renditions of same/similar meaning in three Chinese regions	126
5.3	One or more different foreign source term(s) with different renditions of different meanings in three Chinese regions	127

Figures

4.1	Students' responses to the question 'To what extent did the presentation on contract law terminology help you acquire the translation skills for rendering judgments?' at the end of the semester	84
4.2	Students' responses to the question 'Speaking overall, to what extent did this course that centres on contract law terminology (translating contracts, ordinances relating to contract law concepts, etc.) help you acquire legal translation skills?' at the end of the semester	85
4.3	Students' responses to the question 'To what extent did you gain knowledge of legal Chinese and enhance translation competency?' at the end of the semester	92

Preface

Since Hong Kong's enactment of its first bilingual ordinance in 1989, this is the first English book to describe the bilingual city's legal translation and bilingual law drafting activities and their interaction with Mainland China and Taiwan from a cross-disciplinary perspective. Underlining the significance of the legal translation of Western laws to modernising China, the book focuses on bridging the gap between language and law in the context of Hong Kong, which has returned to China after a century and a half of British rule. The purpose of the book is three-fold. First, to legal professionals, legal translators, students, teachers, and all those who are interested in the field in Hong Kong, the book presents a systemic account of the important events in the past 30 years of the development of the bilingual legal system. The discussion centres on the translation of English legislation and bilingual law drafting starting in the 1980s, the translation of judgments starting in the 1990s, and the exchange of legal terminology between Hong Kong, Mainland China and Taiwan. The text makes ample use of examples to illustrate translation techniques in legal texts. Given that Hong Kong legal professionals receive education entirely in English but have started using Chinese at work more frequently in recent decades, the book aspires to arouse their interest in legal translation and legal Chinese by raising their awareness of the key issues. It also pays tribute to the hard work of legal translators and all practitioners engaging in legal translation, thus promoting their professional status in the long term.

Second, the book aims to demonstrate to academics in legal translation and legal linguistics in other Chinese regions and the world the uniqueness of the bilingual legal system in Hong Kong, which is based on English and Chinese, languages that have enormous grammatical differences. The issues arising from English-Chinese translation have implications for the entire Chinese world. As long as the Hong Kong legal system continues to be based on the English common law, appropriate methods and approaches must be employed to represent it in Chinese. The path is not as smooth as in the bijural, bilingual and multilingual jurisdictions in the West where the greater commonalities between languages facilitate natural translation. In recent decades, a new challenge to Hong Kong is the confusion between similar concepts from the common law and civil law systems, which is further complicated by variations in the Modern Written Chinese of Hong Kong, Mainland China and Taiwan. Now that Hong Kong is part of China and the three regions have closer ties than ever before, Classical Chinese, which is the common basis of the regions' languages, can serve as a unifying factor. In this book, hence, the use of more 'classical' Modern Chinese is one of the solutions suggested for rendering complicated English laws into Chinese and creating future Chinese legal terms.

Third and more importantly, to researchers in the relevant fields, including scholars of legal translation, legal linguists and jurists, the book aims to explore new directions in legal translation and bilingual law drafting in Hong Kong and their implications for other Chinese regions and for the world. Currently, there is only a small circle of researchers working on legal translation and bilingual law drafting in Hong Kong. I have therefore taken this opportunity to revise and reorganise my past work to target a wider readership, enriching it with perspectives from a wide range of previously unconsidered literature. On one hand, my intention is to review what has happened and learn from the experience of the past 30 years of the bilingual legal system, a substantial period that makes such research worthwhile and necessary. On the other hand, based on existing scholarship, I hope to find a new vision that can take the field forward to the next stage. I was enlightened by every piece of literature encountered in the process and trust that the reflections made in this study will be of similar value to those working in this area in other jurisdictions.

The book is divided into six chapters, organised more or less on a chronological basis. Chapter 1 sets forth the background against which legal translation has taken place in China since the Qing Dynasty. It also offers an overview of the translation of Western and international laws into Chinese in Hong Kong, Mainland China and Taiwan in recent decades. Chapter 2 probes into Hong Kong's translation of common law into Chinese and bilingual law drafting from a language perspective. The main issue is the European influence on the Chinese language, which is illustrated by different texts including legislation, judgments, legal documents and legal translation books in Hong Kong. Chapter 3 investigates the legal challenges in translating foreign laws into Chinese, with the aim of examining the central issues of equivalence and the legal knowledge of translators. The discussion first analyses different translation scenarios across the three Chinese regions in general, then presents a case study that compares the translations of one term in an international intellectual property agreement in Mainland China and Taiwan, and the intellectual property law in Hong Kong.

Chapter 4 explores the capacity of education to meet the language and legal challenges in legal translation and bilingual law drafting in Hong Kong. It proposes to broaden the horizons of law and translation students by presenting two case studies: one on the incorporation of legal concepts in a legal translation course and the other on Chinese and translation training for law students. There is also discussion of training issues for practicing lawyers and legal translators. Chapter 5 explores the capacity of research to meet the language and legal challenges. Two major future research areas are proposed, that is, the enhancement of Chinese language quality for bilingual legislation and judgments, and the comparative study of legal terminology and compilation of a legal glossary of Chinese terms from the three

Chinese communities. Chapter 6 evaluates the continuing efforts in education and research that aim to put in place a systematic conceptual comparison of Chinese legal terms and train more personnel with cross-disciplinary competency. It proposes that the field focus on the new direction of translating judgments and continue its leading role in terminology creation in the Chinese world.

In the years to come, it is expected that experts in the field will continue my undertaking and provide this study with open and constructive feedback. This book is expected to appear on the market around the middle of this year. I hope by then the novel coronavirus will be contained to a large extent and most people in the world will return to normal life. In the post-coronavirus era, it is anticipated that legal translation is going to play a more important role in reconnecting and revitalising the world.

Hong Kong, April 2020

Acknowledgments

I would like to express my gratitude to those who have helped and encouraged me in producing this book. Professor Sin King-kui, Professor Benjamin T'sou Ka Yin, Professor Zhu Chunshen, Professor Chan Sin-wai, Professor Emily Poon Wai-yee and Professor Ester Leung Sin-man have given me great insights and inspiration in my recent years of scholarly work. I should also acknowledge Dr Elvis Lee, who invited me to participate in his recent book project with the Hong Kong University Press, as I learnt a great deal from him, his co-editor Edmund Cham and the other authors. I would also like to express my gratitude to Professor Gilbert Fong and Professor Shelby Chan, who have invited me to serve as an external reviewer for their MA Programme in Translation (Business and Legal), so that I can keep abreast of Hong Kong's translation education while teaching in Shenzhen. I am indebted to my PhD supervisor, Professor Chen Ping, who guided me to the studies of Modern Chinese, which provided me with the necessary foundation to investigate Chinese legal language. I am also grateful to my Dean, Professor Fan Xitao, and Associate Dean, Professor Wang Lidi, who gave me enormous support by granting special leave for the last stage of this study during the summer of 2019. I would also like to thank from the bottom of my heart the 30 Hong Kong lawyers and translators who participated in the mini-survey, most of whom I have not met in person. This list includes (in alphabetical order by surname) Kay Chan, William Chan, Andy Hung, Matty Kwong, Joshua Li and Alex Tang, as well as a number of people who preferred to remain anonymous. I thank the following persons for their work in liaising with many of these participants: Martin Ko, Dominic Lai and my former students, Morency Mak and another who preferred to remain anonymous; these latter two also participated in the survey.

I am also indebted to international experts who have provided me with assistance and insights in my work. Invited by Professor Laura Ervo and Professor Anne Wagner, I had great pleasure in attending the Ninetieth International Roundtable for the Semiotics of Law in Örebro, Sweden, in May 2018. Under the special theme 'Law and Arts in Crime Settings', I was introduced to more interdisciplinary perspectives and received inspiring advice on this study from Professor Wagner during conference free time. Thanks to Professor Jean-Claude Gémar, who sent me his works on the Canadian legal system after our chat at the University of Geneva conference in June 2018. At other conferences, I had the pleasure of meeting Professor Łucja Biel and Professor Aleksandra Matulewska, who are active members from Poland in the field of legal linguistics in Europe. They have provided great support through publishing my work in their journals. I am honoured that Professor Marcus Galdia has given me useful advice on various parts of the manuscript. His recent books *Legal Discourse* and *Lectures on Legal Linguistics* have enlightened this study and remain a subject of continual inquiry for me. Thanks also go to Dr Henry Liao Shu-Hsien, who shared with me his views on issues of Chinese legal terminology, especially those of Taiwan.

For the production of the book, special acknowledgment is made to Professor Sin King-kui, Professor Albert Chen Hung-yee and former Secretary of Justice and Senior Counsel Rimsky Yuen Kwok-keung, who kindly contributed their words of endorsement. I am most grateful to my former research assistants Ryan Poon Wing-keung, Vivi Xu Ruowei, Samuel Li Zhiyuan Han Kunmei and my current assistant Bella Xian Yongqi, who conducted data collection; my university's librarian, Yin Meng, who searched for various publications; and my Australian colleague Malcolm Skewis, who proofread the entire manuscript. My colleague Matthew Morgan-James kindly provided English assistance in a timely manner. I would like to express my gratitude to Professor Chris Shei, the editor of the book series, Andrea Hartill, Ellie Auton, Claire Margerison and all other members of the Routledge editorial team, and Kevin Kelsey and all the copyeditors in his team. Thank you so much for your professionalism and patience with me in the long process of engineering this book. Last but not least, I would like to give thanks to God and the 'angel-like friends' He sent to help and support me during my work in the different Chinese regions. My teaching experience has motivated me to identify the future needs of Hong Kong and the neighbouring Chinese regions. There are indeed many talented translation and law students who have great potential to become cross-disciplinary practitioners.

1 Introduction
About this book

1.1 Background and purpose

1.1.1 Legal translation in Modern China

Legal translation has played and continues to play a significant role in the modernisation of China. The Chinese legal system has innovated and reformed itself through continued emulation of foreign laws. In other words, the modernisation of the Chinese legal system is closely linked to legal translation. It is believed that China's first contact with and introduction of Western laws was through the imperial commissioner Lin Zexu (1785–1850) during the Qing Dynasty (1644–1911). Before the First Sino-British War (1839–1842) began, Lin organised the translation of E. De Vattel (1985–1850)'s *The Law of Nations* into Chinese, that is, *Geguo Lüli* (《各國律例》), which was later published in *Haiguo Tuzhi* (《海國圖志》). However, the translated book was not widely disseminated among the public. After its defeat in the Second Sino-British War (1858–1860), the Qing Empire launched the Self-strengthening Movement (1861–1895) to imitate Western science and technology. Chinese personnel were sent abroad for further studies, and Western missionaries came to China engaging in newspaper, education and translation work. In 1864, the missionary W. A. P. Martin (1827–1916) produced the translation *Wanguo Gongfa* (《萬國公法》), based on *Elements of International Laws: With a Sketch of the History of the Science* by Henry Wheaton (1785–1848). This book was the first translated work on public law. During this reform period, *Tianyan Lun*《天演論》was translated from Montesquieu's *De l'esprit des lois* (*The Spirit of Laws*) by Yan Fu, a prominent translator and translation thinker who has had great influence on the later development of Chinese translation studies (Cao 2004: 161–162; Qu 2013: 23–27; Teng and Fairbank 1982: 142).

After its defeat in the First Sino-Japanese War (1894–1895), the Qing Empire founded the law-drafting institution *Xiuding Falü Guan* (修訂法律館) (Law Revision Agency) in 1904. Shen Jiaben (1840–1913), as the minister of the Law Reform Bureau, initiated the modernisation of the Qing Dynasty's Constitution and other laws through the large-scale borrowing of foreign laws (He 2011: 1904). The transplantation and codification processes were facilitated by the medium of

Japanese language and law developed in Japan during the Meiji Period (1868–1914). During the Republican Era, legal drafting relied heavily on the Chinese translation of European continental law, with reference to the Anglo-American tradition. The Six Laws (*Liufa Quanshu*《六法全書》), that is, the constitution, civil law, criminal law, civil procedure, criminal procedure and administrative law, were promulgated at that stage and have been retained in Taiwan (Chen 2011: 29). The Mainland law professor Qu Wensheng (2013: 32) summarises the above legal history of China as follows:

> Legal translation started from the translation of 'The Law of Nations'—from books on public law to books on different areas of law, from missionary translation to translation by Chinese on their own, from translation by common people to officially organised translation, from translation from Anglo-Saxon laws to translation from Japanese laws—it marks the beginning and end of the modernisation of Chinese law. Legal translation has two values. First, it promotes the modernisation of the legal system, remodeling Chinese law, and second, it furthers the development of Chinese language and translation studies.
>
> (English translation by the author)

In 1949, the old laws on the Mainland were abolished, and the laws of the People's Republic of China (PRC), which were borrowed from the Soviet Union, were promulgated. From 1957, the 'Anti-Rightist Campaign' and 'Cultural Revolution' were responsible for a hiatus in legal enactment and implementation, which lasted until 1978 (Chen 2011: 36–41). However, in the last two decades of the twentieth century, much English legislation and numerous academic writings were translated into Chinese, and much new terminology from English jurisdictions was introduced into the PRC legal system (Zhang, Zhao and Yu 2005: 15). During this period the law-making authorities passed more than 450 laws and regulations, of which 350 were economic laws and 100 relevant to foreign investment and technology importation. For example, the tax system was heavily influenced by its US counterpart (Wang and Mo 1999: 3). As time went by, the Westernisation of law has played an important role in modernising China.

Entering the twenty-first century, the role of legal translation is becoming even more important with the intensifying trend towards globalisation and the ongoing trend towards Westernisation of the Chinese legal system. This book aims to discuss the general challenges facing the translation of Western and international laws into Chinese mainly in Hong Kong, a British colony for more than 150 years, and its neighbouring regions, Mainland China and Taiwan, in the context of legal transplantation and growing trade and economic ties with the international world mainly over the past couple of decades.

1.1.2 Legal translation in Hong Kong

The case of Hong Kong is rather special, because the change of sovereignty, when it returned to China as the Hong Kong Special Administrative Region

(SAR) of the PRC in 1997, has prompted three decades (starting from the 1980s) of wholesale translation of English common law-based legislation into Chinese. A translation professor in Hong Kong (Sin 2018: 317–318) who participated in the project states:

> The meaning of the work can be studied in two aspects.... First, it is a milestone in several large-scale translation activities since the translation of Buddhist scripture in the second year of the reign of Emperor Huan in the Eastern Han Dynasty (A.D. 148), and also a systematic attempt by China to absorb Western law (common law) for the building of a regional legal system (the Hong Kong SAR). Second ... we should study what we can learn from others' translation experience and research, and what is worth others learning from us.
>
> (English translation by the author)

Early on, with the Tianjing Treaty of 1856, English was given 'superior status' over Chinese in the legal domain (Lord and T'sou 1985: 15). For most of the 150 years of British rule, English was the sole official language of Hong Kong. With very high social status, the English language has been used widely in government, business, the workplace in general, and even as the main medium of instruction in schools. To meet the needs of the predominantly Cantonese-speaking population, who mostly use Chinese in daily life, it has been the practice of the Hong Kong Government and businesses to translate English documents into Chinese, so that more of the population can understand them. Since the 1980s, the Hong Kong Government has aimed at developing a bilingual system, which is defined by Chen (1991: 15) in two senses: 'First, bilingual texts for legislation should be made available. Secondly, parties in court proceedings should have the right to choose which of the two official languages they want to use'. Bob Allcock, the former Solicitor-General, explains: 'Legislation was also passed enabling all courts to operate in either English or Chinese, at the choice of the court itself. Even where English is used, translation to and from Chinese is of course available where a party or witness needs it' (Government Information Services Department, 9 November 2004). Poon (2018: 449) notes that a judge can choose the language to be used in the court proceeding 'based on the nature of a case and the parties involved'. The judgment language is also based on the language used in the court proceeding.

Of the 'two types of translated domestic legislation' described by Cao (2007: 101, 128), Hong Kong, as a new bilingual jurisdiction, falls into the first type with Canada and Switzerland, which consists of 'bilingual and multilingual jurisdictions where two or more languages are the official legal languages'. Mainland China and Taiwan fall into the second type, which includes 'any monolingual country where its laws are translated into a foreign language or languages for information purposes'. The main challenges facing legal translation in Hong Kong lie in two aspects, language and law. The language challenge mainly refers to the so-called Europeanisation of Chinese terminology and syntax that often occurs during translation, especially given that legal translation usually adopts a faithful approach. The ultimate goal of this solution is to create legal Chinese that naturally accommodates common law concepts and principles. Such Europeanised structures also appear in the bilingual legislation drafted in accordance with the newly-adopted plain language guide. The legal challenge is mainly concerned with the differences between the common law system (adopted by Hong Kong) and the civil law system (adopted by Mainland China and Taiwan), which attach different meanings to Chinese legal terms that are mostly translated from foreign laws. This 'systemic difference' further highlights the ever-important equivalence issue that arises in translating legal terminology from one language to another, and it demonstrates the necessity for research to evaluate the equivalence of translated terms from the three Chinese communities.

Given the author's common law training and substantial teaching experience in Hong Kong, Mainland China and Taiwan, this book focuses on the language problems of Hong Kong's common law system with its emphasis on bilingual legislation, and from there, it discusses its legal differences between that system and the civil law systems of the Mainland and Taiwan. As Europeanised features are prevalent in the Chinese language which has been under English influence, the first part on language has strong implications for the texts of all English-Chinese legal translations in the Chinese world. The second part on law covers comparison of the legal terms currently in use by Hong Kong, Mainland China and Taiwan, which includes the detailed comparison of a term in Mainland and Taiwanese translations of an international agreement, and its counterpart version in Hong Kong. This interdisciplinary study also suggests approaches and ways to meet the challenges and solve problems encountered. It offers the insight of combining language and law as a way forward in twenty-first century legal translation. The suggestions made in the book all target exchange between different legal systems. While some of them are based on the situation in Hong Kong, they are also applicable to the Mainland, Taiwan and other jurisdictions, especially those that draft laws in more than one language.

Roebuck and Sin (1993: 209) note, 'Minds trained in language and law can provide for Hong Kong the law the people want and need. A law which can be known can be better respected and the people's respect for the law is the best safeguard of the rule of law in Hong Kong's future'. This book on language and law contains details from broad approaches to be adopted in teaching translation and law, compiling legal glossaries and dictionaries, and ultimately comparing systematically all Chinese legal terms from the three regions. Through an examination of the past three decades, which includes the historic return of Hong Kong to China's sovereignty in 1997, the book aims to identify the hurdles and problems prevalent in legal translation, explore some existing practices and strategies, and open new opportunities and paths to move forward, mainly in Hong Kong with its growing ties with its neighbouring Chinese regions. It is hoped that this research will invite further relevant academic work into this area of growing importance, especially work focusing on Chinese terminology in other legal areas and the translation of Chinese terminology into English, as legal globalisation is vital to all other areas of development and exchange in and among the Chinese regions.

1.2 Review and framework

This section will review the main legal translation activities that have taken place in Hong Kong, Mainland China and Taiwan, and discuss the general linguistic features of legal Chinese and the issue of equivalence in Chinese legal terminology.

Just before the handover ceremony held on 1 July 1997, Hong Kong rendered all of its legislation that originated from English common law into Chinese in less than a decade. The translation of judgments is up to the present. This enormously difficult project of translation and co-drafting aims to achieve a truly bilingual legal system at both the legislative and judicial levels. The great haste with which the initial translations was carried out resulted in unnatural and awkward Chinese versions of legislation that were strongly influenced by legal English and posed the linguistic challenges mentioned above. Apart from this specifically political reason for the translation of Western laws, all three of the Chinese communities have been under pressure to meet international legal standards. One illustrative example is the constant revision of their intellectual property laws to comply with international law, especially following Mainland China's and Taiwan's admission into the World Trade Organization at the turn of the twenty-first century. This trend towards 'legal globalisation' also manifests in the borrowing of laws from the West to strengthen their legal systems, which is most obvious in Mainland China since its Reform and Opening Up policy of the 1980s. Translation plays an important role in introducing Western concepts, which can create tension between domestic law and international law in the translating process. This legal challenge primarily refers to differences between the common law system and civil law system in expressing the same or similar legal concepts. There are different scenarios, ranging from 'near equivalence', 'partial equivalence' to 'non-equivalence'. In the worst case scenarios, there is an absence of conceptual and terminological correspondence. Mistranslations are also commonplace in all three Chinese regions.

1.2.1 Hong Kong: translation of English laws and bilingual law drafting for the 1997 change of sovereignty

Among the three Chinese communities under study, Hong Kong is probably the best example to illustrate the translation of Western laws, because it was there that, for the first time in human history, the entire common law system appeared in the Chinese language. In accordance with Article 8 of the Basic Law, which has been Hong Kong's constitution after 1 July 1997, common law remains in effect. Article 8 states: 'The laws previously in force in Hong Kong, that is, the common law, rules of equity, ordinances, subordinate legislation and customary law shall be maintained, except for any that contravene this Law, and subject to any amendment by the legislature of the Hong Kong Special Administrative

6 *Introduction*

Region'. In accordance with Article 9 of the Basic Law, both Chinese and English are the official languages: 'In addition to the Chinese language, English may also be used as an official language by the executive authorities, legislature and judiciary of the Hong Kong Special Administrative Region'. Hong Kong has been using the English common law system since the beginning of colonial rule by the United Kingdom in the middle of the nineteenth century. Before Chinese became another official language based on the 1974 amendment to the Official Languages Ordinance, English was the only official language in Hong Kong. Given that the majority of the population is Cantonese-speaking, the signing of the Sino-British Joint Declaration in 1984, which gave Hong Kong a high degree of autonomy under the 'one country, two systems' policy, accelerated the use of Chinese as the legal language (Li 1987: 120).[1]

In 1986, a consultation paper on Laws in Chinese was published, which proposed three underlying principles of an ideal translation, namely 'accurate meaning', 'similar form' and 'good, modern and educated Chinese' (Poon 2002: 76). Based on the 1987 amendments to the Official Languages Ordinance (Cap. 5) and the Interpretation and General Clauses Ordinance (Cap. 1), which stipulated bilingual legislation, the first bilingual ordinance, the Securities and Futures Commission Ordinance (Cap. 24), was enacted in April 1989.[2] Since then, all new principal laws have had to be enacted in both English and Chinese, with both texts to have equal authenticity (Poon 2002: 76; Sin 2000: 196). Section 10B, The Interpretation and General Clauses Ordinance (Cap. 1) stipulates:

(1) The English language text and the Chinese language text of an Ordinance shall be equally authentic, and the Ordinance shall be construed accordingly.
(2) The provisions of an Ordinance are presumed to have the same meaning in each authentic text.[3]

In 1988, the Hong Kong Government started a project to produce Chinese translations of common law-based English legislation that carry equal legal force. The Official Languages (Amendment) Ordinance 1987 created a Bilingual Laws Advisory Committee, which was to 'scrutinise the draft Chinese texts of existing legislation prepared by the Legal Department and thus to advise the Governor in Council on their promulgation as authentic texts' (Chen 1991: 15). The project was finally completed on 16 May 1997, six weeks before the handover ceremony to China on 1 July 1997. A total of 514 ordinances, about 10 million words, were translated into Chinese in nine years (Sin 2000: 196). Tony Yen Yuen-ho (2010: 1), the law draftsman serving between 1994 and 2007, comments: 'This was a mammoth exercise involving the translation into Chinese of over 22,000 pages of legislation, many of which were laws drafted and enacted long time ago'. Michael D. Thomas (1988: 17), the former Attorney General of Hong Kong from 1983 to 1988, articulates the requirements of bilingual legal systems thus: 'The most important principle, in bilingual legislation . . . is that both texts must convey the same legal meaning or legal message'. The participating professors of translation in the Bilingual Laws Advisory Committee described the translation process as one of the most unprecedentedly difficult tasks, full of conflicts between language and law (Jin and Sin 2004: 102–103).

According to the Law Drafting Division (LDD) of the Department of Justice (DOJ), which was responsible for the aforementioned translation project, the work comprised two parts: the translation of the existing English and the co-drafting of new laws, in which the English version was to be drafted first and the Chinese version to follow (Personal communication 13 March 2014). Countries that draft laws in more than one language also use both methods. It has been said that 'translation is the most traditional and the most often used method of drafting in multilingual settings' and that co-drafting methods are employed to preserve 'the principle of language equality and language rights' and to conform to the target language (Doczekalska 2009: 122–129). Both practices have been used in Hong Kong: before 1997, the main method used to produce Chinese legislation was translation of the existing English legislation, and in the period leading up to and following 1997, all new legislation has been drafted in both English and Chinese. However, it is believed that translation is still the predominant method in bilingual legislative drafting in Hong Kong, as the English version precedes the Chinese version. Chan (2012: 127) remarks that 'translation shouldered the mission of creating a new legal Chinese language, namely legal Chinese, for Hong Kong as a common law jurisdiction under China's rule'. Therefore, the linguistic issues relating to bilingual law drafting in Hong Kong, especially those of the Chinese version, are mostly considered translation issues.

Putting an emphasis on the requirement of 'strict legal precision', Yen (2010: 1–4) concluded that law drafters had to confront two main difficulties in both bilingual legislative drafting and in law translation, namely equivalence of expressions and complicated English sentences. He remarks that these difficulties were 'more easily felt in the case of the translation of the 22,000 pages of existing laws than the case of drafting new bilingual laws'. He believes that the solution to the huge linguistic differences between English and Chinese is the 'language engineering' exercise to simplify the language of the English version which started in the 1990s. Drafting the English texts of new legislation in a more modern and plain style would make the Chinese translation work easier. This exercise paved the way for plain legal drafting, which was ultimately adopted by the DOJ in 2012.

In the last two decades, academia has gradually come to accept that legal translation plays a new communicative role in the modern world. It is said that 'Legal translation is not simply linguistic transcoding. . . . It means translation needs to meet two kinds of equivalences: the equivalence of communicative function and the equivalence of legal function or to rephrase it, one is communicative equivalence, the other, legal equivalence' (Cheng and Sin 2008: 37).

1.2.2 Mainland China and Taiwan: legal globalisation

Legal globalisation plays an important function in the process of globalisation. By definition, globalisation is primarily economic, but covers virtually all major human activity. Auby (2008: 211) remarks:

> Globalization is a set of phenomena which is transforming our world by leading it from segmentation to intermingling, from separation to transitivity,

from a territory-based organization to despatialization, from a state-centred configuration to a less state-centred arrangement. Its main manifestation is economic and is related to the dramatic growth of international commerce, the development of increasingly powerful transnational economic actors, and the international liberation of various markets, primarily the financial ones.

In a wider scope, Rundell and Fox (2002: 603) define globalisation as 'the idea that the world is developing a single economy and culture as a result of improved technology and communications and the influence of very large MULTINATIONAL companies'.

For continuity, globalisation needs to be substantiated by law. This can be regarded as legal globalisation, which practically 'takes the forms of internationalisation of domestic laws and domestication of international laws' (Zhu 2010: 2). With regard to the former, there have been two historical tides of legal globalisation movements in the world. The first movement happened in private law fields, from the middle of the nineteenth century to the twentieth century, represented by the transplantation of French and German civil codes to other countries. The second started after the Second World War, represented by the establishment of constitutional courts, constitutional councils and judicial review systems (Zhu 2010: 4). With regard to the latter, strictly speaking, the localisation of international laws is the typical form that legal globalisation takes.

China experienced both forms of legal globalisation in the twentieth century. In terms of the 'internationalisation of domestic laws', the government of the Qing Dynasty commenced the translation and transplantation of foreign laws from the first decade of the nineteenth century. The achievements of the transplantation movement include the enactment of the Six Laws and other important legislation such as Company Law, Copyright Law and Trademark Law (He 2011: 44). After the establishment of the PRC in 1949, the imitation of and learning from foreign law continued. In the 1950s, the PRC adopted a Soviet-style legal system as part of its efforts to construct a socialist society. For example, the first Constitution of the PRC 1954 was highly influenced by the Soviet Union's constitution, and as such is regarded as 'a product of the international socialist movement' (Chen 2011: 33–34). However, the imitation of Soviet law gradually receded after 1956, due to the deterioration of Sino-Soviet relations and the 'anti-rightist' movement. In 1978, after the Cultural Revolution, China embarked on the study and transplantation of Western law. In order to improve the integrity of the PRC legal system, China is continuously learning from foreign countries' legislation, and has enacted various laws, such as the Environment Protection Law, Company Law, Insolvency Law, Administrative Procedure Law and some tax laws. This economic-related legislation has been enacted with study and reference to foreign legal institutions (Zhou 2010: 54).

With regard to the 'localisation of international laws', the PRC joined many international organisations and signed many international treaties during the implementation of the Reform and Opening Up policy starting in 1978. In order to conform to the stipulations of these international laws, China enacted and amended many domestic laws and regulations. For example, since becoming a member of the World Intellectual Property Organization (WIPO) and World Trade Organization (WTO) in 1980 and 2001 respectively, the PRC has amended its Copyright Law, Trademark Law and Patent Law several times to meet the requirements of the convention establishing the WIPO Copyright Treaty, the Agreement on Trade-Related Aspects of Intellectual Property Rights (TRIPS) and other relevant treaties. The localisation of international laws also manifests in the area of public law. For instance, after joining the World Health Organization, PRC enacted the Law on Prevention and Treatment of Infectious Diseases and Regulation on the Urgent Handling of Public Health Emergencies (Zhu 2010: 7–8).

Taiwan participated in the 'internationalisation of domestic laws' process by 'passively' inheriting laws from Japan and China in different historical periods. Taiwan was occupied and governed by Japan under the Treaty of Shimonoseki from 1895 to 1945, during which period Japanese laws and legal experience were imported into Taiwan. Between 1923 and 1945 in the colonial era, Taiwan adopted many Japanese laws, which were actually Westernised legal codes that Japan had compiled during the Meiji period. The result was that Taiwan absorbed many Western laws through the medium of Japanese law (Wang 2005: 6–8). After the end of the Second World War, Taiwan was returned to China, and as a result, the legal system and laws of the Republic of China were implemented in Taiwan. Given that from the late nineteenth century to the first half of the twentieth century both Japan and China had largely modelled their laws on the European continental law system, Taiwan has accommodated the European legal tradition for a long time. In addition to the transplantation of continental law, Taiwan also imported US law in commercial and corporate law areas from the 1960s. Due to its tight economic nexus with the US, Taiwan has studied and opened up to common law institutions from the 1990s onward, as evidenced by the importation of the trust regime (Wang 2006: 156).

On the other hand, Taiwan also localised international law to domestic legislation during the second half of the twentieth century. Take the example of intellectual property (IP) law. Previously, Taiwan paid little attention to the developments of internationalised IP law and did not sign the highly influential Berne and Paris Conventions. However, in order to meet the requirements of joining the WTO, Taiwan actively reviewed 55 bills concerning IP law amendments from 1997 to 2002. Becoming a member of the WTO in 2002, Taiwan completed all major legislation amendments in accordance with TRIPS (Wang 2006: 206).

In this process of legal globalisation, which in practicality 'takes the forms of internationalisation of domestic laws and domestication of international laws' (Zhu 2010: 2), translation plays a vital role in introducing Western and international laws and legal concepts and globalising national laws. International law is regarded as a set of objective valid norms that regulates the mutual behavior of states (Kelsen 1967). It is binding on sovereign states, and the effects of international treaties are implemented through the enactment of domestic legislation.

10 *Introduction*

While in legal translation 'equivalence' is always important to producing the same legal effects, there are two general difficulties in translating international legal terminology into local law, as described by Cao (2004: 170) in the following:

> In legal translation, there are two competing interests or concerns . . . very often SL [source language] and TL [target language] concepts not totally identical are treated and translated as equivalent. In other cases, seemingly equivalent SL and TL concepts must be distinguished and are not or should not be translated as equivalent, to avoid confusing different legal operations.

China has always been introducing legal concepts from other countries, although it is said that these have generally been adapted to work within the confines of local culture (Potter 2001: 4–15; Zhu 2010: 4–8). The effects of international treaties are implemented through the enactment of domestic legislation.

1.3 Terminology

1.3.1 Legal Chinese

The language of law is characterised by the presupposition of a legal system and particular rules of law, from which legal language derives its meanings (Hart 1954: 41–45). The legal Chinese under study is part of Modern Written Chinese, the standardised form of written Chinese currently in use in the four major Chinese communities: Mainland China, Taiwan, Hong Kong and Singapore. Since the adoption of *baihua* (written vernacular Chinese) as its base in 1919, Modern Written Chinese has relied on Northern Mandarin, in particular the Beijing dialect, for norms of grammar and vocabulary. According to Chen (1999: 82–88), Modern Written Chinese has changed considerably since the 1920s, subject to three sources of influence: *wenyan* (classical literary Chinese), non-Northern Mandarin dialects and foreign languages, of which the last one is considered the most significant. There are also regional variations in the grammatical and lexical norms in the four major Chinese communities.

Qu (2013: 44) describes the Chinese legal language in use today is 'one that has been entirely saturated with new foreign words and theories'. Nevertheless, the Chinese language is considered incapable of expressing common law concepts. Cao (1997: 662) remarks:

> In the case of Chinese and English legal language, English is more sophisticated in terms of legal terminology and legal systems whereas Chinese is a less developed technical language of law. This results in the frequent nonexistence of corresponding or equivalent legal terminologies in Chinese.

In its quest to become a precise and user-friendly technical language of law, legal Chinese has become embedded with stylistic and linguistic problems, as well as those relating to the fundamental principles of 'terminological equivalence' in legal translation. In the case of Hong Kong's legislation, which originated from the English common law system, legal professionals, legislators and the general public faced great difficulties in using this 'youthful' Chinese legal language that has a special style. Since Chinese became one of the two official legal languages of Hong Kong in the late 1980s, legal Chinese has essentially been a translation product consisting of 'translationese', with many novel coinages and a heavily Europeanised grammatical style.

In Taiwan legal Chinese is not as influenced by translation as in Hong Kong. A leading legal scholar in Taiwan, Zheng Yi-Zhe (2007), nevertheless distinguishes 'legal Chinese' from 'ordinary Chinese' owing to the constant and artificial changes of meanings made behind legal language and legal terms. He states (Zheng 2007: 132):

> 'Legal Chinese' and 'ordinary Chinese' are not the same language just because they both use the same writing system. This is like the different European languages not being the same language because they use the same alphabetic system. . . . In contrast to 'ordinary language' which can be called 'natural language' as it is based on 'voluntary customs', legal Chinese is unnatural and so 'artificial'.
>
> (English translation by the author)

Therefore, he points out, even in Taiwan, which is a monolingual jurisdiction, legal students have to make special efforts to learn legal Chinese, which is different from the Chinese used in daily life. His view is comparable to the situation with legal English in the English-speaking world.

1.3.2 Chinese legal terminology

The paramount importance of 'equivalence' of terms in legal translation raises challenging issues for Chinese. As Cheng and Sin (2008: 34–35) note, 'the concept of equivalence has always been an essential issue in translation theories as well as in translation studies', and 'a problem in legal translation therefore arises at the outset if a translator aims at finding exact terminological equivalence, which does not imply exact equivalence for a legal term is an impossible task, though it is always difficult'. There are two levels of related discussion in the context of the three Chinese communities. In Hong Kong, on the one hand, 'terminological incongruity' is prevalent when translating English common law terminology into Chinese, which 'has never functioned as a legal language' in Hong Kong (Poon 2002: 77). Wong (1997: 63) states that 'an inherent and inevitable link exists between the Common Law and English'. On the other hand, recognising that it is an impossible mission to find Chinese equivalents for 'culture-laden common law concepts', Sin and Roebuck (1996: 248) propose the approach of 'total equivalence'. They state, 'Since the law of the SAR [Special Administrative Region] is stipulated to be common law, all common law terms in Chinese, however they are produced, must accordingly be understood with reference to the common law'.

Cheng and Sin (2008: 33) also remark that 'total equivalence can be achieved via meta-lingual adjustment, because a sign is not born with meaning but invested with reference by a sign user'. This 'total equivalence' approach makes translation of Hong Kong common law from English into Chinese possible and sensible because the 'semantic reference system' is always fixed in common law. Nevertheless, the translated Chinese legal terms in Hong Kong have met with strong disapproval from lawyers due to their poor readability and Anglicised style. As the methods of translating legal terms have been the focus of criticism, these will be examined in the next chapter.

The second level of discussion lies in the 'systemic' differences between the world's two major legal systems. Generally speaking, the laws of Mainland China and Taiwan are based on civil law, while Hong Kong law is based on English common law.

In essence, civil law is based on statutes. Two authoritative definitions of civil law can be found in *Black's Law Dictionary* (Garner 2009: 280): the first being 'one of the two prominent legal systems in the Western World, originally administered in the Roman Empire and still influential in continental Europe, Latin America, Scotland, and Louisiana, among other parts of the world', and the second 'in reference to Romans, *civil law* (commonly referred to as *jus civile*) denotes the whole body of Roman law, from whatever source derived. But it is also to denote that part of Roman law peculiar to the Romans, as opposed to the common law of all peoples (*jus gentium*)'.

In contrast, the common law system is based on case law. It is defined as 'the body of law derived from judicial decisions, rather than from statutes or constitutions . . . [common law is] the body of law based on the English legal system, as distinct from a civil-law system' (Garner 2009: 313).

In view of the differences between the two systems, there is a constant need to differentiate the specialised meanings of similar legal terms that are commonly used in both systems. In the Chinese communities, the situation is complicated by the fact that identical Chinese legal terms from different systems have different meanings. Šarčević (1997: 273) comments:

> The conceptual, structural, historical and ideological differences between the common law of capitalist Hong Kong and the socialist system of communist China based on civil law make it extremely difficult and often impossible to find adequate legal equivalents. . . . The situation is complicated even more by the fact that the written and spoken Chinese of Hong Kong differs from that of the P.R. of China, not to mention Taiwan and Macao.

In Chinese linguistics, Modern Written Chinese remains essentially the same in Hong Kong, Mainland China and Taiwan, with greater lexical differences than grammatical ones, and the main obstacles to terminology standardisation lie in the cultural and social habits as well as in the translation methods used. 'Such variations constitute a main source of difficulty and misunderstanding when Chinese read publications from the other areas' (Chen 1999: 106).

These variations among lexical norms in Mainland China, Taiwan and Hong Kong have been on the decrease since the implementation of the 'open-door policy' by Mainland China in the late 1970s (Chen 1999: 106–108). In the last two decades, there has been a tendency for the regions to influence one another due to frequent trade, closer economic ties and the relationship between Hong Kong and the Mainland under the 'one country, two systems' policy.

Due to the long separation of the three regions, however, much of the legal terminology translation is done separately, with little regard for their other Chinese counterparts. In order to observe, anticipate and regulate the future development of Chinese legal terminology, the problems and strategies of translation activities deserve scholarly study. It is suggested that solid groundwork be undertaken to solve terminological problems in each and every legal area of the three Chinese regions, beginning with those areas of frequent contact such as commerce and intellectual property rights. Cao (2004: 170) explains the two objectives of this groundwork:

> In legal translation, there are two competing interests or concerns . . . very often SL and TL concepts not totally identical are treated and translated as equivalent. In other cases, seemingly equivalent SL and TL concepts must be distinguished and are not or should not be translated as equivalent, to avoid confusing different legal operations.

In sum, scholars should attempt to clarify confusion in legal differences to 'establish which terms from the two legal traditions are equivalent and to differentiate those which are not'. When the translation of terminology is clarified through an examination of legal differences, hopefully Chinese legal terms that have identical or similar meaning can be standardised through 'meta-lingual adjustment', despite the different 'semantic reference systems' (Chan 2011: 251).

1.3.3 Legal translation

In the field of legal translation, it is generally recognised that the basic approach is literal translation, that is, to follow the letter of the source text. Šarčević (1997: 16) notes:

> Convinced that the main goal of legal translation is to reproduce the content of the source text as accurately as possible, both lawyers and linguists agreed that legal texts had to be translated literally. For the sake of preserving the letter of the law, the main guideline for legal translation was fidelity to the source text.

Against this background, Šarčević (1997: 80–110) believes that legal translation is not a simple decoding process, but rather 'an act of communication within the mechanism of law', with the legal translator as a 'co-drafter'. She argues that a legal translator should achieve equivalence of the 'legal intent' to be interpreted by the court: 'the translator can best preserve the unity of the single instrument by striving to produce a text that will be interpreted and applied by the courts in the same manner as the other parallel texts of that instrument, particularly the original' (Šarčević 1997: 72). However, by citing examples of ambiguities in the court interpretations of the law in Hong Kong, Poon (2005: 322–323) believes that translators 'can often only produce a semantically and syntactically literal translation so as not to affect the substance of the source text, and leave the court to interpret the text according to the nature of different cases'.

As a subfield of translation studies, the nature of legal translation has been changing, which relates to the scope of legal texts.

In their overview of the development of legal translation, Biel and Engberg (2013: 1) state that language in legal settings is one of the areas that 'has boasted the highest degree of interest in recent years'. There have been two key areas of research on legal translation. Traditionally, the main study area is terminological equivalence, which is 'closely related to terminography and is informed by practically-oriented research into legal terms for translation purposes such as the preparation of legal dictionaries or terminological databases' (Biel and Engberg 2013: 1). Thanks to the momentum provided by 'interdisciplinarity', including the catalysts of legal studies, comparative law, terminology and linguistics, a second key area has been taking shape in the field that has 'shifted the focus from the traditional areas of investigation, such as the incongruity of legal terms and the limits of translatability, to the communicative, pragmatic, cognitive and social aspects of legal translation' (Biel and Engberg 2013: 8).

This discussion is highly relevant to the next subsection that concerns the organisation of this book. Due to an 'interdisciplinary turn' in translation studies, legal translation studies is recognised as a major interdisciplinary study within translation studies (Gentzler 2003; Prieto Ramos 2014). This interdisciplinary study is concerned with 'all aspects of translation of legal texts, including processes, products and agents', and a legal language that is 'not a uniform language', where 'legal translators need to discriminate the features of the different styles reflected in original texts as part of translation oriented analysis' (Prieto Ramos 2014: 261). Covering three major groups of texts, namely normative texts, judicial texts and legal scholarly texts, the 'hybridity of legal texts' deals with all aspects of life (Prieto Ramos 2014: 263). Nevertheless, some ordinary texts used in legal settings and worked on by legal translators are not considered legal texts, as they are not written by legal professionals in legal language. These ordinary texts include 'business or personal correspondence, records and certificates, witness statements and expert reports' (Cao 2007: 11–12).

The Hong Kong translation scholar Sin (2018: 102) basically echoes these views when defining legal translation as 'one of the subject-matters of the sociolinguistics of law', influenced by various social factors. In his sociolinguistic analysis of some legal translation issues in Hong Kong, he explains that 'legal translation is an umbrella term covering translation in all types of legal settings', in both narrow and broad senses:

> The source texts involved are hard to classify neatly and exhaustively. Typical texts are those of a legal nature, such as international treaties, domestic statutes, judicial decisions (judgments/opinions), legal notices, contracts, wills and scholarly legal works. Texts which are not of a legal nature in themselves but involved in legal proceedings, either criminal or civil, can become the source texts of legal translation in the broad sense, such as a suicide note, a media report, an advertisement, a poem of the triad society, in fact, anything.

In sum, legal translation deals with all kinds of texts, with those of a legal nature at its core. Sin's definition corresponds with the view that law is a 'discursive social practice', which means that 'law depends on discursiveness for its creation and its application' and 'law is created and applied with the help of linguistic means, i.e. discursively' (Galdia 2017: 33).

1.4 Organisation and technicalities

1.4.1 Structure and limitations

This book will concentrate on legal translation in the narrow sense, that is, legal texts and primarily legislation, which is where the bilingualism of the Hong Kong legal system commenced and developed. Judgments, contracts and international treaties will also be covered. These different text types actually share common linguistic issues, for example, the various Europeanised Chinese features discussed in legislation also appear in judgments, contracts, international treaties and so on. The linguistic issues also affect English-Chinese translation activities in all other Chinese-speaking regions, as the grammatical structure of Modern Written Chinese is basically the same in all the regions. The two key study areas in legal translation mentioned by Biel and Engberg (2013: 8), that is, terminological equivalence and communicative function of legal translation and bilingual law drafting, are the topics under investigation.

The following is the outline of the six chapters of the book.

Chapter 1 first sets forth the background against which legal translation has taken place in China since the Qing Dynasty. It provides an overview of the translation of Western and international laws into Chinese in recent decades, first in Hong Kong, which uses the common law system, and then in Mainland China and Taiwan, which are both considered to use the civil law system. Against the background of growing legal globalisation, which intensifies the process of legal translation, this chapter describes the features of legal Chinese and Chinese legal terminology, both as a tool to introduce foreign laws and as a translation product. The chapter also includes a review of the literature on the scope of legal translation and legal texts, in which the structure and limitations of this book are explained.

16   *Introduction*

Chapter 2 investigates Hong Kong's translation of common law into Chinese and bilingual law drafting from a language perspective. The discussion starts with the Europeanised influence on the Chinese language in general since the May Fourth Movement, and elaborates on its influence on the legislation, judgments, legal documents and legal translation reference books in Hong Kong. The Europeanised influence on Chinese includes its grammatical structures, lexicon and terminology in the process of translation. The discussion ends with the early responses to the governmental translation project of legislation from different sectors, including lawyers, legislators and legal and translation scholars.

Chapter 3 illustrates the legal challenges in translating foreign laws into Chinese, with the aim of discussing the central issues of equivalence and the legal knowledge of translators, which are crucial in translation between different legal systems. The discussion is divided into two main parts. The first part analyses different translation scenarios, that is, the different Chinese options available as translations for the same or similar source words, their different meanings in the two major legal systems, and the level of equivalence among the candidates. The second part is a case study that compares the translations of one term in an international intellectual property agreement in Mainland China and Taiwan, and the intellectual property law in Hong Kong.

Chapter 4 explores the capacity of education to meet the language and legal challenges in legal translation and bilingual law drafting in Hong Kong. It suggests broadening the horizons of students of both law and translation by giving them opportunities to explore each other's knowledge. Therefore, two case studies are presented, one on the incorporation of legal concepts in a legal translation course for students who basically have no legal knowledge or backgrounds, and another on Chinese and translation training for law students who study law entirely in English. Lastly, the discussion highlights some issues around the training of government law drafters, lawyers and legal translators, supported by a mini-survey conducted among 30 practitioners in the field.

Chapter 5 explores the capacity of research to meet the language and legal challenges in legal translation and bilingual law drafting in Hong Kong. Two major future research areas are proposed, that is, the enhancement of Chinese language quality for bilingual legislation and judgments, and the comparative study of legal terminology and compilation of a common legal glossary of Chinese terms from the three Chinese communities. The first area concerns the cultivation of good knowledge and practice of the Chinese language in the legal profession. In the second area, the summary of a chapter on the term 'contract' taken from a book on contract law terms from the three Chinese communities is given, with the aim to enhancing mutual understanding.

Chapter 6 concludes with the macro philosophy of balancing language and law in order to enhance legal translation into Chinese, and offers suggestions for the future development of legal translation and bilingual law drafting in Hong Kong. Continuing efforts in education and research will put in place a systematic conceptual comparison of Chinese legal terms and train increasing numbers of personnel with cross-disciplinary competency. Obstacles mainly arise from the relatively low status of translation and legal translation in Hong Kong. This book proposes that the field focus on the new direction of translating judgments and continue its leading role in terminology creation in the Chinese world.

Owing to the frequent contact between Hong Kong, Mainland China and Taiwan that occurs primarily in the commercial domain, this book concentrates more on civil law including contract law, property law, intellectual property law and company law than on criminal law. The six chapters in the book are organised more or less on a chronological basis. Chapters 1–3 focus on a brief background history of the importation of Western laws since the Qing Dynasty, the ceding of Hong Kong to Britain, efforts towards legal globalisation by Mainland China and Taiwan, and the three decades of the Hong Kong bilingual legal system, starting from the launch of bilingual legislation translation and co-drafting in the 1980s and the responses from the professions and society up to around 2010. Chapters 4–6 focus on the latest developments in the past decade, with suggestions for future directions. Besides this limitation of the focus on civil law rather than criminal law, the book also focuses on legislation rather than judgments. There are two main reasons for this: First, the bilingualism of Hong Kong's legal system started with legislation, and translation of judgments is still an ongoing task, proceeding according to degree of importance; second, most past research and social discussion was also prompted by and centres on bilingual legislation.

1.4.2 Romanisation and convention

This subsection will explain conventions used, romanisation and other technicalities with the history and rationale behind these choices. To remain aligned with the Hong Kong practice of using British English and traditional Chinese characters in official and business writing, this book adopts traditional Chinese characters and British English spellings. In the Chinese writing system, traditional characters are used in Hong Kong and Taiwan, and simplified characters in Mainland China. For the sake of consistency, traditional characters are also adopted for the laws and other data from the Mainland, which are all originally written in simplified characters. In the text body, the Chinese words, terms, laws and sentences cited are presented in Mandarin romanisation (*pinyin*) followed by Chinese characters, and the English translation is provided immediately after or somewhere in the immediate context. The *pinyin* system has been advocated by the PRC since the 1950s, and now is the official form of Chinese transliteration adopted by the United Nations. The English translation is presented with a combination of idiomatic and literal approaches. In this book with many titles of laws, the bilingual Hong Kong law under investigation are presented first in English followed by *pinyin* and Chinese characters, as for the most part are the Chinese laws of the Mainland and Taiwan. Some laws not being under study are presented in English only. This is to enhance the ease of reading this book, which is written in English to target an international audience, including bilingual intellectuals in all the Chinese-speaking regions, and Hong Kong lawyers and legal translators who mostly receive secondary school education in English. However, exceptions are made where the discussion closely relates to the lexical or literal meaning of the legislation titles, in which cases *pinyin* and Chinese characters are presented before the English translation. When citing Hong Kong legislation, this book will follow the usual practice of including the chapter number in parentheses after the title, for instance, the Sale of Goods Ordinance (Cap. 26). The year of the enactment or amendment of legislation is indicated only where there is a need to make distinctions in the text.

In the stand-alone examples (sentences marked with consecutive numbers in each chapter), bilingual laws from Hong Kong will be presented with the English text first, followed by the Chinese text. In contrast, Chinese laws from the Mainland will present the Chinese text first, followed by the English translation. It is noted that in Mainland China and Taiwan, Chinese is the only official language and only the Chinese version of the legislation has legal force, while the English version is for reference only. In most cases, The English translations of the PRC laws are cited from LawInfoChina, Peking University (www.pkulaw.cn), and those of Taiwan's laws from the Law and Regulations Database, Ministry of Justice, Taiwan (https://law.moj.gov.tw). For examples that consist of materials other than legislation, the original text is placed before the translated text, and the author will state if it is her own translation. When there are two or more Chinese translations or drafted versions of the same English source, in most cases the second is the author's suggested preferred alternative. The relationship between different versions of the same example is indicated by the addition of letters to the number, as in (1a), (1b) and (1c). In such example sentences, all the focal points of discussion are underlined.

In this book, which focuses on the field of legal translation, the use of 'field' refers to 'the field of legal translation' or 'the fields of legal translation and bilingual law drafting', depending on the context. 'Hong Kong' and 'Hong Kong Special Administrative Region' established in 1997 are used interchangeably. While 'Mainland China', 'the Mainland', the 'People's Republic of China' and its abbreviation 'PRC' are used interchangeably, 'China' is used in the discussion relating to the country as a whole, mostly before the PRC was established in 1949. Accordingly, the Copyright Law of the PRC, for example, means the Copyright Law enacted in Mainland China, which only applies to Mainland China. Despite the fact the Hong Kong is now part of the PRC, PRC law does not apply to Hong Kong in accordance with the Basic Law of Hong Kong. Article 18 of the Basic Law in principle states that no national law is applied to Hong Kong except the Annex III of the Basic Law: 'National laws shall not be applied in the Hong Kong Special Administrative Region except for those listed in Annex III to this Law. The laws listed therein shall be applied locally by way of promulgation or legislation by the Region'. As stipulated in Article 2 of the Basic Law, Hong Kong is entitled to 'exercise a high degree of autonomy and enjoy executive, legislative and independent judicial power, including that of final adjudication'.

All Chinese people's names are romanised according to the different romanisation systems of the different Chinese regions, with the order of the family name and given name retained. The Chinese characters are not shown. If the Chinese person adopts a Western first name that is widely known to the public, that name is also added. For example, in the name of the Hong Kong barrister and former legislator Margaret Ng Ngoi-yee, Ng is the family name, Ngoi-yee is the Chinese given name and Margaret is the Western given name.

Notes

1 Cantonese is a Chinese dialect originating from Canton city and its surrounding area in Southeastern China. As the second strongest Chinese dialect to the Northern Mandarin, it is the dominant spoken language used in Hong Kong, Macao and overseas Chinese communities. Given that Chinese is a tonal language, Cantonese has nine tones, while Putonghua (普通話), the common standard language in Mainland China, and the similar Taiwanese Mandarin Guoyu (國語), have four tones. Cantonese and Putonghua are considered distinct and mutually intelligible by linguists. General speaking, foreign Chinese learners find tones in Chinese difficult. While Cantonese is the mother-tongue of most Hong Kong people, students are taught Modern Written Chinese in school based on ancient and modern Chinese literature. Modern Written Chinese remains basically the same, especially in terms of its grammar, among Hong Kong, Mainland China, Taiwan and Singapore. The written Chinese mainly vary in lexicon and style across the Chinese regions.
2 Securities and Futures Commission Ordinance (Cap. 24) (*Zhengquan ji Qihuo Shiwu Jiancha Weiyuanhui Tiaoli*《證券及期貨事務監察委員會條例》(第24章)) has been repealed.
3 Concerning 'presumption of same meaning', Sin (2018: 318–346) states that it is the foundation of all bilingual and multilingual legal systems. As soon as the legislative branch passes a bilingual or multilingual law, its texts will enjoy the same legal status, and be presumed to have the same meaning. This presumption, though controversial as it relates to whether immemorial debates of equivalence and what is translatable and what is not, is intended to ease worries that there is always a discrepancy among the bilingual and multilingual texts of law. There have been studies of the methods on bridging the gap of court interpretations of the bilingual laws of Hong Kong. In the recent study by Cheung (2019), the court compares the meaning of the modal verb 'shall' with the Chinese copular verb *wei* (為) in the preamble of the Chinese University of Hong Kong Ordinance (Cap. 1109) (Xianggang Zhongwen Daxue Tiaoli《香港中文大學條例》(第1109章)) (*Li Yiu Lee v The Chinese University of Hong Kong* [2010] HKCA 218; CACV 93/2009), with the understanding that there is a difference between the bilingual laws due to the absence of a modal verb before *wei* (為). However, in the Chinese legislation of PRC and Taiwan, it is commonplace to express compulsoriness without using modal verbs such as *yingdang* (應當), *ying* (應) or *xu* (須). For example, Article 33 of the Constitution of the PRC states *Zhonghua Renmin Gongheguo gongmin zai Falü mianqian yilü pingdeng* (中華人民共和國公民在法律面前一律平等) (All the citizens of the People's Republic of China [shall be] equal before the law). This indicates that some Hong Kong judges lack familiarity with the usage of Chinese legal words and terms due to their lack of experience in the Hong Kong historical context.

English references

Auby, Jean-Bernard (2008). Is Legal Globalization Regulated? Memling and the Business of Baking Camels. *Utrecht Law Review 4*(3): 210–217.
Biel, Łucja and Engberg, Jan (2013). Research Models and Methods in Legal Translation. *Linguistica Antverpiensia, New Series—Themes in Translation Studies 12*: 1–11.
Cao, Deborah (1997). Consideration in Translating English/Chinese Contracts. *Meta: Translators' Journal 42*(4): 661–669.

Cao, Deborah (2004). *Chinese Law*. Aldershot, Hants: Ashgate.
Cao, Deborah (2007). *Translating Law*. Clevedon: Multilingual Matters Ltd.
Chan, Clara Ho-yan (2011). The Use and Translation of Chinese Legal Terminology in the Property Laws of Mainland China and Hong Kong: Problems, Strategies and Future Development. *Terminology: International Journal of Theoretical and Applied Issues in Specialized Communication 17*(2): 249–273.
Chan, Clara Ho-yan (2012). Bridging the Gap Between Language and Law: Translational Issues in Creating Legal Chinese in Hong Kong. *Babel: International Journal of Translation 58*(2): 127–144.
Chen, Albert Hung-yee (1991). The Bilingual Legal System in Hong Kong: A Gloomy Future. *Hong Kong Law Journal 21*(1): 14–18.
Chen, Albert Hung-yee (2011). *An Introduction to the Legal System of the People's Republic of China* (4th Ed.). Hong Kong: LexisNexis.
Chen, Ping (1999). *Modern Chinese: History and Sociolinguistics*. Cambridge: Cambridge University Press.
Cheng, Le and Sin, King-kui (2008). Terminological Equivalence in Legal Translation: A Semiotic Approach. *Semiotica 172*(1): 33–45.
Doczekalska, Agnieszka (2009). Drafting or Translation – Production of Multilingual Legal Texts. In Olsen, Frances, Lorz, Alexander and Stein, Dieter (Eds.), *Translation Issues in Language and Law* (pp. 116–135). Basingstoke and New York: Palgrave Macmillan.
Galdia, Marcus (2017). *Lectures on Legal Linguistics*. Frankfurt: Peter Lang.
Garner, Bryan A. (Ed.) (2009). *Black's Law Dictionary* (9th Ed.). St. Paul, MN: West.
Gentzler, Edwin (2003). Interdisciplinary Connections. *Perspectives 11*(1): 11–24.
Government Information Services (2004). *Speech by Solicitor-General* (Press release), November 9. Retrieved from: www.info.gov.hk/gia/general/200411/09/1109202.htm.
Hart, Herbert L. A. (1954). Definition and Theory in Jurisprudence. *The Law Quarterly Review 70*: 37–60.
Kelsen, Hans (1967). *Pure Theory of Law*. Berkeley: University of California Press.
Lord, Robert and T'sou, Benjamin Ka-yin (1985). *The Language Bomb: The Language Issue in Hong Kong*. Hong Kong: Longman.
Poon, Emily Wai-yee (2002). The Pitfalls of Linguistic Equivalence: The Challenge for Legal Translation. *Target: International Journal of Translation Studies 14*(1): 75–106.
Poon, Emily Wai-yee (2005). The Cultural Transfer in Legal Translation. *International Journal for the Semiotics of Law 18*: 307–323.
Poon, Emily Wai-yee (2018). Sex and Gender in Legal Translation. In Shei, Chris and Gao, Zhao-Ming (Eds.), *The Routledge Handbook of Chinese Translation*. London and New York: Routledge.
Potter, Pitman B. (2001). *The Chinese Legal System: Globalization and Local Legal Culture*. London: Routledge.
Prieto Ramos, Fernando (2014). Legal Translation Studies as Interdiscipline: Scope and Evolution. *Meta: Translators' Journal 59*(2): 260–277.
Roebuck, Derek and Sin, King-kui (1993). The Ego and I and Ngo: Theoretical Problems in the Translation of the Common Law into Chinese. In Wacks, Raymond (Ed.), *Hong Kong, China and 1997: Essays in Legal Theory* (pp. 185–210). Hong Kong: Hong Kong University Press.
Rundell, Michael and Fox, Gwyneth (2002). *Macmillan English Dictionary for Advanced Learners*. London: Palgrave Macmillan.
Šarčević, Susan (1997). *New Approach to Legal Translation*. The Hague: Kluwer Law International.

Sin, King-kui. (2000). The Missing Link Between Language and Law: Problems of Legislative Translation in Hong Kong. In Herberts, Kjell and Turi, Joseph G. (Eds.), *Multilingual Cities and Language Policies* (pp. 195–210). Abo: Abo Akademi University Social Science Research Unit.

Sin, King-kui. (2018). Language, Law, Translation, and Society: The Sociolinguistics of Translating Hong Kong Laws. In Chan, Sin-wai (Ed.), *An Encyclopedia of Practical Translation and Interpreting* (pp. 101–134). Hong Kong: The Chinese University Press.

Sin, King-kui and Roebuck, Derek (1996). Language Engineering for Legal Transplantation: Conceptual Problems in Creating Common Law Chinese. *Language and Communication 16*(3): 235–254.

Teng, Ssu-yü and Fairbank, John K. (1982). *China's Response to the West: A Documentary Survey, 1939–1923*. Cambridge: Harvard University Press.

Thomas, Michael D. (1988). The Development of a Bilingual Legal System in Hong Kong. *Hong Kong Law Journal 18*(1): 15–24.

Wang, Guiguo and Mo, John (Eds.) (1999). *Chinese Law*. Hague and Boston: Kluwer Law International.

Wong, Derry (1997). Securing a Bilingual Legal System for Hong Kong. *Asia Pacific Law Review 5*(2): 63–75.

Yen, Tony (2010). *Hong Kong's Bilingual Legislative Drafting and Translation of Legislation*. Hong Kong Institute of Legal Translation Limited. Retrieved from: www.hkilt.com/news/58_Tony%20Yen.pdf.

Chinese references

Cheung, Anna 張善喻 (2019). 〈淺談香港法院如何解決雙語法例的分歧〉 (How Hong Kong Courts Resolve Differences in Bilingual Legislation?). In Cham, Edmund Shu Kay 湛樹基 and Lee, Elvis Kim Hung 李劍雄 (Eds.), 《香港雙語法制: 語言與翻譯》 (*Bilingual Legal System in Hong Kong: Language and Translation*) (pp. 20–48). Hong Kong: Hong Kong University Press.

He, Qinhua 何勤華 (2011). 〈法的國際化與本地化：以中國近代移植外國法實踐為中心的思考〉 (Legal Globalisation and Localisation: Thinking on Legal Transplantation of Foreign Laws in Modern China). 《中國法學》 (*China Legal Science*) 4: 43–52.

Jin, Serena Sheng Hwa 金聖華 and Sin, King-kui 冼景炬 (2004). 〈香港法例中譯的幾個問題〉 (Some Problems in the Chinese Translation of Hong Kong Legal Provisions). 《翻譯學報》 (*Journal of Translation Studies*) 9: 89–103.

Li, Zonge 李宗鍔 (1987). 〈香港建立雙語法制的前景和困難—對評「香港合約法與公司法」的回應〉 (The Prospects and Difficulties in Building a Bilingual Legal System in Hong Kong: A Response to the Comments on 'Hong Kong's Contract Law and Company Law'). 《信報財經月刊》 (*Hong Kong Economic Journal Monthly*) 10(10): 120–127.

Qu, Wensheng 屈文生 (2013). 《從詞典出發：法律術語譯名統一與規範化的翻譯史研究》 (*Lexicography: A Study of Unification and Standardisation of Translated Legal Terms*). Shanghai: Shanghai Renmin Press.

Sin, King-kui 冼景炬 (2018). 〈從佛經翻譯到雙語法制的建立：香港法例翻譯的啓示〉 (From the Translation of Buddhist Scriptures to the Establishment of the Bilingual Legal System: Inspirations from the Translation of Hong Kong Legislation). In Qu, Wensheng 屈文生 (Ed.), 《法律翻譯研究》 (*Legal Translation Studies*) (pp. 316–394). Shanghai: Shanghai Renmin Press.

Wang, Tai-sheng 王泰升 (2005).《臺灣法的世紀變革》 (*A Century of Changes in Taiwanese Law*). Taipei: Angle Publishing.

Wang, Tai-sheng 王泰升, Hsueh, Hua-Yuan 薛化元 and Huang, Shijie 黃世杰 (2006). 《追尋臺灣法律的足跡: 事件百選與法律史研究》 (*Tracing the Course of Taiwanese Law: a Hundred selected Events and Studies in Legal History*). Taipei: Wu-Nan Book.

Zhang, Yue 張越, Zhao, Ruihong 趙瑞紅 and Yu, Juan 余娟 (Eds.) (2005). 《法學翻譯與中國法的現代化—「美國法律文庫暨法學翻譯與法律變遷」研討會紀實》 (*Legal Translation and Modernisation of Chinese Law: 'American Law Library and Legal Translation and Legal Transformation' Seminar Reports*). Beijing: China University of Political Science and Law Press.

Zheng, Yi-Zhe 鄭逸哲 (2007) 〈法律人的雙語世界 談日常語言和法律語言的併用〉 (The Bilingual World of Judicial Persons: The Merge of Folk- and Legal-language). In Liu, Hsing-I 劉幸義 (Ed.), 《東亞法律漢字用語之整合》 (*On Integration of Chinese Legal Terms in East Asia*). Taipei: New Sharing Publication.

Zhou, Shizhong 周世中 (2010). 《比較法學》 (*Comparative Law*). Beijing: China Renmin University Press.

Zhu, Jingwen 朱景文 (2010). 〈國內法的國際化和國際法的國內化：關於法律和全球化研究的基本理論〉 Guoneifa de Guojihua he Guojifa de Guoneihua: Guanyu Falü he Quanqiuhua Yanjiu de Jiben Lilun (Internationalisation of Domestic Laws and Domestication of International Laws: Several Fundamental Theories on Law and Globalisation Studies). In Chiu, Man-chung 趙文宗 (Ed.) 《中華法哲學發展：全球化與本地化之間》 (*The Development of Legal Philosophy in Greater China: Beyond Globalisation and Localisation*) (pp. 2–13). Hong Kong: Red Corporation Limited.

2 Challenges in legal translation

A language perspective

The lexical and grammatical features of today's Chinese legal language, which is primarily a translated language, are essentially a continuation of the radical changes to the Chinese language of the past century. This chapter will describe the historical background of the Westernisation or Europeanisation of Chinese intended to 'strengthen the country', so as to lay a good understanding of the properties of legal Chinese developed in Hong Kong through legal transplantation and reform. Based on *baihua*, Modern Standard Chinese was born out of the drastic social, political and economic changes that occurred as part of China's modernisation. In 1919, the May Fourth Movement broke out in China as a protest against the unfair treaties signed with Western powers at the end of the First World War. The advocates of the Movement, who were a group of Western-trained intellectuals, also started the New Culture Movement with the aim of strengthening China by helping the masses to learn written Chinese. They proposed replacing classical literary Chinese, *wenyan* (文言), with the new written language, *baihua* (白話), as the basis of standard written Chinese. Modern Standard Chinese was intended as a tool to save China from illiteracy and backwardness. Li and Luk (2017: 99) remark that since the twentieth century, Chinese writers tended to use the 'norms of *baihua*', so that this new style of written Chinese became a vernacular language:

> New ideas across a wide range of topics and genres written in foreign languages were introduced to Chinese readers via translation, for example, novels, short stories, poetry, essays, dramas, and literary theories. Aspiring young intellectuals took advantage of burgeoning newspapers and magazines as platforms to reach out to the general public. This encouraged the experimentation of literary writing in as well as translation into *baihua*... were all eager to experiment with new vocabulary and morpho-syntactic features that were inspired by their reading and appreciation of original works written in various foreign languages, notably English.

Overall speaking, the intelligentsia aimed to transform Chinese so that it could '"carry" or express novel ideas, in keeping with the spirit of and advances in the modern era' (Li and Luk 2017: 99). Zhou Zuoren (1922), one of the New

24 *Challenges in legal translation*

Culture Movement pioneers, proposed that in order to make Chinese a sophisticated vehicle capable of expressing subtle sentiments and thoughts, the language must be reformed through the incorporation of the old language and dialects, new vocabulary and increased precision of grammar through Europeanisation. Chen (1999: 82–88) suggests that the same three avenues of influence have continued to be active in the formation and enrichment of the Chinese language, namely, Old Chinese *wenyan*, non-Northern Mandarin dialects and foreign languages. Today, while non-Northern Mandarin dialects have impact on written Chinese in all three Chinese communities, they differ with respect to the degree of influence of Classical Chinese. Taiwan has retained the most classical elements, and Mainland China the fewest, with Hong Kong standing between the two. Since the years leading up to the 1997 handover, Hong Kong Chinese has gradually changed its classical style to follow the vernacular style employed in official writing on the Mainland (Lee 1999; Tung 2012). The most compelling force in changing Modern Chinese is foreign languages, which will be dealt with in detail in the following sections.

2.1 Europeanisation of Chinese

Of these three influences, foreign languages have exerted the most important influence on the development of Modern Written Chinese (Chen 1999: 85). Extensive studies have been undertaken to investigate Western influence, many of them using the terminology 'Europeanisation of Chinese', 'Westernisation of Chinese' or 'Anglicisation of Chinese' (Gunn 1991; Hsu 1994; Kubler 1985; Li 1962; Li and Luk 2017: 110; Tse 1990; Wang 1984, 1985). By definition, 'Europeanization refers to the influence of European languages on local languages at the lexical and morpho-syntactic levels' (Li and Luk 2017: 110). Details are as follows.

2.1.1 Lexical changes

The lexical system of languages is highly subject to outside influence, in order to satisfy practical needs (Zdenka 1967: 613). Ma (1963: 54) states that the rapid growth of new vocabulary in Modern Standard Chinese was 'due to the coinage of new terms to describe new situations or to replace old terms, and the use of traditional, colloquial or regional terms used in a new sense'. Of the three main channels for the importation of new vocabulary, namely, Classical Chinese, non-Northern Mandarin dialects and foreign languages, the most important influence is also foreign languages, mainly through translation. Since the Opium War in the nineteenth century, vocabulary across all levels of life has undergone substantial changes, with foreign influence accelerating the transformation of Chinese words from monomorphemic to polymorphemic constructions, and creating a wealth of compounds (Kratochvil 1968: 139; Li 1962: 9–20; Norman 1988: 56). Two common examples are the replacement of *mei* (美) with *meili* (美麗) (beautiful), and *shi* (使) and *yong* (用) with *shiyong* (使用) (use) (Kratochvil 1968: 141). Japanese and European languages, mainly English, are two major sources of foreign influence, although terms from French, German and Russian have also been borrowed

(Liu 1995: 284–301, 343–378). In Taiwan, some words borrowed from Japanese during colonial rule have become everyday words, for example, *biandang* (便當) (box meal), *shiyou* (室友) (roommate) and *fuzhi* (福祉) (welfare).

Li and Luk (2017: 100–101) note two ways to create new Chinese words. The first is through transliteration, for example, *gelangma* (葛朗瑪) (grammar), which preceded its being semantically translated as *wenfa* (文法) and *yufa* (語法). The other way is by combining existing monosyllabic verbs and adjectives to translate English nouns, for example, *yuejian* (約見) ('arrange-see', meaning 'appointment') and *chenji* (沉寂) ('deep-lonely', meaning 'stillness'). Chen (1999: 103–107) lists five main translation methods, namely, loan translation, semantic translation, phonetic transcription, juxtaposition of semantic translation and phonetic transcription, and a combination of semantic translation and phonetic transcription. The main trend is towards loan translation, semantic translation and using names commonly used in Northern Mandarin areas. There is great dialectal variation between the respective lexical items of the Mainland, Taiwan and Hong Kong, and the differences lie mainly in the source of borrowing and the translation methods. For example, after a long period of separation since the founding of the PRC in 1949, Taiwan and Mainland China have adopted different names for many common objects. Examples include *cundi* (存底) (reserve), *jiaoliudao* (交流道) (over-pass) and *taikongren* (太空人) (astronaut) used in Taiwan, as distinct from *chubei* (儲備), *lijiaoqiao* (立交橋) and *yuhangyuan* (宇航員) used on the Mainland. However, due to the growing contact and exchange among the three areas, the variation in lexical norms has been diminishing.

2.1.2 Morpho-syntactic changes

Li (1962: 71), in describing the grammatical changes in Modern Standard Chinese, states that Chinese grammarians unintentionally molded the Chinese language on the basis of the linguistic principles of Indo-European languages:

> Thus they encourage the use of 'grammatically complete' sentences, the demarcation of word classes, and development of features which may look similar to morphology of inflectional languages and increased uses of prepositions and conjunctions, which are alien to traditional Chinese idioms, result[ing] only in linguistic artificialities.

This goal of 'grammatically complete' sentences has elicited plentiful new patterns and markers, some of which are excessively used. It is believed that all of these new grammatical elements have entered Modern Standard Chinese as by-products of translation (Hsu 1994; Kachru 1994; Wang 1984: 501), creating a novel literary style (Gunn 1991). With frequent use of markers that combine grammar and logic, the Chinese sentence structure has become stricter (Wang 1990: 476–488). With the progression of time, these linguistic additions have penetrated into Chinese grammar and spoken language (Kratochvil 1968: 141). Tse (1990) identifies seven types of 'beneficial Europeanisation' and ten types of 'adverse Europeanisation', and Li and Luk (2017) refer to most of them in their English book on Chinese-English contrastive grammar. They listed six trends that they as well as the above-mentioned scholars observed as follows.

2.1.2.1 Affixation

At the morphological level, there are a number of affix-like morphemes in Chinese that play a similar role to prefixes and suffixes in English. Examples are *fei-* (非) (non-), *fan-* (反) (anti-), *fu-* (副) (vice-), *hou-* (後) (post-); and *-zhe* (者) (-er, -or), *-jia* (家) (-ist), *-zhuyi* (主義) (-ism), *xing* (性) (-tion, -ity, -ness), *-hua* (化) (-ise, -ify), *-du* (度) (-th). Among these, *-xing* (性) and *-hua* (化) have gained the most popularity and are considered 'adverse Europeanisation'. Prominent instances are *keduxing* (可讀性) (readability) and *yanzhongxing* (嚴重性) (seriousness) (Hsu 1994: 171; Li and Luk 2017: 112). According to Kubler (1985: 73), *xing* (性) is used 'either to form attributives indicating quality or capacity, or to form abstract nouns meaning state, condition, or quality, somewhat like the English morphemes *-tion*, *-ity*, and *-ness*'. There are also the pluraliser *-men* (們), the adverbial suffix *-de* (地), and the verbal suffixes or aspect markers *-le* (了), *-zhe* (者), *-guo* (過) to mark 'perfective aspect, imperfective aspect, and experiential aspect, respectively' (Li and Luk 2017: 102).

2.1.2.2 Conjunctions

Traditionally, Chinese tends to link clauses in temporal sequence. Chinese is described as a 'disconnected' language with infrequent use of conjunctions (Tsai 1995: 243). Under the influence of English, conjunctions such as *yinwei* (因爲) (because), *ruguo* (如果) (if), *yaoshi* (要是) (provided), *zhiyao* (只要) (as long as or if only), *suiran* (雖然) (although) and *chufei* (除非) (unless) are in widespread use to 'disambiguate intended speaker/writer meanings' (Li and Luk 2017: 106). Chinese now also contains a greater number of conjunctive phrases such as *tongyang* (同樣) (in the same fashion), *yuci tongshi* (與此同時) (in the meantime), *zuihou* (最後) (finally), *youyu* (由於) (because of), *weile* (爲了) (for the sake of), *fanguolaishuo* (反過來說) (conversely), *zai ci zhong qingkuang xia* (在此種情況下) (under these circumstances) (Chou and Liu 1996: 313; Gunn 1991: 275–276). Some frequently-used expressions such as . . . *zhi yi* (. . . 之一) (one of the . . .), *shishi shang* (事實上) (actually), *jiben shang* (基本上) (basically) and *bijiao lai shuo* (比較來說) (comparatively speaking) are regarded as 'beneficial Europeanisation', to present views 'more objectively, logistically, and/or precisely' (Li and Luk 2017: 110). However, it is considered adverse Europeanisation to overuse coordinating conjunctions such as *he* (和), especially in Chinese set phrases and idioms. Similarly, some Chinese linguists observe more frequent use of the copula verb *shi* (是) (to be) to connect sentences (Chou and Liu 1996: 313; Shi and Zhu 2000; Tsai 1995: 244; Tse 2001: 18, 202; Wang 1984: 447–449). The overuse of *shi* (是) has developed a 'discontinuous structure' *shi* . . . *de* (是 . . . 的) to function as a descriptive or judgement sentence in Chinese, another type of 'adverse Europeanisation' (Li and Luk 2017: 121).

2.1.2.3 *Pronouns*

Under the influence of the pronouns *he*, *she* and *it* in English, the Chinese third person pronoun has experienced a gender differentiation into orthographic forms of masculine *ta* (他), feminine *ta* (她) and neuter *ta* (它), as well as their corresponding plural forms, masculine *tamen* (他們), feminine *tamen* (她們) and neuter *tamen* (它們). Furthermore, Tse (1990: 80–83), Wang (1984: 478–481) and Taiwanese poet Yu Kwang-Chung (1979: 2) note that pronouns have been used more frequently than Chinese was influenced by Western languages in subject and object positions, and as possessive adjectives with *de* (的). In particular, overuse of the neuter *ta* (它) has resulted in significant changes to the Chinese sentence structure as shown in the following examples:

(1)
他不管有多傷心，他都會生活下去。
No matter how upset he is, he will live on.

(2)
快把你的槍放下。
Put down your gun quickly.

As the meaning of both sentences is 'contextually clear' without personal or possessive pronouns, they can be omitted in Chinese, which is characterised by terseness (Li and Luk 2017: 114).

2.1.2.4 *Pre-nominal modifiers and embedding levels*

At the sentential level, there is lengthening of sentences due to the increased use of pre-nominal modifiers with pronouns and proper nouns. Such modifiers are linked to the head noun by the subordinating particle *de* (的), and may function as attributes at one or more levels of embedding (Gunn 1991: 225–227). Simple examples are *mai de dongxi* (賣的東西) (things being sold) and *mai dongxi de ren* (賣東西的人) (persons selling things) derived from *mai dongxi* (賣東西) (sell things) (Li and Luk 2017: 121). New embedded structures have also been introduced into general writing habits. Examples cited in Gunn (1991: 227–231) include *zui* . . . *zhi yi* (最 . . . 之一) (one of the most . . .), *zai* . . . (*de*) *tongshi* (在 . . . (的) 同時) (at the same time as), *yi* . . . *wei* . . . *de* (head) (以 . . . 為 . . . 的(中心詞)) (to regard . . . as), *yue* . . . *yue* . . . *de* (head) (越 . . . 越 . . . 的 (中心詞)) (more and more) and *you* . . . *de biyao* (有 . . . 的必要) (having the necessity of). However, the overuse of prepositions and prepositional phrases produces convoluted structures. Consider the following two examples taken from Li and Luk (118–119):

(3)
當她十六歲的時候，就從鄉下到了上海。
<u>At</u> age 16/<u>When</u> she was 16 years old, she went from the countryside to Shanghai.

(4)
關於他的申請，你看過了沒有？
<u>About</u> his application, have you seen it?

The prepositional phrase and the preposition in the first and second sentences should be ellipted in Chinese, thus producing more succinct and natural structures, that is, *Ta shiliusui jiu cong xiangxia daole Shanghai* (她十六歲就從鄉下到了上海, She, 16 years old, went from the countryside to Shanghai), and *Ta de shenqing, ni kanguole meiyou* (他的申請，你看過了沒有？His application, have you seen?).

2.1.2.5 Passive voice

In Chinese, traditionally, the passive voice was used only in unpleasant situations (Gunn 1991: 219–220; Hsu 1994: 177–179; Kubler 1985: 88–98; Tsao 1978: 47–48). However, through more frequent use of the syntactic marker *bei* (被), the passive voice is now free to refer to positive situations. According to Li and Luk (2017: 120), there are *bei zanshang* (被讚賞) (be praised), *bei timing wei daibiao* (被提名為代表) (be nominated as representative), and *bei xuan wei yiyuan* (被選為議員) (be elected as councilor). In the following two examples, the passive marker *bei* (被) is 'syntactically redundant', as it contravenes the conciseness that is characteristic of Chinese:

(5)
犯人已<u>被</u>押到。
The convict has been escorted here.

(6)
你們都該<u>被</u>罰。
You should all be punished.

2.1.2.6 Other types of syntactic change

Due to the influence of indefinite articles in Western languages, the composition of *yi zhong* (一種) and *yi ge* (一個) as the 'numeral + classifier' NPs are also used excessively (Li and Luk 2017: 117; Peyraube 2000: 8; Tsai 1995: 244; Tsao 1978: 48–49). Tsao (1978: 49) exemplifies this category with non-count nouns such as *yi zhong jimo* (一種寂寞) (a kind of loneliness), *yi zhong fengdu* (一種風度) (a kind of graceful manner), and Li and Luk (2017: 118) cite plural nouns such as *yi ge renmin* (一個人民) (a 'people') and *yi ge qunzhong* (一個群衆) (a 'mass'). Scholars also note 'empty verbs' placed before verb phrases, for example, *jiayi* (加以), *yuyi* (予以), *jinxing* (進行), *geiyu* (給予), *zuochu* (作出) and *zuo* (作) (Gunn 1991: 188; Yu 1979: 3). In analysing the phrase *zuochu jueding* (作出決定) (make a decision), Yu Kwang-Chung remarks that this kind of empty verb construction, composed of the empty verb *zuochu* (作出) (make) and an abstract noun *jueding* (決定) (decision), is a weak expression because *jueding* (決定) (decision) can stand on its own as an active verb meaning 'to decide' (Yu 1979: 3). Tsai (1995) also discusses the excessive appearance of nouns in Chinese.

2.2 Europeanisation of legal Chinese

In the government efforts to create bilingual legislation in the decade before 1997, the Chinese version of the Laws of Hong Kong, which carries equal legal force, was essentially prepared through translation from the English legislation. There is a general belief among translators that legal translation should remain faithful to the original, and so language is sacrificed for legal meaning or legal effects (Šarčević 1997: 71; Wagner 2003: 177). Sin King-kui, one of the participating professors in the bilingual law translation project, emphasises the importance of accuracy versus fluency thus: 'In translating the laws of Hong Kong, the translation team did encounter cases where the English text was capable of being rendered accurately in clear, fluent Chinese, but where both aims were in conflict, accuracy prevailed over easy reading'.

Therefore, the Chinese version naturally carries with it all the issues typical of the so-called 'translationese' style, that is, translated text that has been so influenced by the grammar of the source that it contains awkward and unnatural expressions that clearly identify it as a translation. The current state of affairs is that most Chinese in Hong Kong, including lawyers, legislators and members of the public, are dissatisfied with the terminology and syntax of the Chinese version of the Laws of Hong Kong. Two places where these issues commonly arise will now be discussed: legislation and legal documents, and some suggestions towards resolving the related problems will be offered.

2.2.1 Legislation

2.2.1.1 Lexicon

Following the Chinese language's century-long trend of borrowing, the legal Chinese created in Hong Kong has also imported many new terms through translation. Terminology is the aspect of language that is most likely to be influenced by contact with another language (Zdenka 1967: 613). Poon (2002: 78–84) summarises the four methods used by the LDD to create new Chinese legal terminology during the bilingual translation project before 1997. They are (i) literal translation, e.g. 'common assault' as *putong xiji* (普通襲擊); (ii) explaining the

30 *Challenges in legal translation*

intended meaning, e.g. 'slander' as *duanzan xingshi feibang* (短暫形式誹謗) (temporary form defamation) or 'libel' as *yongjiu xingshi feibang* (永久形式誹謗), (permanent form defamation); (iii) coining new words and terms with new meanings based on existing morphemes, e.g. 'aircraft' as *hangkongqi* (航空器) (aero instrument) to refer to any kind of machine, instead of the frequently-used translation *feiji* (飛機) (flying machine); and (iv) borrowing from similar legal terms in Mainland China and Taiwan, e.g. 'indecent assault' as *weixie qinfan* (猥褻侵犯), instead of *feili* (非禮) (no manners), a compound word originating from the Classic *Lunyu*《論語》(*The Analects*) of Confucius.

This discussion will further illustrate (ii)–(iv) of these four methods, as they were used in drafting the recent Companies Ordinance (Cap. 622) (*Gongsi Tiaoli*《公司條例》(第622章)). The second of these methods (explaining the intended meaning) is often employed to translate terms with underlying common law culture or tradition, which cannot be delivered by a literal translation. Consider this example:

(7)
Company may have <u>common seal</u> etc. (Section 124, Companies Ordinance (Cap. 622))
公司可備有<u>法團印章</u>等。(《公司條例》(第622章) 第124條)

'Common seal' is translated as *fatuan yinzhang* (法團印章), adding the meaning of 'body corporate' to the Chinese term to indicate the property of a common seal; that is, that the common seal shall be owned and used by a body corporate.

For method (iii) (coinage of words and terms based on existing morphemes), the following example shows that the Chinese version of the term conveys the legal meaning using a natural compounding of two morphemes.

(8)
Registrar must <u>keep</u> records of companies. (Section 27, Companies Ordinance (Cap. 622))
處長須<u>備存</u>關於公司的紀錄。(《公司條例》(第622章) 第27條)

Beicun (備存) (prepare and save), with the meaning of *zhunbei* (準備) (prepare) and *baocun* (保存) (save), is a natural and logical compound. It is derived from two existing similar Chinese words that normally combine with the same object (*an*), *bei* (備) in *bei'an* (備案) (prepare record) and *cun* (存) in *cun'an* (存案) (save record). According to Section 28 of the Companies Ordinance (Cap. 622), *bei* (備) indicates a purpose of keeping companies' records to be retrieved and inspected later. Thus, *beicun* (備存) (prepare and save) is used instead of the daily-use compound *baocun* (保存) (save).

However, not all coinages are plain and natural. To precisely deliver the legal concept in common law, which is an important goal of the underlying translation policy, translated Chinese legal terms may give a specified meaning to the ordinary word. In the example from Section 113 of the Companies Ordinance

(Cap. 622) shown next, the meaning of a term in the Chinese version is qualified to express the legal concept behind the English term.

(9)
The body corporate is a member of the company as a trustee, and the holding company or any of its subsidiaries is not <u>beneficially interested</u> under the trust. (Section 113 (2)(b), Companies Ordinance (Cap. 622))
該法人團體是以受託人身分作為該公司的成員，而有關控權公司或其任何附屬公司並無根據有關信託享有實益權益。(《公司條例》(第622章)第113(2)(b)條)

'Beneficial interest' is translated as *shiyi quanyi* (實益權益) (real beneficial interest) instead of the literal translation *liyi quanyi* (利益權益) (beneficial interest) in order to differentiate it from the concept of 'legal interest'. According to Section 2 of the New Territories Land Exchange Entitlements (Redemption) Ordinance (Cap. 495), 'legal ownership' (*falü shang de yongyouquan* 法律上的擁有權) means legal ownership of a land exchange entitlement, which is distinct from 'beneficial ownership' of the land exchange entitlement. Thus, it is a commonly-used method to delimit the scope of meaning in order to precisely express the legal concept.

Alongside borrowing similar terms from the Mainland and Taiwan, most of which are words used in everyday Chinese, the DOJ also commonly uses the method of giving legal meanings to ordinary words. The advantage of this approach is that it maintains the readability of ordinary words while expressing the legal meaning through interpretation. The use of the term *zhenzheng* (真誠) (in good faith) from Section 162 of the Companies Ordinance (Cap. 622) is a typical example of this method.

(10)
Genuine purchaser (真正購買者), in relation to shares, means –
(a) a person (other than a person to whom a new certificate for the shares is issued under this Division) who purchases the shares <u>in good faith</u> for value and without notice of any defect in the title of the seller; or . . . (Section 162, Companies Ordinance (Cap. 622))
真正購買者 (genuine purchaser) 就股份而言，指 –
(a) 在不知悉售賣人的所有權欠妥的情況下，<u>真誠地</u>付出價值購買該等股份的人(但屬該等股份的新股份證明書根據本分部發出的對象的人除外)；或 ... (《公司條例》(第622章) 第162條)

'In good faith', an expression commonly used in legal texts, contains the legal meaning of 'fair dealing'. The Chinese translation *zhencheng* (真誠) (true and sincere) is a frequently-used word in daily life. By assigning a legal meaning to *zhencheng* (真誠), a term was created that applies that meaning into the legal concept and culture of the common law.

Of all the methods illustrated, it is the new coinages that have attracted the most antipathy, the ones in which the DOJ have utilised the flexibility of the Chinese language to form new terminologies by compounding morphemes. Examples include *guanyou* (管有) (possession) formed by combining *guanli* (管理) (manage) and *yongyou* (擁有) (own), *zhuanyi* (轉易) (conveyance) from *zhuanrang* (轉讓) (transfer) and *jiaoyi* (交易) (transaction), *yaojian* (要件) (condition) from *zhongyao* (重要) (important) and *tiaojian* (條件) (condition), and *xinna* (信納) (satisfy) from a combination of *xiangxin* (相信) (believe) and *jiena* (接納) (accept) (Ng 2009: D05; Tso 2002: 70). Another important example is the Chinese translation of 'charge' *yaji* (押記) (pledge mark), in which the morpheme *ya* (押) does not normally collocate with *ji* (記), and for which the general translation used in daily life is *diya* (抵押) (Poon 2002: 80–81). The barrister and former legislator Margaret Ng (2009: D05), who opposes this method, commented in the Hong Kong Chinese newspaper *Ming Pao Daily* that:

> Before 1997, they rushed to create a Chinese version of Hong Kong law, intending to translate over 440 statutes into Chinese. They coined new words when they couldn't find existing terms. Those experts created *xinna*, thinking that 'satisfy' conveys the legal meanings of believing and accepting. . . . At present, legal terminology has already passed into daily usage in Hong Kong, so poisoning legal Chinese is also poisoning everyday Chinese.
>
> (English translation by the author)

Coinage does not appear to be a wise approach to translation, given that most people do not have good legal knowledge. The compounds so created hinder rather than facilitate people's comprehension of law. In this regard, Chan (2012) suggests a three-level approach. The first level is English terms that have an existing Chinese counterpart that carries half or more of the intended common law meaning; in these it is preferable not to coin a new term by compounding two legal concepts. For example, the ordinary Chinese translation of 'possession' *cangyou* (藏有) (hide and possess) is recommended for use in criminal law since the word *cang* (藏) (hide) implies the illegal retention of something. At the second level the existing Chinese translation carries less than half of the common law meaning; in these cases a new term is justifiable and the ideal method is to add a technical meaning to an existing Chinese term. An example of this is 'consideration', which in contract law means 'price' with the definition of 'something bargained for and received by a promisor from a promise that motivates one to engage in a legal act' (Garner 2009: 579). The meaning of the ordinary Chinese translation of 'to consider' is *kaolü* (考慮), but that is quite distinct from the English legal meaning. Thus adapting the term *daijia* (代價) (cost) is preferable, as it is a close, though not so natural, equivalent. At the third level the English presents totally new concept, principle or system; in these instances when there is no suitable domestic candidate, a brand-new coinage is acceptable. The term 'equity', for example, is a new common law concept in Chinese. The novel Chinese semantic translation *hangpingfa* (衡平法)

(the law of balance and fairness) adequately expresses the core English meaning in simple language, that is, 'the body of principles constituting what is fair and right' (Garner 2009: 619). For another new concept, 'estoppel', which means 'stop' in common law (an idiomatic expression), the four-word structure *burong fanhui* (不容反悔) (no allowance for going back on a promise) was found and was ideal.

In contrast to Margaret Ng's view, Tse (1997: 136) holds a 'developmental' view of the new coinages in Chinese: 'When the Chinese term is first introduced, it will not make sense to many people. It takes time and frequent use to develop the representational link. . . . The rest is basically about currency and popularity'. After two decades of use, some new Chinese coinages in Hong Kong, have obviously taken root, although their meaning may not yet be fully understood. For example, *guanyou* (管有) (possession) is now a familiar word to use in the everyday life of Hong Kong. A search by the author using the Google search engine on 17 August 2018 produced 12 results, of which six appeared in the Hong Kong media, in both print and audio forms. Further study is needed to investigate whether users understand its legal meaning, that is, *guanli* (管理) (manage) and *yongyou* (擁有) (own). Poon (2010: 83) holds a similar opinion in her endorsement of 'the consistent use of standardized Chinese terms in courts and their ease of use by general users', so semantic equivalence of a term is not attained 'through a literal translation of an English term'; rather 'how a term is defined in both statute law and case law must also be taken into consideration'.

To educate Hong Kong people in legal knowledge, Poon (2010: 93) proposes a three-step method for creating a bilingual legal dictionary:

> The first step requires a lexicographer to select the most representative cases that best convey the meaning of a legal term, and then summarize and translate the brief facts of the cases as well as the *ratio decidendi* into Chinese. The next step is to find out the definition of a legal term from statute and authorities. . . . Finally, a lexicographer has to render the terminology according to the meaning assigned by statute and case law, a translation that could more accurately reflect the legal meaning.

Therefore, ongoing lexicographical work is vital to refinement of the translated legal terminology as its definitions change.

All of the current translated terms adopted by the DOJ based on the bilingual legislation can be found in their two publications, namely three volumes of *English-Chinese Glossary of Legal Terms* (*Yinghan Falü Cihui* 《英漢法律詞彙》 (4th Ed.), 2004), and the *Chinese-English Glossary of Legal Terms* (*Hanying Falü Cihui*, 《漢英法律詞彙》, 1999). According to the introduction to these publications by the DOJ, the former has 32,000 entries (volumes 1–2) and lists of English-Chinese short titles and citations, serial numbers and names of government organisations (volume 3), and the latter has 11,500 entries (www.doj.gov.hk/sc/public/pub20030007.html). The contents of these books can be accessed on the

Hong Kong e-Legislation 《電子版香港法例》 website of the DOJ (www.elegislation.gov.hk/glossary/chi (Chinese-English glossary) and www.elegislation.gov.hk/glossary/en (English-Chinese glossary)).[1] These free materials are useful for legal practice, legal translation and academic research and teaching in Hong Kong and in the Chinese regions.

The next subsection will discuss the Europeanised syntax of legislation.

2.2.1.2 Syntax

We have discussed previously how, for the past 100 or so years, Chinese has been absorbing various linguistic features of the English language, mainly through translation. Examples of these features have included overuse of affixation, pre-nominal modifiers, passive voice and conjunctions in a language that is otherwise known for its brevity and conciseness. Another aspect of that influence has emerged: shifting the structures of the Chinese sentences. When translating, one unavoidably imitates and transfers the structures of the source language into the target language. Tsai (1995: 242) notes, 'The source language of a translation seems reluctant to make its exit; it prefers to seek reincarnation in the target language. If it is English, it will prevail upon the translator to anglicize Chinese, if the target language is Chinese'. Traditionally, translators of legal statutes have also adopted the literal and faithful approach, thus transferring foreign syntactic features as well as lexical ones to the target language. Chan (2007: 27–38), in analysing the 62 sections of the Chinese version of the Sale of Goods Ordinance (Cap. 26) (《貨品售賣條例》(第26章)), describes a number of Europeanised features. These are discussed in the following examples (i)–(vi), along with various suggestions to improve the lengthy and complicated sentence structures.

(I) *HUO* (或) (OR) . . . *HUO* (或) (OR)

(11)

In this section, "necessaries" (必需品) means goods suitable to the condition in life of <u>such infant or minor or other person</u>, and to his actual requirements at the time of the sale and delivery. (Section 4(2), Sale of Goods Ordinance (Cap. 26))

在本條中，"必需品" (necessaries) 指適合<u>幼年人或未成年人或其他人士</u>的生活狀況，且在售賣和交付時是適合其實際需要的貨品。(《貨品售賣條例》(第26章) 第4(2)條)

The pattern in the Chinese version, with the three noun phrases linked with the conjunctions *huo* (或) (or), is an exact copy of that of the English version. It is a common feature in legal English to make *conjoined phrases* with *and* and *or*, with the property of recursion leading to 'the possibilities of creating tremendously long phrases and sentences' (Tiersma 1999: 62).

(II) PREPOSITIONS AND PREPOSITIONAL PHRASES

In the Chinese version of Cap 26, there is frequent use of prepositional phrases borrowed from the English original texts. Consider this example:

(12)
there is an implied condition that the bulk shall correspond with the sample <u>in quality</u> (Section 17(2)(a), Sale of Goods Ordinance (Cap. 26))
整批貨品須<u>在品質上</u>與樣本相符；(《貨品售賣條例》(第26章) 第17(2) (a)條)

It is suggested that the prepositional phrase *zai pinzhi shang* (在品質上), which corresponds to 'in quality', be eliminated and the sentence rewritten in the more concise form *zhengpi <u>huopin pinzhi</u> xu yu yangben xiangfu* (整批<u>貨品品質</u>須與樣本相符), which attaches the head word *pinzhi* (品質) (quality) to the subject *huopin* (貨品) (goods). There are many other instances of prepositional phrases in the Ordinance: *zai maifang zantong xia* (在買方贊同下) (with the assent of the seller) (Section 20 Rule 5), *zai gaideng huopin de yongyouren tongyi xia* (在該等貨品的擁有人同意下) (with the consent of the owner) (Section 27(2)), *zai . . . yaoqiu xia* (在 . . . 要求下) (on request) (Section 36(2)), and *zai yixia qingkuang xia* (在以下情況下) (in the following cases) (Section 43(1)). Also, *jie* (藉) has become the standard translation of the English preposition 'by'. Examples are *jie qude dui huopin de shiji guanyou* (<u>藉</u>取得對貨品的實際管有) (<u>by</u> taking actual possession of the goods (Section 48(1)), *jie mingding de xieyi, huo jie shuangfang jiaoyi guocheng, huo jie guanli* (<u>藉</u>明訂的協議，或<u>藉</u>雙方交易過程，或<u>藉</u>慣例) (<u>by</u> express agreement, or <u>by</u> the course of dealing between the parties, or <u>by</u> usage) (Section 57(1)).

(III) UNDERPUNCTUATION

Underpunctuation is common practice in the legal genre (Duff 1995: 1109). The following two examples are both more than 40 characters in length and contain no punctuation. Each example is followed by a version with suggested punctuation marks (in parentheses) for easier comprehension.

(13a)
Capacity to buy and sell is regulated by the general law concerning capacity to contract, and to transfer and acquire property: (Section 4(1), Sale of Goods Ordinance (Cap. 26))

(13b)
買賣的行為能力受與訂立合約的行為能力及轉讓和取得產權的行為能力有關的一般法律規管：(《貨品售賣條例》(第26章) 第4(1)條)

(13c)
買賣的行為能力 [,] 受與訂立合約的行為能力及轉讓和取得產權的行為能力有關的一般法律規管：(《貨品售賣條例》(第26章) 第4(1)條)

(14a)

The unpaid seller of goods loses his lien or right of retention thereon –
(a) when he delivers the goods to a carrier or other bailee for the purpose of transmission to the buyer, without reserving the right of disposal of the goods; ...
(Section 45(1), Sale of Goods Ordinance (Cap. 26))

(14b)

未獲付款的賣方在以下情況下喪失其對貨品的留置權或保留權 —
(a) 他將貨品交付承運人或其他受寄人以轉交買方而並無保留對貨品的處置權利；...
(《貨品售賣條例》(第26章) 第45(1) 條)

(14c)

未獲付款的賣方在以下情況下[,] 喪失其對貨品的留置權或保留權 —
(a) 他將貨品交付承運人或其他受寄人以轉交買方[,]而並無保留對貨品的處置權利；...
(《貨品售賣條例》(第26章) 第45(1) 條)

In Example 13, an 'expletive comma' can be inserted after the subject *maimai de xingwei nengli* (買賣的行為能力) (capacity to buy and sell). In Example 14, commas can be inserted after the prepositional phrase *zai yixia qingkuang xia* (在以下情況下) (under the circumstance) and *yi zhuanjiao maifang* (以轉交買方) (for the purpose of transmission to the buyer).

(IV) 'EMPTY VERB' CONSTRUCTION

(15)

Unless otherwise agreed, the goods remain at the seller's risk until the property therein is transferred to the buyer, but when the property therein is transferred to the buyer the goods are at the buyer's risk, whether <u>delivery has been made</u> or not ... (Section 22, Sale of Goods Ordinance (Cap. 26))

除另有議定外，貨品的風險由賣方承擔，直至貨品的產權轉讓給買方為止，但貨品的產權一旦轉讓給買方，則不論有否<u>作出交付</u>，貨品的風險由買方承擔 ... (第26章《貨品售賣條例》第22條)

This is an empty verb construction *zuochu jiaofu* (作出交付), composed of the empty verb *zuochu* (作出) (make) and an abstract noun *jiaofu* (交付) (delivery, deliver), imitating the original 'delivery has been made'. There are other examples in the Ordinance: *zuochu guzhi* (作出估值) (make the valuation) (Section (11)(2)), *zuochu panjue* (作出判決) (make a judgment) (Section 54), and *zuochu gaizhong chuli* (作出該種處理) (such thing be done) (Section 20 Rule 2). For another empty verb *yuyi* (予以), there are *yuyi liding* (予以釐定) (may be determined), *yuyi queding* (予以確定) (must be ascertained) (Section 18 Heading, Sections 52(3) and 53(3)) and *yuyi fouding huo biangeng* (予以否定或變更) (be negated or varied) (Section 57(1)). In the examples *zuochu mouzhong chuli* (作出某種處理) (to do something) (Section 20 Rule 2) and *bu jiayi fouding* (不加以否定) (does not negate) (Section 57 Part VI (2)), the structure of empty verbs is formed without the influence of English.

(V) *SHI . . . DE* (是 . . . 的)/*WEI . . . DE* (為 . . . 的) CONSTRUCTION

As noted, the frequent use of the copular verb *shi* (是) (to be) to connect sentences is recognised as a Europeanised feature of Modern Written Chinese, resulting in a descriptive or judgmental sentence (Wang 1984: 447–449). There are also the 'discontinuous' constructions of *shi . . . de* (是 . . . 的) and *wei . . . de* (為 . . . 的) (to describe or opine on something), where *wei* (為) is a classical word serving as a copular verb. The construction is omissible in Chinese. Consider the following example:

(16)
A contract of sale <u>may be</u> absolute or conditional. (Section 3(2), Sale of Goods Ordinance, Cap. 26)
售賣合約<u>可為</u>不附帶條件<u>的</u>，亦<u>可為</u>附帶條件<u>的</u>。(《貨品售賣條例》(第26章) 第3(2)條)

(17)
or that <u>it is unreasonable</u> for him to rely, on the seller's skill or judgment. (Section 16(3), Sale of Goods Ordinance (Cap. 26))
或顯示買方依靠賣方的技能或判斷<u>是不合理的</u>，則不在此限。(《貨品售賣條例》(第26章) 第16(3)條)

(VI) EXCESSIVE USE OF NOUNS

There are a number of abstract nouns formed with the suffix *xing* (性) in Cap. 26. For example, there are *shiyongxing* (適用性) that is equivalent to 'fit' (Section 2(5)(a)) and to 'fitness' (Sections 16(1) and 16(4)); and *youxiaoxing* (有效性) that is equivalent to 'validity' (Section 23(2)(b)). In addition, a number of Chinese verbs that are usually not used as nouns have been converted to nouns, for instance, the verb *shoumai* (售賣) (to sell) in *yi zong shoumai* (一宗售賣) (a sale) (e.g. Sections 3(3) and 14(1)(a)) and *yi zong huopin de shoumai* (一宗貨品的售賣) (a sale of goods) (Section 15(2)). Other examples are the verbs *zhuanshou* (轉售) (sub-sale) and *chuzhi* (處置) (disposition) (Section 37(6)), *bujiu* (補救) (remedies) (Section 42), *guanyou* (管有) (possession) (e.g. Sections 2(1), 14(1)(b), 27(2), 31(1), 31(3) and 43(1)). The conversion of these verbs into nouns is ungrammatical in the Chinese language.

Following are two prominent examples of Europeanised structures in other Hong Kong ordinances. First, Chan (2012) provides an example of underpunctuation from the Copyright Ordinance (Cap. 83) (*Banquan Tiaoli* 《版權條例》(第83章)). In the following section, commas included in the English text are not added to the Chinese text, causing enormous difficulty to Chinese readers:

(18a)
A body designated under subsection (3) may, <u>for the purpose of providing people who are deaf or hard of hearing, or physically or mentally handicapped in other ways, with copies which are sub-titled or otherwise modified for their special needs,</u> make copies of television broadcasts or cable programmes and

issue and make available copies to the public, without infringing any copyright in the broadcasts or cable programmes or works included in them. (Section 83(1), Copyright Ordinance (Cap. 83))

(18b)
<u>為了將附有字幕或在其他方面經變通以切合失聰或聽覺有問題的人或身體上或精神上有其他方面殘障的人的特殊需要的電視廣播或有線傳播節目的複製品提供予該等人士</u>，根據第(3)款而指定的任何機構均可製作該等複製品並向公眾發放及提供該等複製品，而不屬侵犯該等廣播或有線傳播節目或其所包括的作品的版權。(《版權條例》(第83章)第83(1)條)

The first Chinese clause containing the modified noun phrase *dianshi guangbo huo youxian chuanbo jiemu de fuzhipin* (電視廣播或有線傳播節目的複製品) (copies of television broadcasts or cable programmes) consists of 74 characters without a comma. For easier comprehension, two commas can be conveniently inserted at exactly the same position as in the English original, that is, after the two prepositional phrases, as follows:

(18c)
<u>為了將附有字幕或在其他方面經變通 [，] 以切合失聰或聽覺有問題的人 [，] 或身體上或精神上有其他方面殘障的人的特殊需要的電視廣播或有線傳播節目的複製品提供予該等人士</u>，根據第(3)款而指定的任何機構均可製作該等複製品並向公眾發放及提供該等複製品，而不屬侵犯該等廣播或有線傳播節目或其所包括的作品的版權。(《版權條例》(第83章)第83(1)條)

Second, Leung (2015: 7–8) exemplifies the copying of English sentence structures into Chinese with a section of the Sexual Offences Ordinance, that results in 'absurd Chinese'.

(19)
(4) It is hereby declared that if at a trial for a rape offence the jury has to consider whether a man believed that a woman was consenting to sexual intercourse, the presence or absence of reasonable grounds for such a belief is a matter to which the jury is to have regard, in conjunction with any other relevant matters, in considering whether he so believed. (Added 25 of 1978 s.3)
現予聲明，在強姦罪行的審訊中，陪審團如須考慮一名男子是否相信一名女子同意性交，<u>則在考慮此事時</u>，除須顧及其他有關事項，亦須顧及該名男子是否有合理理由相信該名女子同意性交。（由1978年第25號第3條增補）

Leung states that the sentence is 'anglicized' in that it is 'rendered into Chinese in the exact order of the English sentence structure', with the addition of 'but when considering this matter' (則在考慮此事時) which has a contrastive meaning to the second clause, and in which the subject of *cishi* (此事) is ambiguous. Such an addition also relates to the repetition habit and excessive use of grammatical markers discussed earlier.

2.2.2 Judgments

In 1995, the first translated Chinese judgment appeared (i.e. 孫爾娖 訴 盧靜及另二人 [1996] 1 HKC 1, with English translation *Sun Er-jo v Lo Ching and Others* [1996] 1 HKC 1)). In their analysis of the Chinese language of judgments, Wong and Sin (2002) note that based on the 'limited number' of texts since 1995, the improper use includes the Europeanised structure, the Cantonese lexicon, the ungrammatical structures and the collocation errors. Consider the following Example 20a of Europeanised structure in Chinese taken from this first judgment, which is revised with the splitting technique in Example 20b (Wong and Sin 2002: 198):

(20a)
該傳統觀念最近亦受英國上訴法庭在一九九三年每週法律年報第一冊第一千三百六十一頁之些利地方議會對比道路住屋有限公司之案例獲得重新確認。(*Surrey County Council v Bredero Homes Ltd* (1993) I, W.L.R.1361)
This traditional concept has recently been reaffirmed in *Surrey County Council v Bredero Homes Ltd.* [1993] 1 WLR 1361.

(20b)
最近英國上訴法庭在一案例中重新確認傳統觀念。該案例見一九九三年每週法律年報第一冊第一千三百六十一頁，些利地方議會對比道路住屋有限公司案。
This traditional concept has recently been reaffirmed in a case. The case is *Surrey County Council v Bredero Homes Ltd.* [1993] 1 WLR 1361.

In advocating plain language use in translating judgments, Poon (2006: 224–225) cites the following sentence to illustrate the distinction between translation in the Europeanised style and that in natural Chinese.

(21a)
I am also satisfied that the Judge [Sears, J.] was in error in ordering that damages should be payable by the Hong Kong Government for the breach of the promise it had allegedly made.

(21b)
本席亦信納施偉文法官命令香港政府須為違反其被指稱的承諾而作出損害賠償的判決實屬錯誤。

The Chinese translation imitates the subordination structure in the English source version, that is, placing the long modifier *Shi Weiwen Faguan mingling Xianggang Zhengfu xu wei weifan qi bei zhicheng de chengnuo er zuochu sunhai peichang* (施偉文法官命令香港政府須為違反其被指稱的承諾而作出損害賠償) and the subordinating particle *de* (的) before *panjue* (判決). This is a long attribute embedded in a long sentence *Benxi yi xinna . . . shishu cuowu* (本席亦信納 . . .

實屬錯誤). In revising the sentence, Poon adopts the 'paratactic structure' of the Chinese language, in which the long sentence is broken down into two clauses and organised in chronological order. This shows that the plain language principle includes the principle of conforming to the target language habits and customs.

(21c)
施偉文法官命令香港政府須為違反其被指稱的承諾而作出損害賠償，本席信納此項的判決實屬錯誤。

Despite the call, Poon (2006: 220) maintains that literal translation is the main method in legal translation, which is defined as: 'In translating legal texts, it is desirable to render, in addition to the contextual meaning, the grammatical and stylistic pattern of the source text as closely as the semantic and syntactic structure of the target language allow'. For example, 'The court has to consider the natural and ordinary meaning which the words convey to ordinary reasonable persons' can be literally translated as *Fating xu kaolü, youguan yanci de ziran ji yiban hanyi dui yiban heli de ren suo chuanda de yisi* (法庭須考慮，有關言詞的自然及一般含義對一般合理的人所傳達的意思) (*Charles Sin Cho Chiu v Tin Tin Publication Development Ltd. And Another* [2001] HKCFI 1019; HCA 6662/1997 (3 December 2001)). Chapter 5 will discuss the translation of English judgments with regard to future research directions.

2.2.3 Legal documents

Apart from the legislative and judicial writings, other types of legal texts also display the same Europeanised or Westernised features in their Chinese versions, primarily in their complicated sentence structures with insufficient punctuation and frequent use of pronouns and conjunctions. Consider the following clauses from a Hong Kong bilingual tenancy agreement:[2]

(22)
Preamble
The Landlord shall let and the Tenant shall take the Premises for the Term and at the Rent as more particularly described in Schedule I and both parties agree to observe and perform the terms and conditions as follow:-
業主及租客雙方以詳列於附表一的租期及租金分別租出及租入詳列於附表一的物業，並同意遵守及履行下列條款：-

In this example, the first long sentence is formed by the use of two instances of *ji* (及) (and) that connect the two nouns *zuqi* (租期) (term) and *zujin* (租金) (rent) and the two verbs *zuchu* (租出) (let) and *zuru* (租入) (take), and the use of two pre-nominal modifiers linked to the head noun by the subordinating particle *de* (的), that is, two instances of *xianglie yu fubiao yi de* (詳列於附表一的) (as more particularly described in Schedule I).

(23)
Clause 1
The Tenant shall pay to the Landlord the Rent in advance on the first day of each and every calendar month during the Term. If the Tenant shall fail to pay the Rent within 7 days from the due date, the Landlord shall have right to institute appropriate action to recover the Rent and <u>all costs, expenses and other outgoings so incurred by the Landlord in relation to such action shall be a debt owed by the Tenant to the Landlord</u> and shall be recoverable in full by the Landlord.

租客須在租期內每個月份第一天上期繳付指定的租金予業主。倘租客於應繳租金之日的七天內仍未清付該租金，則業主有權採取適當行動追討租客所欠的租金<u>而由此而引起的一切費用及開支將構成租客所欠業主的債項</u>，業主將有權向租客一併追討所欠款項全數。

In this example, there is the unnecessary addition of the conjunction *ze* (則) (but) in the second clause, where there is no contrastive meaning. There are two methods to enhance the readability: insert a comma before the clause *er youci er yinqi de yiqie feiyong ji kaizhi jiang goucheng zuke suo qian yezhu de zhaixiang* (而由此而引起的一切費用及開支將構成租客所欠業主的債項) (all costs, expenses and other outgoings so incurred by the Landlord in relation to such action shall be a debt owed by the Tenant to the Landlord), or delete the conjunction *er* (而) and add a full stop to start this clause.

(24)
Clause 6
The Tenant shall during the Term keep the interior of the Premises in good and tenantable repair and condition (fair wear and tear and damage caused by inherent defects excepted) and shall deliver up vacant possession of the Premises in the same repair and condition on the expiration or sooner determination of this Agreement.

租客須在租約期內保持物業內部的維修狀態良好(自然損耗及因固有的缺陷所產生的損壞除外)並須於租約期滿或終止時將物業在同樣維修狀態下交吉交回業主。

This is a typical example of an underpunctuated legal sentence. The original English clause is 54 words long without a comma, and is rendered into a 70-word long Chinese sentence also without a comma. To improve the readability, a comma can be easily inserted before the second clause of this sentence starting with the conjunction *bing* (並) (and).

2.2.4 Legal translation textbook

In a book on teaching legal translation in Hong Kong, some useful translation techniques in English-Chinese legal translation are taught (Wang 2006: 88–100).

Yet even there many Europeanised features remain in the example sentences he has chosen. Consider the following:

(25a)

There is a recognized distinction between general and regional rules of international law, that is to say between, <u>on the one hand</u>, rules which, practically speaking, are of universal application, and, <u>on the other hand</u>, rules which have developed in a particular region of the world as between the states there located, without becoming rules of a universal character.

(25b)

在國際法的一般性規則和地區性規則之間存在一種公認的差別；也就是說，一般性規則實際上具有普遍適用性，<u>而</u>地區性規則是在位於世界的某個特定地區內的國家之間發展起來的，因此不具有普遍適用性特點。

This sentence is intended to illustrate the 'omission' technique in using the Chinese conjunction *er* (而) (and, but) to refer to the contrastive meaning of 'on the one hand' and 'on the other hand' in the source text. Nevertheless, there are a number of Europeanised grammatical markers and structures. The first is the suffix *xing* (性) (-tion, -ty, -ness) as used in *yibanxing guize* (一般性規則) (general rules), *diquxing guize* (地區性規則) (regional rules) and *pubian shiyongxing* (普遍適用性) (universal application). The second is *yi zhong* (一種), a 'numeral + classifier' NP, as in *yi zhong gongren de chabie* (一種公認的差別) (a recognised distinction). A third feature is use of the 'discontinuous structure' *shi . . . de* (是 . . . 的) to function as a descriptive or judgment sentence in Chinese, as in *shi zai weiyu shijie de mouge teding diqu nei de guojia zhijian fazhan qilai de* (是在位於世界的某個特定地區內的國家之間發展起來的) (which have developed in a particular region of the world as between the states located there).

The following revised translation demonstrates how these markers can be removed:

(25c)

在國際法之<u>一般規則</u>和<u>地區規則</u>間，有<u>一</u>公認之差別。即是，一般規則能實際<u>用於全球各國</u>，而<u>地區規則</u>只發展於世界某地區國家之間，不能<u>廣泛使用</u>。

In the following example Wang aims to illustrate the repetition method commonly used in legal translation. However, the Chinese translation contains redundancies with three counts of *dongshihui renwei shidangde* (董事會認為適當的) (as deemed appropriate by the Board of Directors), and is too long with no punctuation.

(26a)

The Company shall purchase other insurance policies at such time and in such amounts and with such terms <u>as deemed appropriate by the Board of Directors</u>.

(26b)
合作公司應在董事會認為適當的時候以董事會認為適當的金額及董事會認為適當的條款購買其他保單。

This sentence can be made more concise by removing repetition and adding punctuation as follows:

(26c)
合作公司應按董事會認為適當的時間、金額及條款，購買其他保單。

In the following example, Wang intended to offer instruction in shifting the negative meaning from the subject in English to the verb in Chinese. Yet the resultant sentence is also quite long, contains redundant repetition of *youguan ben xieyi de* (有關本協議的) (regarding this agreement) and has no punctuation. The second and third counts of 'any' are exactly reproduced as *renhe* (任何).

(27a)
No party shall issue or make any public announcement or disclose any information regarding this agreement.

(27b)
任何一方均不得發出或作出有關本協議的任何公告或披露有關本協議的任何資料。

The sentence is made more succinct with the use of only one instance of *jiu ben xieyi de* (就本協議的) (regarding this agreement), and addition of a comma.

(27c)
任何一方均不得就本協議發出或作出任何公告，或披露任何資料。

The further omission of two counts of *renhe* (任何) (any) will result in an even more succinct sentence with the exact same meaning.

(27d)
任何一方均不得就本協議發出或作出公告，或披露資料。

The following example sentence is mainly intended to illustrate the restructuring technique that is frequently used in English-Chinese translation. First, the English sentence, which is written in passive voice, is transformed into active voice in the Chinese translation. Second, the word order is rearranged, with the subordinate clause placed before the main clause. However, the sentence still retains Westernised features, namely, the passive marker *bei* (被) and the empty verb construction *zuochu peichang* (作出賠償) (make compensation). The expressions *falü shang* (法律上) (legal) and *shishi shang* (事實上) (factual) can be considered 'beneficial Europeanisation'.

44 *Challenges in legal translation*

(28a)

This Agreement may be immediately terminated by one of the Parties, without compensation from either side, in case of bankruptcy, winding up, or legal or factual, direct or indirect, taking over by a third party of the other party.

(28b)

如果一方破產、結束營業或在法律上或事實上直接或間接地被第三方所接管，另一方可立即終止本協議，任何一方無須就此作出賠償。

The sentence can be further improved by replacing the marker *bei* (被) with *wei* (為), and removing the empty verb *zuochu* (作出) (make).

(28c)

如果一方破產、結業或在法律或事實上直接或間接地為第三方所接管，另一方可立即終止本協議，任何一方毋須賠償。

Having discussed the Europeanised Chinese resulting from translation in various legal texts in Hong Kong, the chapter will conclude with a discussion of the responses and recommendations regarding this tendency.

2.2.5 *Responses from different sectors*

As briefly mentioned earlier, the early development of legal bilingualism for legislation has elicited feedback, suggestions and criticism from many fronts in Hong Kong, including lawyers, legislators and scholars. Most of the issues relate to the philosophy behind and methods of legislative drafting that affect ease of the translation work into Chinese. Judgments, which to date remain mostly untranslated, also face the same issue of having convoluted structures.

Barrister and jurist Derry Wong expresses his disapproval of the drafting procedures for bilingual legislation thus (Wong 1997: 66):

> Bilingual legislation in Hong Kong originates in the Drafting Division of the Attorney-General's Chambers where monolingual anglophone drafting counsel, and occasionally bilingual sinophone drafting counsel, draft legislation in English. These are very often copied from statutes of other Common Law jurisdictions. Such drafts are then literally translated into Chinese by language translation officers who have had no legal training, and then reviewed by bilingual sinophone counsel. They are also reviewed by the Bilingual Legislative Advisory Committee, which consists of both lawyers and lay persons, some of whom are linguists, but who have no legal training.

He notes that the 'degree of literalism in the translation' involves a close pursuit of the English text 'nearly clause by clause, phrase by phrase and expression by expression', that renders the Chinese text unintelligible. Noting that the government has no plan to translate case law, he claims such treatment violates Article 22 of Hong Kong Bill of Rights Ordinance (Cap. 383) (*Xianggang Renquan Fa'an*

Tiaoli 《香港人權法案條例》(第 383 章)) that provides that all people are equal before the law, which 'shall prohibit any discrimination and guarantee to all persons equal and effective protection against discrimination on any ground such as race, colour, sex, language . . .'.

Traditionally, clarity is the main goal in drafting legislation. Bhatia (2010: 38) remarks, 'Legislative rules, as far as possible, should have clarity of expression'. However, there are difference voices from the legal profession in recent decades. In his opening speech for the Legal Year 2006, Philip Dykes, Chairman of the Hong Kong Bar Association, urged Hong Kong to learn from Singapore in using 'linguistic economy and clear syntax' for legal drafting, to overcome the widespread problems of underpunctuation and the embedded sentence structure in the English version of the Laws of Hong Kong (Dykes 2006: 3).

Legislators have also shown concern over the bilingual drafting policy. As a Legislative Council panel paper in 2009 shows, during the scrutiny of the Securities and Future Bill in 2000, the Bills Committee queried discrepancies between the English and Chinese parallel texts that could result in different interpretations. Up to 2009, in the meetings of special Financial Committee and the Panel on Administration of Justice and Legal Services, questions were raised over the quality of the law drafting. The DOJ replied that they would draft English law in plain language and improve the textual style, including reducing the number of cross-references and complex definitions. The simplified English text could assist the co-drafting of the Chinese law. An English language expert would also be recruited to review grammar and syntax in law drafting in order to enhance the language flow of legislation (Legislative Council Secretariat 2009: 2–3). In 2011, an outspoken legislator, Raymond Wong Yuk-man, criticised the Europeanised sentences and rigid collocation of words in the Chinese version of the Food and Safety Bill. He stressed that legal Chinese is crucial to Hong Kong's rule of law and urged the DOJ to set up a working group to enhance its standards (Wong 2011).

Law professor Zhao Yuhong (2000a: 23–24) suggested linguistic revisions to the Securities and Futures Bill that align with the development of the communicative approach in translation theories that has gone on elsewhere for decades. She proposed various Chinese law drafting techniques, most importantly in the parallel co-drafting process, where, she believed, English texts with long and complicated sentence structures should also be revised. Based on the beliefs that translation is a communicative act and legal translation should produce texts that are easily comprehensible to the general public, Zhao proposed the use of more punctuation and simple structures in the Chinese legislation. She remarked, 'Legislation can serve its function in prescribing social behaviour only when it is effectively communicated to the addressees, particularly the regulated community' (Zhao 2000b: 41).

Adding weight to her argument, legal translation scholar Emily Poon Wai-yee (2002: 99) also promoted plain language as the solution to these linguistic issues in Chinese legal texts. She urged that archaic English provisions be redrafted in plain English and with simpler sentence structures, in order to help translators understand and correctly render the texts into modern Chinese. In turn, the Chinese versions would be more easily understood by general readers. In her thesis, she also advocated for the use of plain language in the Chinese translations of judgments, and argued that more translated Chinese judgments would enable greater use of Chinese in court proceedings. She proposed adopting plain language in translating the 'facts' of a case in particular (Poon 2006: 196–237). Similarly, commenting on their translation of Hong Kong criminal cases, Luk and Hui (2003: xxiii–xxiv) contend that the goals of case translation include both accuracy and readability. A translated case, like a translated literary work, should use idiomatic Chinese phrases and rhetorical devices:

> Besides being as accurate as possible, the translated cases are also expected to be fluent and expressive, reading like idiomatic Chinese, in line with the functions and wide readership of this book. Thus, provided that the contexts and common law concepts allow, the translation text is rendered in local Chinese as far as possible.
>
> Guided by this principle, 'reasonable man', an important common law concept, is rendered as *mingli de ren* (明理的人) (a person who understands reason), not *heli de ren* (合理的人) (reasonable man) as adopted by the DOJ.
> (English translation by the author)

Once they were aware of these criticisms, the governmental law drafters were more aware of the production of Chinese and English laws that would be both accurate and stylish in line with the 'worldwide trend of plain legal language' (Law Drafting Division of Department of Justice 2001: 5). In Chinese law drafting, they try to develop skills such as the omission of redundant words, more careful choice of words and adding definitions. These stylistic differences are kept to a minimum of 1–2% of the provisions (Law Drafting Division of Department of Justice 2001: 3–4 and Annex). Most important of all, the Division recommended, an English text drafted in long and complicated sentence structure should be revised in the parallel drafting process (Zhao 2000a: 23–24). To achieve this, it was proposed to reduce the number of cross-references and complex definitions, and to recruit an English language expert to review grammar and syntax in law drafting (Legislative Council Secretariat 2009: 2–3). Since all these Chinese drafting skills are targeted towards the readability and acceptability of the Chinese text, they are motivated by the growing communicative function in translation achieved by the translator. Hatim and Mason (1997: 12) early on had urged attention to that when they remarked in their work *The Translator as Communicator*:

> Yet, it is this very quest for the successful exchange of meanings that is at the heart of what we pursue as professional or trainee translators, teachers or critics of translation. Typically, one might say of translators that they are constantly exchanging something, not only by engaging in a dialogue with a source text producer and a likely target text receiver, but also by brokering

a deal between the two parties to communicate across both linguistic and cultural boundaries.

The introduction of new Chinese drafting techniques such as word omission, careful diction and reducing cross-references are intentional efforts towards achieving a communicative text. Whether the translator's role in the creation of the Chinese version of legislation is assumed by a legal translator or a lawyer, the communicative value is the ideal that is being pursued in the current reform in simplifying the syntactic structure of legislation. The following chapters will expand on these early responses and new initiatives that have grown out of them.

Notes

1 The homepage of the bilingual website in three versions (English, traditional Chinese and simplified Chinese) states: 'Hong Kong e-Legislation (HKeL) is the official database of Hong Kong legislation. It provides free online access to current and past versions of consolidated legislation dating back to 30 June 1997 and PDF copies marked "verified copy" have official legal status. Different searching and viewing modes are available to facilitate access to law. The database is maintained by the Department of Justice'. This new website replaced the old website named Bilingual Legislation Information System (BLIS) (《雙語法例資料系統》) (www.legislation.gov.hk), which discontinued its service on 1 July 2018. According to a government press release, the HKeL, launched on February 2017, was enhanced with new functions, 'for example, the Chapter Number Index was enhanced so that users could conveniently download PDF copies of different chapters using the Index. A progress bar was also added to the "view legislation" page to show users the loading progress of a chapter' (www.info.gov.hk/gia/general/201805/25/P2018052500343.htm?fontSize=1).
2 The bilingual tenancy agreement has been used by the author as teaching material for more than five years. Currently, a very similar version is accessible on the website of the Student Housing and Residential Life Office, the Hong Kong University of Science and Technology (http://shrl.ust.hk/upload/files/tenancy_agreement_b.pdf).

English references

Bhatia, Vijay (2010). Legal Writing: Specificity: Specification in Legislative Writing: Accessibility, Transparency, Power and Control. In Coulthard, Malcolm and Johnson, Alison (Eds.), *The Routledge Handbook of Forensic Linguistics* (pp. 37–50). Abingdon, Oxon, and New York: Routledge.

Chan, Clara Ho-yan (2007). Translated Chinese as a Legal Language in Hong Kong Legislation. *Journal of Specialized Translation* 7: 25–41.

Chan, Clara Ho-yan (2012). Bridging the Gap Between Language and Law: Translational Issues in Creating Legal Chinese in Hong Kong. *Babel: International Journal of Translation* 58(2): 127–144.

Chen, Ping (1999). *Modern Chinese: History and Sociolinguistics*. Cambridge: Cambridge University Press.

Duff, Alan M. (1995). Undertranslation. In Chan, Sin-wai and Pollard, David E. (Eds.), *An Encyclopedia of Translation* (pp. 1108–1117). Hong Kong: The Chinese University Press.

Dykes, Philip (2006). Speech for Opening of the Legal Year 2006. *Hong Kong Bar Association* 1–5. Retrieved from: www.hkba.org/events-publication/speeches-articles.

Garner, Bryan A. (Ed.) (2009). *Black's Law Dictionary* (9th Ed.). St. Paul, MN: West.

Gunn, Edward (1991). *Rewriting Chinese: Style and Innovation in Twentieth-Century Chinese Prose*. Stanford: Stanford University Press.

Hatim, Basil and Mason, Ian (1997). *Discourse and the Translator*. London: Longman Group Limited.

Hsu, Jia-Ling (1994). Englishization and Language Change in Modern Chinese in Taiwan. *World Englishes 13*(2): 167–184.

Kachru, Braj B. (1994). Englishization and Contact Linguists. *World Englishes 13*(2): 135–154.

Kratochvil, Paul (1968). *The Chinese Language Today: Features of an Emerging Standard*. London: Hutchinson University Library.

Kubler, Cornelius C. (1985). *A Study of Europeanized Grammar in Modern Written Chinese*. Taipei: Student Book.

Law Drafting Division, Department of Justice (2001). Information Paper on Drafting Policy on Bilingual Legislation for LegCo Panel on Administration of Justice and Legal Services Meeting on 20 March 2001. *The Legislative Council Library, Hong Kong Special Administrative Region of the People's Republic of China* 1–5 + Annex. Retrieved from: http://sc.legco.gov.hk/sc/library.legco.gov.hk:1080/search*cht/X?SEARCH=m%3A%28drafting+policy+on+bilingual+legislation%29&searchscope=10&l=&m=&Da=&Db=&SORT=D.

Legislative Council Secretariat (2009). Background Brief for Panel on Administration of Justice and Legal Services Meeting on 15 December 2009. *The Legislative Council Library, Hong Kong Special Administrative Region of the People's Republic of China* 1–6 + Appendix. Retrieved from: http://sc.legco.gov.hk/sc/library.legco.gov.hk:1080/search*cht/Xdrafting+of+legislation&SORT=D/Xdrafting+of+legislation&SORT=D&extended=0&SBKEY=drafting%20of%20legislation/1%2C2%2C2%2CB/frameset&FF=Xdrafting+of+legislation&SORT=D&2%2C2%2C.

Leung, Ester Sin-man (2015). What Can a Bilingual Corpus Tell Us About the Translation and Interpretation of Rape Trials? *International Journal for the Semiotics of Law 28*(3): 469–483.

Li, Chi (1962). New Features in Chinese Grammatical Usage. *Studies in Chinese Communist Terminology 9*: 1–76.

Li, David C. S. and Luk, Zoe Pei-sui (2017). *Chinese-English Contrastive Grammar: An Introduction*. Hong Kong: Hong Kong University Press.

Liu, Lydia H. (1995). *Translingual Practice: Literature, National Culture, and Translated Modernity—China, 1900–1937*. Stanford: Stanford University Press.

Ma, Meng (1963). Recent Changes in the Chinese Language. *Journal of the Hong Kong Branch of the Royal Asiatic Society 3*: 51–59.

Norman, Jerry (1988). *Chinese*. Cambridge: Cambridge University Press.

Peyraube, Alain (2000). Westernization of the Chinese Grammar in the twentieth century: Myth or Reality? *Journal of Chinese Linguistics 28*(1): 1–25.

Poon, Emily Wai-yee (2002). The Pitfalls of Linguistic Equivalence: The Challenge for Legal Translation. *Target: International Journal of Translation Studies 14*(1): 75–106.

Poon, Emily Wai-yee (2006). *The Effectiveness of Plain Language in the Translation of Statutes and Judgments*. Doctoral Dissertation, The HKU Scholar Hub, The University of Hong Kong, Pokfulam, Hong Kong. Retrieved from: http://dx.doi.org/10.5353/th_b4501564.

Poon, Emily Wai-yee (2010). Strategies for Creating a Bilingual Legal Dictionary. *International Journal of Lexicography 23*(1): 83–103.
Šarčević, Susan (1997). *New Approach to Legal Translation*. The Hague: Kluwer Law International.
Tiersma, Peter M. (1999). *Legal Language*. Chicago: The University of Chicago Press.
Tsai, Frederick (1995). Europeanized Structure in English-Chinese Translation. In Chan, Sin-wai and Pollard, David E. (Eds.), *An Encyclopaedia of Translation: Chinese-English, English-Chinese* (pp. 242–248). Hong Kong: The Chinese University Press.
Tsao, Feng-Fu (1978). Anglicization of Chinese Morphology and Syntax in the Past Two Hundred Years. *Studies in English Literature and Linguistics* April: 41–54.
Tse, Alan Chung (1997). Conceptual Equivalence and Translation: Translating Common-Law Terms into Chinese. In Klaudy, Kinga and Kohn, János (Eds.), *Transferre Necesse Est: Proceedings of the Second International Conference on Current Trends in Studies of Translation and Interpreting, Budapest, 5–7 September, 1996* (pp. 134–139). Budapest: Scholastica.
Wagner, Anne (2003). Translation of the Language of the Common Law into Legal French: Myth or Reality. *International Journal for the Semiotics of Law 16*(2): 177–193.
Wong, Derry (1997). Securing a Bilingual Legal System for Hong Kong. *Asia Pacific Law Review 5*(2): 63–75.
Zdenka, Novontná (1967). Contribution to the Study of Loan Words and Hybrid Words in Modern Chinese. *Archiv Orientalni 35*: 613–648.
Zhao, Yuhong (2000a). Drafting Policy on Bilingual Legislation: Comments on the Hong Kong Securities and Futures Bill. *The Legislative Council Library, Hong Kong Special Administrative Region of the People's Republic of China* 1–25. Retrieved from: http://sc.legco.gov.hk/sc/library.legco.gov.hk:1080/search*cht/X?SEARCH=m%3A%28drafting+policy+on+bilingual+legislation%29&searchscope=10&l=&m=&Da=&Db=&SORT=D.
Zhao, Yuhong (2000b). Legal Legislation in the Legislative Genre. *Journal of Translation Studies 4*: 19–41.

Chinese references

Chou, Kuang-Ching 周光慶 and Liu, Wei 劉瑋 (1996). 《漢語與中國新文化啟蒙》 (*Chinese Language and the New Cultural Awakening of China*). Taipei: Tung-Ta Books Co.
Lee, Chi-ming 李志明 (1999). 〈香港政府公函文體要求的改變〉 (Changing Requirements of Hong Kong Government Correspondence) 《中國語文通訊》 (*Newsletter of Chinese Language*) *49*: 12–20.
Luk, Angelina 陸文慧 and Hui, Eleanor 許趣怡 (2003). 《雙語普通法：刑事案例摘錄》 (*Bilingual Common Law: Extracts from Criminal Cases*). Hong Kong: Sweet & Maxwell Asia.
Ng, Margaret Ngoi-yee 吳靄儀 (2009). 〈救救法律中文〉 (Please Save Legal Chinese). *Ming Pao Daily* D05, October 26.
Shi, Dingxu 石定栩 and Zhu, Zhiyu 朱志瑜 (2000). 〈英語與香港書面漢語〉 (English and Hong Kong Written Chinese). 《外語教學與研究》 (*Foreign Language Teaching and Research*) *32*(3): 200–206.
Tse, Yiu-kay 謝耀基 (1990). 《現代漢語歐法概論》 (*Outline of the Europeanised Modern Chinese*). Hong Kong: Kwong Ming Books.
Tse, Yiu-kay 謝耀基 (2001). 〈漢語語法歐化綜述〉 (Survey of the Europeanisation of Modern Chinese Grammar). 《語文研究》 (*Research on Chinese Language*) *1*: 17–22.

Tso, Wing-keung 曹永強 (2002). 〈法律英語結構〉 (The Structure of Legal English). In Luk Man-wai, Angelina 陸文慧 (Ed.), 《法律翻譯：從實踐出發》 (*Legal Translation in Practice*). Hong Kong: Chung Hwa Book Co.

Tung, Chiao 董橋 (2012). 〈公文救命〉 (Please Save Official Writing). In Tung, Chiao 董橋 《英華浮沉錄》(五) (*Swimming in the Seas of English and Chinese*) (pp. 234–237). Oxford: Oxford University Press.

Wang, Daogeng 王道庚 (2006). 《法律翻譯—理論與實踐》 (*Legal Translation: Theory and Practice*). Hong Kong: City University of Hong Kong.

Wang, Li 王力 (1984). 《王力文集》 (*Collected Essays of Wang Li*) (Vol. 1). Shandong: Shandong Education Press.

Wang, Li 王力 (1985). 《王力文集》 (*Collected Essays of Wang Li*) (Vol. 2). Shandong: Shandong Education Press.

Wang, Li 王力 (1990). 《王力文集》 (*Collected Essays of Wang Li*) (Vol. 11). Shandong: Shandong Education Press.

Wong, Pui-kwong 王培光 and Sin, King-kui 冼景炬 (2002). 〈香港中文判決書的語言問題〉 (Language Issues in Hong Kong Chinese Judgments). In Zhou, Qingsheng 周慶生, Wang, Jie 王潔 and Su, Jinzhi 蘇金智 (Eds.), 《語言與法律研究的新視野—語言與法律首屆學術研討會論文集》 (*New Perspectives in Studies of Language and Law: Proceedings of the First Conference on Language and Law*) (pp. 193–201). Beijing: Law Press.

Wong, Raymond Yuk-man 黃毓民 (2011). 〈法律中文亟待改進〉 (*Legal Chinese Has Great Room for Improvement*). Speech at Legislative Council, March 30. Retrieved from: www.yukman.hk/wp/works/record/1128.

Yu, Kwang-Chung 余光中 (1979). 〈從西而不化到西而化之〉 (On the Process of Westernisation). 《明報月刊》 (*Ming Pao Monthly*) *164*: 2–7.

Zhou, Zuoren 周作人 (1922). 〈國語改造的意見〉 (Comments on the Reform of the National Language). 《東方雜誌》 (*Eastern Miscellany*) *19*(17): 7–15.

3 Challenges in legal translation
A legal perspective

This chapter first provides a general illustration of the equivalence issue as it relates to legal terms, citing examples from English laws and laws from Hong Kong, the Mainland and Taiwan. This is followed by a discussion of the five categories of translated Chinese terminology in terms of their equivalence to the Western source terms. And last, there is an in-depth case study of translations of a single term in an international agreement on intellectual property law, which provides in the Chinese context the first step in applying a functional theory in assessing the equivalence of terms, a most complicated issue in legal translation.

3.1 'Equivalence' in Hong Kong bilingual legal terminology

In theory, due to the use of the same common law system, there is no equivalence issue between the English legal terms and their Chinese counterparts in Hong Kong. In contrast, such issues do exist between the Chinese terms used in Hong Kong and their counterparts from Mainland China and Taiwan. Consider the following examples of the term 'theft' from the Theft Act and its Chinese translation *daoqiezui* (盜竊罪) from Hong Kong's Theft Ordinance (Cap. 210) (*Daoqiezui Tiaoli*《盜竊罪條例》(第210章)):

(1)
English law:
A person is guilty of <u>theft</u> if he dishonestly appropriates property belonging to another with the intention of permanently depriving the other of it; and "thief" and "steal" shall be construed accordingly. (Section 1(1), Theft Act 1968)

(2)
Hong Kong bilingual law:
A person commits <u>theft</u> if he dishonestly appropriates property belonging to another with the intention of permanently depriving the other of it; and 'thief' (竊賊) and 'steal' (偷竊) shall be construed accordingly. (Section 2, Theft Ordinance (Cap. 210))

如任何人不誠實地挪佔屬於另一人的財產，意圖永久地剝奪該另一人的財產，即屬犯<u>盜竊罪</u>，而"竊賊" (thief) 及"偷竊" (steal) 亦須據此解釋。(《盜竊罪條例》(第210章)第2條)

To convict under the Theft Act 1968 in the UK, both *actus reas* (guilty act) and *mens rea* (guilty mind) must be proved. There are five elements under the Theft Act 1968, which correspond to those in the Theft Ordinance (Cap. 210) of the Laws of Hong Kong Law. For *actus reas*, they are 'appropriation', 'property' and 'belonging to another' in the UK law, which respectively correspond to *nuozhan* (挪佔), *caichan* (財產) and *shuyu lingyiren* (屬於另一人) in the Hong Kong law. In terms of *mens rea*, there is 'dishonestly' and 'with the intention of permanently depriving' in the UK law, which correspond to *bu chengshidi* (不誠實地) and *yitu yongjiude boduo* (意圖永久地剝奪). Containing the exact same five elements, the Chinese term *daoqiezui* (盜竊罪) in the Theft Ordinance (Cap. 210) of Hong Kong is therefore regarded as an *absolute equivalent* to the term 'theft' in the English common law.

On the other hand, the Mainland Chinese term *daoqiezui* (盜竊罪) has a different legal definition.

(3)
> 盜竊公私財物，數額較大的，或者多次盜竊、入戶盜竊、攜帶兇器盜竊、扒竊的，處三年以下有期徒刑、拘役或者管制，並處或者單處罰金；數額巨大或者有其他嚴重情節的，處三年以上十年以下有期徒刑，並處罰金；數額特別巨大或者有其他特別嚴重情節的，處十年以上有期徒刑或者無期徒刑，並處罰金或者沒收財產。（《中華人民共和國刑法》第264條）

> Whoever steals a relatively large amount of public or private property, commits thefts many times, commits a burglary or carries a lethal weapon to steal or pick pockets shall be sentenced to imprisonment of not more than 3 years, criminal detention or control and/or a fine; if the amount involved is huge or there is any other serious circumstance, shall be sentenced to imprisonment of not less than 3 years but not more than 10 years and a fine; or if the amount involved is especially huge or there is any other especially serious circumstance, shall be sentenced to imprisonment of not less than 10 years or life imprisonment and a fine or forfeiture of property.

(English translation, Criminal Law of the PRC)

According to Interpretation for Several Issues Concerning the Specific Application of Law in the Trial of Theft Cases) (*Guanyu Shenli Daoqie Anjian Juti Yingyong Falü Ruogan Wenti de Jieshi* 《關於審理盜竊案件具體應用法律若干問題的解釋》) issued by the Supreme People's Court of the PRC on 4 November 1997, 'a relatively large amount' means 500–2,000 yuan, and 'multiple thefts' means break-in theft or theft in a public place for three or more times within one year. Despite these differences in legal definitions, the Hong Kong term *daoqiezui* (盜竊罪) and the Mainland term *daoqiezui* (盜竊罪) can be considered 'functional equivalents' in legal translation, as the identical Chinese terms serve similar communicative purposes and are defined to produce similar legal effects in their respective jurisdictions.

3.2 Equivalence in Chinese legal terminology in three Chinese regions

Based on these illustrations, the problems in using legal terminology across different jurisdictions or legal systems essentially exist at the level of law. Thus, legal language is system-bound, and the differences between legal terms from the common law and civil law systems present a challenge to Hong Kong lawyers and legal translators. Such equivalence issues may long persist. Legal professionals should be able to familiarise themselves with the basic similarities and differences in frequently used concepts and terminology. For example, there are different expressions for the important English terms 'judge' (Hong Kong: *dafaguan* (大法官) vs Mainland: *shenpanyuan* (審判員), *faguan* (法官), for 'claim' (Hong Kong: *shensuo* (申索) vs Mainland: *suopei* (索賠)), and for 'imprisonment' (Hong Kong: *zhongshen jianjin* (終身監禁) vs Mainland: *wuqi tuxing* (無期徒刑)) (Li and Zhang 2006: 183–184).

Since most Chinese legal terms are translations from Western legal systems, they are subject to the general problems of translation. Overall speaking, when a new term from the Western world enters the Chinese world, different translations arise due to the different historical, cultural and dialectal backgrounds of the three regions, and the different translation methods applied. Legal terminology is more complicated in that the three communities can have different legal sources. Therefore, the translation of Chinese legal terminology across the three communities can be divided into the following five non-exclusive categories. They can be classified into 'near equivalents', 'partial equivalents' and 'non-equivalents' based on Šarčević's (1997, 1989) measurement of functional equivalence. The five categories are:

(a) Category 1 (near equivalents)
One or more similar term(s) from a foreign source with the same renditions of same/similar meaning in both languages

(b) Category 2 (near equivalents)
One or more similar term(s) from a foreign source with different renditions of same/similar meaning in the two languages

(c) Category 3 (partial or non-equivalents)
One or more similar term(s) from a foreign source with different renditions of different meaning in the two languages

(d) Category 4 (partial or non-equivalents)
Different terms from a foreign source with different renditions of different meanings

(e) Category 5 (non-equivalents)
Mistranslation

There are several key factors behind the division into these five categories, all of which influence and complicate the development of the Chinese legal terminology. First, there has been linguistic borrowing of the Chinese terminology between the three communities due to closer economic ties, and such borrowing may involve only the linguistic form, or the linguistic form together with a legal meaning. Hence, it is not an easy task to determine whether terms carry the same, similar or different meanings, and their division is based on a comparative sense. Second, owing to frequent English-Chinese and Chinese-English translation activities in the Chinese communities, it may be difficult to determine the foreign term that is the source of a translated Chinese term, especially for Mainland and Taiwanese terms where Chinese-English translation is dominant. Thus, when speaking of 'a foreign source term' as in Categories 1–3, there may be more than one. Third, since the written Chinese language is mutually intelligible across the three communities, the Chinese people can accept and tolerate the existence of different translations of the same foreign term, and sometimes even endeavour to make co-existing terms equivalent.

3.2.1 Five translation categories in terms of equivalence

Based on the author's previous work (Chan 2011, 2010), the following subsections will elaborate on and provide examples of the five categories where they occur in two civil law areas, property law (or real right law in the civil law system) and intellectual property law. The analysis is mainly based on the following data:

Hong Kong:

(i) Conveyancing and Property Ordinance (Cap. 219)
    Wuye Zhuanyi ji Caichan Tiaoli 《物業轉易及財產條例》(第219章)
(ii) Copyright Ordinance (Cap. 528)
    Banquan Tiaoli 《版權條例》(第528章)
(iii) Prevention of Copyright Piracy Ordinance (Cap. 544)
    Fangzhi Daoyong Banquan Tiaoli 《防止盜用版權條例》(第544章)

Mainland China:

(i) Real Right Law of the PRC (2007)
    Zhonghua Renmin Gongheguo Wuquan Fa 《中華人民共和國物權法》(2007)
(ii) Copyright Law of the PRC (2010 Amendment)
    Zhonghua Renmin Gongheguo Zhuzuoquan Fa 《中華人民共和國著作權法》(2010 修正)
(iii) Trademark Law of the PRC (2001 Amendment)
    Zhonghua Renmin Gongheguo Shanbiao Fa Tourism Law of the PRC (2001修正)

(iv) Guarantee Law of the PRC (1995)
Zhonghua Remin Gongheguo Danbaofa 《中華人民共和國擔保法》
(v) Chinese translation of 'Agreement on Trade-Related Aspects of Intellectual Property Rights' (TRIPS) (State Intellectual Property Office of the PRC, www.sipo.gov.cn/zcfg/gjty/1063142.htm; publication date: 29 March 2007)
Yu Maoyi Youguan de Zhishi Chanquan Xieyi 《與貿易有關的知識產權協議》

Taiwan:

(i) Copyright Act of Taiwan (2010 Amendment)
Taiwan Zhuzuoquan Fa 《臺灣著作權法》(2010 修正)
(ii) Civil Code of Taiwan (2012 Amendment)
Taiwan Minfa 《臺灣民法》(2012修正)
(iii) Chinese translation of 'Agreement on Trade-Related Aspects of Intellectual Property Rights' (TRIPS)
(Intellectual Property Office of Taiwan, www.tipo.gov.tw/ct.asp?xItem=207100&ctNode=6780&mp=1; updated date: 15 November 2016)
Yu Maoyi Youguan zhi Zhihui Caichanquan Xieding 《與貿易有關之智慧財產權協定》

3.2.1.1 Category 1 (near equivalents)—one or more similar foreign source term(s) with same renditions of same/similar meaning

This is the ideal situation, where there are the same renditions for the same foreign terms across the three Chinese regions. Examples are 'easement' (*diyiquan* 地役權) and 'lien' (*liuzhiquan* 留置權) in common law property law (or real right law in civil law system). Easement is defined as 'An interest in land owned by another person, consisting in the right to use or control the land, or an area above or below it, for a specific limited purpose (such as to cross it for access to a public road)' (Garner 2009: 585–586). Lien is defined as 'A legal right or interest that a creditor has in another's property, lasting usu. until a debt or duty that it secures is satisfied' (Garner 2009: 1006). Such concepts are considered 'universal' property concepts that exist in both the civil law and common law systems, so their Chinese translations can be standardised (Chan 2011: 259). Problems mainly lie in Categories 2–4, where there are different translations and different source terms.

3.2.1.2 Category 2 (near equivalents)—one or more similar foreign source term(s) with different renditions of same/similar meaning

Category 2, where a foreign term has different renditions of same/similar meanings, is exemplified by 'possession', which is translated as *guanyou* (管有) in Hong Kong (e.g. Conveyancing and Property Ordinance (Cap. 219)) and *zhanyou* (佔有) in Mainland China and Taiwan (e.g. the real right law of the two regions).

As discussed in Chapter 2, *guanyou* (管有) was created by Hong Kong law drafters as a combination of the two morphemes *guan* (管) (meaning *guanli* 管理, manage) and *you* (有) (meaning *yongyou* 擁有, own). Since its introduction, the term has become widely used in Hong Kong. Sin and Roebuck (1996: 241–242) comment on these legal compounds of free morphemes in Hong Kong: 'Thus, Chinese words are "transparent", i.e. readily comprehensible and hence highly communicative'. Consider the following:

(4)

the grant, disposal or surrender of a lease taking effect in <u>possession</u> for a term not exceeding 3 years (whether or not the lessee is given power to extend the term) at the best rent which can be reasonably obtained without a premium; (Section 4(2)(d), Conveyancing and Property Ordinance (Cap. 219))

任何租契的批出、處置或退回，而該租契是在承租人<u>管有</u>時即生效，且為期不超過3年(不論承租人是否獲賦權將該年期延長)，而租金則為在無須支付額外費用的情況下可合理取得的最佳租金者；(《物業轉易及財產條例》(第219章) 第4(2)(d)條)

In both the Mainland and Taiwan, the similar term *zhanyou* (佔有) is an ordinary word in the Chinese language, in which *zhan* (佔) carries the meaning of *zhanju* (佔據) (occupy), according to the English/Chinese edition of *The Contemporary Chinese Dictionary* (Bilingual Dictionary Subdivision, Linguistics and Dictionary Division, Foreign Language Teaching and Research Press 2002: 2411). In the Mainland, similar to *guanyou* (管有), *zhanyou* (佔有) also carries the meanings of 'control' and 'ownership', as defined in *Law Dictionary* (Law Dictionary Editorial Committee, the Institute of Law, China Academy of Social Sciences 2003: 1828). The related legislation of both the Mainland and Taiwan also contains these two meanings. Consider Article 39 of Real Right Law 2007 of the PRC:

(5)
所有權人對自己的不動產或者動產，依法享有<u>佔有</u>、使用、收益和處分的權利。(《中華人民共和國物權法》第39條)
The owner of a real property or movable property has the rights to <u>possess</u>, use, seek profits from and dispose of the real property or movable property according to law.

(English translation, Article 39, Real Right Law of PRC)

In Taiwan, Article 768 of the Civil Code uses the same term in the same sense:

(6)
以所有之意思，十年間和平、公然、繼續<u>佔有</u>他人之動產者，取得其所有權。(《臺灣民法》第768條)
A person, who has peacefully, publicly and continually <u>possessed</u> another's personal property with the intent of being an owner for ten years, acquires the ownership of such personal property.

(English translation, Article 768, Civil Code of Taiwan)

Challenges in legal translation 57

'Dispose of' is another example under Category 2 relating to a foreign term with different renditions of same/similar meanings. The Chinese translations consist of *chuzhi* (處置) in Hong Kong (e.g. Section 4(2)(d), Conveyancing and Property Ordinance (Cap. 219) as cited previously) and *chufen* (處分) in the Mainland (e.g. Article 39, Real Right Law of PRC as cited previously) and Taiwan (e.g. Article 759 of Civil Code of Taiwan). Consider an article from the Taiwan Civil Code:

(7)
所有人，於法令限制之範圍內，得自由使用、收益、<u>處分</u>其所有物，並排除他人之干涉。(《臺灣民法》第759條)

The owner of a thing has the right, within the limits of the Acts and regulations, to use it, to profit from it, and to <u>dispose of</u> it freely, and to exclude the interference from others.

(English Translation, Article 759, Civil Code of Taiwan)

The term 'dispose' originates from Old French *disposer* and from Latin *disponer* 'arrange' (Feinman 2003: 54). 'Disposition' refers to 'The act of transferring something to another's care or possession, esp by deed or will; the relinquishing of property' (Garner 2009: 539).

3.2.1.3 *Category 3 (partial or non-equivalents)—one or more similar foreign source terms with different renditions of different meanings*

For Category 3, in which a foreign term has different renditions with different meanings, 'intellectual property rights' is illustrative, as its two translations *zhishi chanquan* (知識產權) (knowledge property right) and *zhihui caichanquan* (智慧財產權) (wisdom property rights) reflect different legal traditions. The term *zhishi chanquan* (知識產權) is used in Hong Kong (e.g. Section 129, Copyright Ordinance (Cap. 528)) and Mainland China, while *zhihui caichanquan* (智慧財產權) is used in Taiwan.[1] The term 'intellectual property' originated with the emergence of *Geistiges Eigentum* in Germany in the eighteenth century (*Geistig*: mental, intellectual; *Eigentum*: property) (Zheng 1997: 13). In accordance with the principle of natural law, the Doctrine of *Geistiges Eigentum* emphasised the notion of enjoying the fruits of one's labour (Mostert 1987: 495–497). As pointed out by some Chinese scholars, the translations of *zhihui caichanquan* (智慧財產權) (wisdom property right), *zhili caichanquan* (智力財產權) (intellectual property rights) and even *zhili chanquan* (智力產權) (intellectual property rights) would be more faithful to the original meaning of intellectual property rights than the terms in use in all three regions (Lu 2004: 11; Wang 2005: 118).

In contrast, European people started to realise that intellectual property protection interferes with freedom of competition, and such protection should be based on registration through administrative agencies (Ohly 2010: 373). Following such reasoning, the Doctrine of Incentive was developed and later adopted by the World Intellectual Property Organization in 1967 (Dean 2001: 1). The PRC also adopted this doctrine and its translation *zhishi chanquan* (知識產權), which places emphasis on 'knowledge' and the balance between protecting the creators and knowledge dissemination under socialism (Liu 2003). *Zhishi chanquan* (知識產權) has become a standardised translation in most parts of the Chinese world.

'Copyright' is also a good example of Category 3. This is because its two Chinese translations have different legal meanings, yet efforts have been made to narrow their difference and make the two translations equivalent. The two translations are *banquan* (版權) (right to copy), used in Hong Kong's common law system, and *zhuzuoquan* (著作權) (authorship right), used in Taiwan. The Mainland has been using both Chinese translations. *Banquan* (版權) emphasises the 'right to copy' of the work itself with reference to an extension from 'publishing' to 'copying' in the world of modern technology. Meanwhile, *zhuzuoquan* (著作權) emphasises the concept of 'authorship', the rights of the natural person who owns their creation, with reference to 'authored' literary works such as novels and academic papers (Jiang 2005: 4–5). According to *Black's Law Dictionary* (Garner 2009: 386), copyright is defined as:

> The right to copy; specifically, a property right in an original work of authorship (including literary, musical, dramatic, choreographic, pictorial, graphic, sculptural, and architectural works; motion pictures and other audiovisual works; and sound recording) fixed in any tangible medium of expression, giving the holder the exclusive right to reproduce, adapt, distribute, perform, and display the work.

Based on this definition, the legal concept of copyright involves protecting the right to copy the work, rather than the person who owns such a right. This is closer to the literal meaning of the translation of *banquan* (版權), that is, 'right to copy'. These days, *banquan* (版權) appears to meet the current international convention that grants rights not only to the author but also to *gaibian, fanyi, zhushi, zhengliren* (改編、翻譯、注釋、整理人) (the adapter, translator, annotator or arranger) (Article 12, Copyright Law of the PRC). Despite their legal differences, the two terms *zhuzuoquan* (著作權) and *banquan* (版權) have been made equivalent in the PRC by legislative means. Article 56 of the Copyright Law 2010 stipulates:

(8)
本法所稱的著作權即版權。(《中華人民共和國著作權法》第56條)
For the purposes of this Law, the terms 'zhuzuoquan' is 'banquan'.
(English Translation, Article 56, Copyright Law of the PRC)

Today, the two terms *zhuzuoquan* (著作權) and *banquan* (版權) are even generally considered interchangeable in international law (Jiang 2005: 6). Although the two Chinese translations are significantly different in meaning, for the purposes of communication in a globalised world, they are made equivalent in current use.

Another example of Category 3 is the two Chinese translations of 'mortgage', that is, *anjie* (按揭) in Hong Kong and *diya* (抵押) in Mainland China and Taiwan.

Challenges in legal translation 59

For instance, *anjie* (按揭) is used in Hong Kong as the translation of 'mortgage' in the Chinese version of Part IV Mortgages, Conveyancing and Property Ordinance (Cap. 219), and *diya* (抵押) is translated as 'mortgage' in both Chapter 16 Right to Mortgage, Real Right Law of PRC and Chapter 6 on Mortgage, Civil Code of Taiwan. A compound of Latin *mortum* (everlasting) and the Old French *gage* (security) meaning 'lifetime surety', 'mortgage' is defined in *Black's Law Dictionary* as 'A conveyance of title to property that is given as security for the payment of a debt or the performance of a duty and that will become void upon payment or performance according to the stipulated terms', and 'A lien against property that is granted to secure an obligation (such as a debt) and that is extinguished upon payment or performance according to stipulated terms' (Garner 2009: 1101). *Anjie* (按揭) is a term originating in Hong Kong specifically as the Chinese translation for 'mortgage', and so has acquired the legal meaning (Zhang 2007: 329). In contrast, the term *diya* (抵押) denotes setting certain properties as guarantee to the creditor's rights without transferring the ownership (e.g. Chapter 3, Guarantee Law of the Copyright Law of the PRC). Today the Mainland has borrowed *anjie* (按揭) from Hong Kong but uses it with a similar sense as *diya* (抵押), that is, to transfer possession without transferring the title. All in all, *diya* (抵押) and *anjie* (按揭) can be regarded as partial equivalents, and used interchangeably for translation purposes. In Mainland China, legal translators should translate *diya* (抵押) or *anjie* (按揭) as 'mortgage' in English, with a footnote stipulating that the use of such terms does not include the concept of transfer of ownership (Chan 2011: 264).

3.2.1.4 Category 4 (partial or non-equivalents)—different foreign source terms with different renditions of different meanings (partial or non-equivalents)

Under this category, representative examples from civil law are the Chinese terms *caichanquan* (財產權) and *wuquan* (物權), and their corresponding laws *caichanfa* (財產法) and *wuquanfa* (物權法). There are major differences between the two terms as they have different sources. Originating from a common law term 'property right', *caichanquan* (財產權) is used in Hong Kong, for example, Conveyancing and Property Ordinance (Cap. 219). *Wuquan* (物權), often translated as 'real right', is a civil law concept with narrower connotation than 'property right' in common law. *Wuquan* (物權) is used in the *Wuquanfa* (《物權法》) (translated as 'Real Right Law' as explained below) promulgated in the PRC in 2007, and the Civil Code of Taiwan (Part III Rights in Rem). 'Property' is derived from the Latin phrase *proprius*, meaning 'one's own' (Perrins 2000: 1), whereas 'right in a thing', derived from the phrase *jus reale, jus in re*, is explained by Kant (1887: 86) as 'a Right to the Private Use of a Thing, of which I am in possession—original or derivative—in common with all others'. Real right only refers to tangible assets. Section 90 of the German Civil Code states that 'Only corporeal objects are things as defined by law'. A Mainland law scholar, commenting on real right, which was made an independent area in the German civil law in 1900 (Wang 2001: B1), states that real right is separable from other property rights, whereas 'property right refers to the subject possessing the right of the property value, being a corresponding concept to the right of the person. It comprehensively includes creditor's right, right of things, and intellectual property' (English translation by the author).

In adopting the Real Right Law in 2007, the National People's Congress of the PRC uses the concept of 'real right', which regulates immovable and movables in tangible form, but not intangible form (Law Committee, Standing Committee of the National People's Congress of PRC 2007: 93). Nevertheless, the Mainland legal service provider LawInfoChina provides two translations for the term *wuquan* (物權), that is, 'property right' and 'real right' in their English translations of the Chinese law, so as to help foreigners (especially Americans) to understand the new legislation (Personal communication 20 February 2009). The translation strategy is communicative but may mislead foreigners in their understanding of the law. It is suggested that the translation of 'real right' is used as the title of the law, in order to promote this legal concept's distinctiveness from 'property law' (Chan 2011: 253).

3.2.1.5 Category 5 (non-equivalents)—mistranslation

Mistranslated Chinese legal terms are plentiful and the discussion can proceed at two levels, the lay level and the specialist level. The lay level, with examples taken from Chinese newspapers, is indicative of the lack of legal knowledge among the general public. Whereas the specialist level, with examples from official Chinese translations of the international agreement TRIPS, uncovers underlying reasons for mistranslation. TRIPS (1994), administered by the World Trade Organization (WTO) for its members (www.wto.org/english/docs_e/legal_e/legal_e.htm#TRIPs), has different Chinese translations in Mainland China and Taiwan.

At the first level, consider the term 'intellectual property' in examples taken from Chinese newspaper articles relating to intellectual property news:

(9)
文化部一位官員在接受記者採訪時說，讓文化和資本對接很難。因為文化企業都是"輕資產"，比如版權、知識產權和商標，它們的價值在金融機構那裡很難得到有效論證、評估。(Zhao 17 May 2011)

An official from the Ministry of Culture said in an interview that it was difficult to turn culture into capital. This is because most cultural enterprises are engaged in producing 'light assets', for example, <u>copyrights, intellectual property rights and trademarks</u>, of which the values are hardly assessed by financial institutions in an effective manner.

(English translation by the author)

(10)
他說，商販都應該向商業註冊局註冊，以保護他們在商業活動，特別是知識產權和商標等方面的權益。唯有通過註冊，他們的知識產權和商標將可以獲得保障。(*Guang Ming Daily* (Malaysia) 20 December 2005)

He said that all vendors should register at the Accounting and Corporate Regulatory Authority, so as to protect their commercial activities, especially in terms of <u>intellectual property rights, copyrights</u> and so on. It is only through registration that their intellectual property rights and trademarks can receive protection.

(English translation by the author)

It is a mistake to juxtapose 'intellectual property rights' and 'copyrights'/'trademarks' on the same level, as shown in these examples. 'Intellectual property' is the umbrella term covering different rights. According to Garner (2009: 881), 'intellectual property' is defined as 'a category of intangible rights protecting commercially valuable products of the human intellect. The category comprises primarily trademark, copyright, and patent rights, but also includes trade-secret rights, publicity rights, moral rights, and rights against unfair competition'.

Below is another mistranslation from a news report relating to 'geographical indications', a category under intellectual property:

(11)
一、智慧財產權
智慧財產權 (Intellectual property) 即大陸所謂的知識產權，為法律所創設的一種權利，係指人類精神活動之成果，而能產生財產上價值者。按「與貿易有關之智慧財產權協定，簡稱TRIPS」之定義，係包括著作權及相關權利、商標權、<u>產地標示</u>、工業設計、專利權、積體電路布局、未公開資料之保護（營業秘密）以及契約授權衍生反競爭行為之防制（公平交易法），大致如圖一所示。(Hsieh 2011 April 26)

1 Intellectual Property
Zhihui caichanquan (Intellectual property) is equivalent to *zhishi chanquan* as called in the Mainland China. A legal right, intellectual property refers to the fruits of human intellectual activities that generate economic value. According to the definition in the 'Agreement on Trade-Related Aspects of Intellectual Property Rights' (TRIPS), intellectual property comprises Copyright and Related Rights, Trademarks, <u>Place of Origin</u>, Industrial Designs, Patents, Layout-Designs (Topographies) of Integrated Circuits, Protection of Undisclosed Information, and Control of Anti-Competitive Practices in Contractual Licences. General details are shown in Diagram 1.

(English translation by the author)

The underlined phrase *chandi biaoshi* (產地標示) (place of origin), as an intellectual property right under the TRIPS protection, is a mistranslated term. In Part II, Standards Concerning the Availability, Scope and Use of Intellectual Property Rights of TRIPS, the original English term is 'geographical indications', which refers to goods with the characteristics of a particular geographical origin. This is defined in Article 22(1) thus: 'Geographical indications are, for the purposes of this Agreement, indications which identify a good as originating in the territory of a Member, or a region or locality in that territory, where a given quality, reputation

62 *Challenges in legal translation*

or other characteristic of the good is essentially attributable to its geographical origin'. Therefore, to translate this as 'place of origin', that is, where the product is made, indicates a total misunderstanding. The newspaper editors could find the correct translation in Taiwan's translation of TRIPS, that is, *dili biaoshi* (地理標示). A similar term *dili biaozhi* (地理標誌) is also used in Article 16(1) of the Trademark Law of the PRC:

(12)
商標中有商品的<u>地理標誌</u>，而該商品並非來源於該標誌所標示的地區，誤導公眾的，不予註冊並禁止使用；但是，已經善意取得註冊的繼續有效。(《中華人民共和國商標法》第16(1)條)

If a trademark contains the <u>geographic mark</u> of the commodities while the commodities don't come from the region indicated by that mark, and thus misleads the public, the trademark shall not be registered and shall be prohibited from use; however, those that have been registered in good faith shall continue to be valid.

(English translation, Article 16(1), Trademark Law of the PRC)

Here the 'geographic mark' refers to the 'geographical indications', the term used in the TRIPS where the entire Section 3 expands on its details.

This illustrates the general lack of legal knowledge in the media with the public as the target readers.

The following example will show how the preference for a domestic term rather than an international term can cause mistranslation. The two Chinese translations of the term 'copyright piracy' in TRIPS, one of which is a mistranslation, represent the difference between the terms used in international and national laws, and the openness of a nation to absorb new legal terms for use in domestic laws and translations of international conventions. In Article 61 of TRIPS, the term 'copyright piracy' is translated as *daoban* (盜版) (pirated copy) in the PRC's version and *qinhai zhuzuoquan* (侵害著作權) (infringement of authorship right) in Taiwan's version.

(13a)
TRIPS original version
Members shall provide for criminal procedures and penalties to be applied at least in cases of wilful trademark counterfeiting or <u>copyright piracy</u> on a commercial scale. (Article 61, TRIPS)

(13b)
TRIPS PRC translation
成員方應規定刑事程式和懲罰，至少適用於具有商業規模的故意的商標仿冒和<u>盜版</u>案件。(《與貿易有關的知識產權協議》第61條)

TRIPS Taiwan translation
會員至少應對具有商業規模而故意仿冒商標或<u>侵害著作權</u>之案件，訂定刑事程式及罰則。(《與貿易有關之智慧財產權協定》第61條)

As discussed above earlier, *zhuzuoquan* (著作權) (authorship) emphasises the natural person who owns the creation, while *banquan* (版權) (copyright) emphasises the work itself. Using *banquan* (版權) to translate 'copyright' in TRIPS (e.g. Article 9(2)), the PRC accordingly translates 'copyright piracy' as *daoban* (盜版) (pirated copy). In international law, the concept of 'copyright', that is, right to copy, is adopted, and 'copyright' is a more familiar term to the general public who use *daoban* (盜版) to mean 'illegal copying' (Qu 2009). The English word 'piracy' is defined as 'reproducing published works or phonograms by any appropriate means for public distribution and also rebroadcasting another's broadcast without proper authorization' (World Intellectual Property Organization 2007: 186), while the PRC term *daoban* (盜版) is defined as the act of reproducing and distributing works with the aim of making profit without the authorisation of the copyright holder (Lü 2006: 56). The two definitions share the common elements that the means of infringement is reproduction and no consent is sought from the copyright owner, but they differ in that PRC requires the profit-making goal. Therefore, 'piracy' and *daoban* (盜版) can be considered close equivalents, and *daoban* (盜版) is more of an international term due to the recognition of 'copyright'.

On the other hand, Taiwan's translation *qinhai zhuzuoquan* (侵害著作權) is more of a domestic term, Originating as a Japanese borrowing during the Qing Dynasty legal reform, *zhuzuoquan* (著作權) is believed to have been used for a long time in China's legislation. The use of this term is in line with the concept of 'author's right' adopted in civil law countries (Qu 2009). In the Copyright Act of Taiwan, *Qinhai zhuzuoquan* (侵害著作權) refers to any infringement of an author's personal or property rights. Therefore, the problem of translating 'piracy' as *qinhai* (侵害) is that the latter has a wider scope, covering other types of copyright infringement such as infringements of the rights to publicly release the work, to indicate the author's name, to publicly perform, and to rent (Article 87, Copyright Act of Taiwan), while 'piracy' only refers to the means of infringement. It should be noted that the term 'copyright piracy' is not in use in the intellectual property codes of the PRC and Taiwan, but it is in Hong Kong, in the Prevention of Copyright Piracy Ordinance (Cap. 544). This indicates that when domestic law adopts a source term from international law, there is a tendency for such translations to take root, and this is assisted in the case of Hong Kong by the official status of English (Chan 2018: 11–13).

3.3 Case study of terminology in international agreements: intellectual property rights in Mainland China, Taiwan and Hong Kong

3.3.1 Introduction and methodology

This case study aims to compare 'layout-design', an intellectual property rights (IPR) term and its translated Chinese terms from the three regions, based on

64 *Challenges in legal translation*

statutes and translations of an international agreement. The analysis will be conducted in the order of Mainland China, Taiwan and Hong Kong since the international agreement under study only has Chinese translations in the former two regions. The Hong Kong translation of 'layout-design' is found in its bilingual law. Illustration of their respective problems, levels of equivalence and translation strategies is mainly based on Susan Šarčević's three criteria for determining a 'functional equivalent': (i) function/structure; (ii) scope of application; and (iii) legal effects as used. The level of functional equivalence is assessed first, and then the three translations are compared and contrasted, so as to elucidate the motivating factors behind certain choices, such as the adoption of terms from domestic codes.

This comparative study is based on the Agreement on Trade-Related Aspects of Intellectual Property Rights (TRIPS) on the protection and enforcement of intellectual property rights among World Trade Organization (WTO) members, its two Chinese official translations from Mainland China and Taiwan, and domestic legislation related to IPR. The original English text of TRIPS was retrieved from the WTO website (www.wto.org/english/docs_e/legal_e/27-trips.doc); the PRC version *Yu Maoyi Youguan de Zhishichanquan Xieyi* 《與貿易有關的知識產權協議》 was retrieved from the website of the State Intellectual Property Office of the PRC; and the Taiwan version *Yu Maoyi Youguan zhi Zhihui Caichanquan Xieding* 《與貿易有關之智慧財產權協定》 from the website of Taiwan's Intellectual Property Office. It is found that there is no official Chinese translation for TRIPS in Hong Kong, so data for this region is collected from the Layout-design (Topography) of Integrated Circuits Ordinance (Cap. 445) (《集成電路的布圖設計(拓樸圖)條例》(第445章)). For the Mainland and Taiwan, the respective domestic legislations are Patent Law of the PRC (*Zhonghua Renmin Gongheguo Zhuanli Fa* 《中華人民共和國專利法》) (2008 Amendment) and Integrated Circuit Layout Protection Act (*Jiti Dianlu Dianlu Buju Baohu Fa* 《積體電路電路布局保護法》) (2002 Amendment).

3.3.2 'Layout-design', its Chinese translations and the measurement of equivalence (waiguan sheji *(外觀設計) vs dianlu buju (電路布局 (拓樸圖)) vs butu sheji (布圖設計 (拓樸圖))*

'Layout-design'[2] is covered in Section 6, Part II of TRIPS, which contains four articles pertaining to the protection of the layout-design of integrated circuits. 'Layout-design' is translated as *waiguan sheji* (外觀設計), *dianlu buju* (電路布局 (拓樸圖)) and *butu sheji* (布圖設計 (拓樸圖)) in Mainland China, Taiwan and Hong Kong, respectively. First consider the term in Article 35 of TRIPS and its respective translations from Mainland China and Taiwan:

(14a)
TRIPS original version
Members agree to provide protection to the layout-designs (topographies) of
    integrated circuits (referred to in this Agreement as "layout-designs") in

accordance with Articles 2 through 7 (other than paragraph 3 of Article 6), Article 12 and paragraph 3 of Article 16 of the Treaty on Intellectual Property in Respect of Integrated Circuits and, in addition, to comply with the following provisions. (Article 35, TRIPS)

(14b)
TRIPS PRC translation
各成員方同意按有關積體電路的智慧財產權條約中第2條至第7條（第6條中第3款除外）、第12條和第16條第3款規定，對積體電路的<u>外觀設計</u>提供保護，此外還服從以下規定。（《與貿易有關的知識產權協議》第35條）

(14c)
TRIPS Taiwan translation
會員同意依照積體電路智慧財產權條約之第二條至第七條（不包括第六條第三項）、第十二條及第十六條第三項保護積體電路<u>電路佈局（拓樸圖）</u>，並遵守下列規定。（《與貿易有關之智慧財產權協定》第61條）

Also consider the bilingual Hong Kong laws:

(15)
'<u>layout-design (topography)</u>' (布圖設計(拓樸圖)) means the 3-dimensional disposition, however expressed, of the elements of an integrated circuit (at least one of which is an active element) and of some or all of the interconnections of an integrated circuit, or such a 3-dimensional disposition prepared for an integrated circuit intended for manufacture; (Section 2(1), Layout-design (Topography) of Integrated Circuits Ordinance (Cap. 445))

'<u>布圖設計(拓樸圖)</u>' (layout-design (topography)) 指集成電路中多個元件(其中至少有一個是有源元件)，和其部分或全部集成電路互連的三維配置，或者是指為集成電路的製造而準備的這樣的三維配置；（《集成電路的布圖設計(拓樸圖)條例》（第445章）第2(1)條）

To evaluate the degree of equivalence of the three Chinese terms to the original, three criteria are used. In terms of the first criterion, 'function/structure', the definitions of each of the terms provide sufficient clues as to their equivalence. Article 35 stipulates that members shall provide protection of layout-designs of integrated circuits in accordance with the Washington Treaty on Intellectual Property in Respect of Integrated Circuits (the 'Washington Treaty'), therefore the definition of 'layout-design' can be sought in that document. As Article 2(ii) of Washington Treaty states, layout-design is 'the three dimensional disposition, however expressed, of the elements, at least one of which is an active element, and of some or all of the interconnections of an integrated circuit, or such a three-dimensional disposition prepared for an integrated circuit intended for manufacture'. Based on this, the function of 'layout-design' is to protect the technical drawing according to which the integrated circuits are manufactured. Structurally speaking, the layout design is the first-class protected intellectual property subject matter under the *sui generis* protection, meaning a special protection in IPR, which enjoys separate-but-equal status to copyrights and patents. In other words, layout design has different characteristics from copyright works and patentable subject matters.

In terms of Šarčević's second criterion, 'applicable scope', the concept of 'layout-design' is only applied to the area of integrated circuits, which comprises a range of products, for example, microprocessors, dynamic memories and programmable logic devices (UNCTAD-ICTSD 2005: 506). This is much narrower than other parallel intellectual property concepts such as copyright.

Using Šarčević's third criterion, from the perspective of 'legal effect', the right holders of 'layout-design', as stipulated in both TRIPS Article 36 and the Washington Treaty Article 6.1, have exclusive rights (a) to reproduce the protected layout-design by incorporation in an integrated circuit or otherwise; and (b) to import, sell and distribute for commercial purposes the protected layout-design or an integrated circuit in which the protected layout-design is incorporated (UNCTAD-ICTSD 2005: 513). TRIPS Article 38 stipulates a minimum ten-year term of protection, beginning from the date of filing an application or from the first commercial exploitation wherever in the world it occurs, or a 15-year protection after the creation of the layout-design.

3.3.2.1 Mainland China: waiguan sheji (外觀設計)

The analysis that follows argues that, based on these same three criteria, the original term 'layout design' in TRIPS and *waiguan sheji* (外觀設計) (exterior design) are 'non-equivalents'. According to Šarčević (1997: 239, 1989: 281), two concepts are non-equivalent when 'only a few or none of the essential features of concepts A and B coincide (intersection) or if concept A contains all of the characteristics of concept B but concept B only a few or none of the essential features of concept A (inclusion)'. In the PRC, *waiguan sheji* (外觀設計), as one of the three categories of a patent (the other two being 'invention' and 'utility model'), refers essentially to the aesthetic design of the product's appearance. This is substantially different from the intension of 'layout-design'. Article 2 of PRC Patent Law defines *waiguan sheji* (外觀設計) thus: 'The term "design" refers to any new design of a product's shape, pattern or a combination thereof, as well as the combination of the color and the shape or pattern of a product, which creates an aesthetic feeling and is fit for industrial application'.

Thus, *waiguan sheji* (外觀設計) and the source term share few characteristics in common. First, in terms of Šarčević's structure/function, *waiguan sheji* (外觀設計) is a subset of patent in the PRC law. Therefore, designs are protected under the regime of patents, which is a different category from 'integrated circuit layout-design', under the special protection of 'Regulations on Protection of Integrated Circuit Layout Design 2001' (*Jicheng Dianlu Butu Sheji Baohu Tiaoli* 《集成電路布圖設計保護條例》).

Second, the applicable scope of *waiguan sheji* (外觀設計) has little overlap with that of layout-design. According to Article 2 of the PRC Patent Law, *waiguan sheji* (外觀設計) is the design of a product's appearance and its suitability for industrial application. Therefore, the concept applies only in the field of industrial

Table 3.1 Measurement of equivalence between 'layout-design' and *waiguan sheji* (外觀設計) used in Mainland China

Terms / Criteria	Layout-design	Waiguan sheji (外觀設計) in Mainland
(i) Function	Technical drawing of integrated circuits	Aesthetic design of industrial products
(ii) Structure	First-class IPR protected subject matter, parallel with patent	Sub-category of patent
Scope of application	Three dimensional design of integrated circuit	Aesthetic exterior design industrial products
Legal effect	Exclusive rights to reproduce, import, sell or distribute for commercial purposes Ten years of protection from the application date or first commercial exploitation; or 15 years after creation	Exclusive rights to make, offer for sale, sell or import Ten years of protection from application date

products (Wang 2011: 268). In contrast, in the Washington Treaty, 'layout-design' is the three-dimensional disposition of integrated circuits (Article 2(ii)). 'Layout-design' only applies to integrated circuits, which is only one category of industrial products.

Third, the legal effect generated by the *waiguan sheji* (外觀設計) regime is in some ways similar to the effects of 'layout design'. According to Article 11 of PRC Patent Law, the right holders have the exclusive right to make, offer for sale, sell or import the product incorporating the patented design for production and business purposes (Wang 2011: 208–209). The period of protection for design patent is ten years, counted from the date of filing an application.

Overall speaking, due to the fact that 'layout-design' and *waiguan sheji* (外觀設計) are essentially two different subject matters under the IP protection, Šarčević's first and second criteria are not met. The two terms are 'non-equivalents', in that the concepts to which they refer share no essential features. The overlap in the third criterion, legal effects, does not have any bearing on their level of equivalence (Table 3.1).

3.3.2.2 *Taiwan: dianlu buju* (電路布局 (拓樸圖))

The Taiwanese translation *dianlu buju* (電路布局) (circuit layout) constitutes 'partial equivalence', which occurs when 'concepts A and B share most of their essential and some of their accidental characteristics (intersection) or when concept A contains all of the characteristics of concept B but concept B only most of the essential and some of the accidental characteristics of concept A' (Šarčević 1997: 238, 1989: 280).

In the Taiwan TRIPS translation, 'layout-design' is rendered as *dianlu buju* (電路布局). It is believed that this term is derived from Taiwan's *Jiti Dianlu*

Dianlu Buju Baohu Fa (積體電路電路布局保護法) (Integrated Circuit Layout Protection Act),[3] promulgated on 11 August 1995 to construct a *sui generis* regime for integrated circuits. The literal English translation of *dianlu buju* (電路布局) is 'circuit layout', which is not the same as the TRIPS term 'layout-design', but has a similar definition. The Taiwan term refers to 'a two-dimensional or three-dimensional design of electronic components and interconnecting leads on an integrated circuit' (Article 2, Integrated Circuit Layout Protection Act). The common essence of these two terms ('circuit layout' and 'layout-design') is that both constitute a type of design on the basis of which integrated circuits are manufactured. The only noticeable difference is that 'layout-design' in TRIPS only refers to three-dimensional disposition, while *dianlu buju* (電路布局) covers both three-dimensional and two-dimensional design. Moreover, as with 'layout-design', *dianlu buju* (電路布局) is a first-class protected subject matter under Taiwanese law, on the same level as patent, trademark and copyright (Lin 2010: 12–13). Based on this analysis, the major characteristics of the two terms, circuit layout and layout deisgn, as judged against the 'function/structure' criterion, are quite similar.

The other two aspects are also similar. Regarding scope of application, like its source term, the concept *dianlu buju* (電路布局) specifically refers to the design of integrated circuits and does not include other industrial product designs. The legal effect of *dianlu buju* (電路布局) is also very close to its source term. Right holders have the exclusive rights (a) to reproduce the circuit layout in whole or in part; and (b) to import or distribute for commercial purpose the circuit layout or an integrated circuit containing the circuit layout (Article 17, Integrated Circuit Layout Protection Act). In short, they have three major rights, namely, right of reproduction, right of import and right of distribution, where 'distribution' includes the act of selling (Article 2, Integrated Circuit Layout Protection Act). The term of protection for *dianlu buju* (電路布局) is ten years commencing from the filing date of the circuit layout registration application or the date of first commercial exploitation (Article 19, Integrated Circuit Layout Protection Act).

The three criteria are well satisfied, apart from the fact the subject matter 'layout-design' in TRIPS covers only three-dimensional disposition, while *dianlu buju* (電路布局) includes both three-dimensional and two-dimensional design. In other words, the function and scope are slightly different from each other. Therefore, the two terms are 'partial equivalents' in that they share most of their essential and some of their accidental characteristics (Table 3.2).

3.3.2.3 Hong Kong: *butu sheji* (布圖設計 (拓撲圖))

The study contends that 'layout-design' and the Hong Kong translation *butu sheji* (布圖設計(拓撲圖)) are 'near equivalents', which is 'when concepts A and B share all of their essential and most of their accidental characteristics (intersection) or when concept A contains all of the characteristics of concept B, and concept B all of the essential and most of the accidental characteristics of concept A (inclusion)' (Šarčević 1997: 238, 1989: 280).

Table 3.2 Measurement of equivalence between 'layout-design' and *dianlu butu* (電路布圖) used in Taiwan

Criteria \ Terms	Layout-design	*Dianlu butu* (電路布圖) *in Taiwan*
(i) Function	Technical drawing of integrated circuits	Design of integrated circuits
(ii) Structure	First-class IPR protected subject matter, parallel with patent	A first-class protected subject matter in intellectual property law, parallel with patent regime
Scope of application	Three dimensional design of integrated circuit	Two or three dimensional design of integrated circuit
Legal effect	Exclusive rights to reproduce, import, sell or distribute for commercial purposes Ten years of protection from the application date or first commercial exploitation; or 15 years after creation	Exclusive rights to reproduce, import or distribute Ten years of protection from the application date or first commercial exploitation

The Hong Kong translation *butu sheji* (布圖設計(拓撲圖)) is taken from the Chinese title of the local Layout-design (Topography) of Integrated Circuits Ordinance (Cap. 445). The function and structure of this term are the same as that of the original term 'layout design' because it was absorbed by Hong Kong laws from TRIPS, and the bilingual texts of law carry the same legal effects. The statutory definition of *butu sheji* (布圖設計(拓撲圖)) can be found in Section 2:

> 'layout-design (topography)' (布圖設計(拓撲圖)) means the 3-dimensional disposition, however expressed, of the elements of an integrated circuit (at least one of which is an active element) and of some or all of the interconnections of an integrated circuit, or such a 3-dimensional disposition prepared for an integrated circuit intended for manufacture.

This is almost exactly the same as the definition of 'layout-design' in TRIPS. Furthermore, *butu sheji* (布圖設計(拓撲圖)) is a first-class intellectual property law concept which in Hong Kong shares the same status as copyright, trademark and patent. The statutory definition also shows that *butu sheji* (布圖設計(拓撲圖)), the three-dimensional design of integrated circuits, has identical scope of application with 'layout-design'.

The legal effects are also identical: under the *sui generis* protective regime established by Layout-design (Topography) of Integrated Circuits Ordinance (Cap. 445), right holders have two major rights:[4] to reproduce and to exploit commercially the protected layout-design (Section 4). The spectrum of 'commercial exploitation' includes (a) to sell, let for hire or otherwise dispose; (b) to offer or expose for sale or hire or otherwise offer to dispose of or expose for the purpose of disposing of; or (c) to import for the purpose of sale, letting for hire

70 *Challenges in legal translation*

Table 3.3 Measurement of equivalence between 'layout-design' and *butu sheji* (布圖設計) used in Hong Kong

Criteria \ Terms	Layout-design	*Butu sheji* (布圖設計) *in Hong Kong*
(i) Function	Technical drawing of integrated circuits	Technical drawing of integrated circuits
(ii) Structure	First-class IPR protected subject matter, parallel with patent	First-class IPR protected subject matter, parallel with patent
Scope of application	Three dimensional design of integrated circuit	Three dimensional design of integrated circuit
Legal effect	Exclusive rights to reproduce, import, sell or distribute for commercial purposes	Exclusive rights to reproduce or commercially exploit
	Ten years of protection from the application date or first commercial exploitation; or 15 years after creation	Ten years of protection from the application date or first commercial exploitation; or 15 years after creation

or other disposition. The term of protection for *butu sheji* (布圖設計 (拓撲圖)) is ten years after the end of the year in which it was first commercially exploited or 15 years after the end of the year in which it was created (Section 6).

In sum, the characteristics of *butu sheji* (布圖設計(拓撲圖)) and 'layout-design (topography)' have substantial intersection, so the former is a faithful and adequate translation that can reflect the original intent of 'layout-design (topography)'. What is more, considering the translation method, the term is a combination of transliteration (*bu* 布 imitates the sounds of the second syllable *po* of 'topography') and semantic translation (*tu* 圖 is 'graphy' and *sheji* 設計 is 'design'). This combination formally resembles the sound of the original while making sense to the target Chinese readers (Table 3.3).

3.3.3 Summary and conclusion

The following summarises the features and translation strategies of the three Chinese terms. First of all, one reason for the three regions' tendency to translate differently possibly lies in translation being done in isolation, without consideration of each other's approaches. Secondly, their translation strategies can vary greatly and produce drastically different effects. The Mainland translation *waiguan sheji* (外觀設計), arguably a term that is 'non-equivalent' to the original, is the weakest translation of the three terms under comparison. This non-equivalence appears to have arisen from the translator adopting a term from the domestic code without considering its legal meaning. The Taiwanese translator also employs a domestic term, *dianlu buju* (電路布局). However, despite the fact that this term covers both two and three dimensional dispositions of integrated circuits, its much closer legal meaning to the original enables it to be considered a 'partial equivalence'. From these contrasting examples, it can be seen that the adoption of terms from domestic legislation is a convenient translation method for rendering terms from international agreements, but doing it without due care can produce contrasting results. As for the Hong Kong translation of *butu sheji* (布圖設計(拓撲圖)), it is considered a 'near equivalent' to the original mainly because the legislative definitions make it the same. Furthermore, the translation is tactfully designed, so that it is faithful to the original both in sound by transliteration (布, *bu* imitating 'topo') and in meaning by literal translation (*sheji* (設計) for 'design', and *tu* (圖) for 'graphy'). Without doubt, its communicative function is the best of the three.

3.4 Concluding remarks

Given the complexity of terminological equivalence in the Chinese regions, a good legal translator should at the very least acquire good legal knowledge in order to avoid mistranslation. It has been strongly advised that legal translators should possess basic legal knowledge as part of their professional competency. Cao (1998: 250) remarks, 'A legal translator, therefore, needs to have a basic understanding of the nature and function of law in society as such a legal knowledge is essential not to interpret or apply the law, but to understand the message and re-present it in another language appropriately'. In particular, 'some basic knowledge of the relevant law and legal concepts and understanding of legal usage will go a long way' (Cao 2002: 337). As a practical matter, translators should read more laws and cross-check the words they are working on so that they know when they have a special legal meaning (Cao 2007: 70). The following chapter on education will elaborate on the issues of training legal translators and bilingual lawyers.

Notes

1 As shown on the homepages of their official bilingual websites, the English and Chinese full names of the authorities responsible for the IPR affairs in Hong Kong, Mainland China and Taiwan are: Intellectual Property Department, The Government of the Hong Kong Administrative Region (香港特別行政區政府知識產權署), retrieved from: www.ipd.gov.hk/eng/home.htm and www.ipd.gov.hk/chi/home.htm; National Intellectual Property Administration (CNIPA), PRC (國家知識產權局), retrieved from: www.sipo.gov.cn and http://english.cnipa.gov.cn; and Intellectual Property Office (IPO), Ministry of Economic Office (經濟部智慧財產局), Taiwan retrieved from: www.tipo.gov.tw/mp.asp?mp=1 and www.tipo.gov.tw/mp.asp?mp=2
2 'Topography', a synonym for 'layout-design', is usually used in European legislation (UNCTAD-ICTSD 2005: 506).
3 This case study uses the original version of Integrated Circuit Layout Protection Act, which was promulgated 11 August 1995, in order to evaluate the Taiwan translation on the basis of laws operating before/around the TRIPS translation in 1995.
4 Layout-design (Topography) of Integrated Circuits Ordinance (Cap. 445) uses the term 'qualified owner' instead of 'right holder'.

English references

Cao, Deborah (1998). The Illocutionary Act in Translating Chinese Legislative Texts. *Babel: International Journal of Translation 44*(3): 244–253.

Cao, Deborah (2002). Finding the Elusive Equivalents in Chinese/English Legal Translation. *Babel: International Journal of Translation 48*(4): 330–341.
Cao, Deborah (2007). *Translating Law*. Clevedon: Multilingual Matters Ltd.
Chan, Clara Ho-yan (2010). Legal Globalization and Law Drafting and Translation: Use of Legal Terms and Technical Words in Intellectual Property Laws of People's Republic of China. *Translation Quarterly 58*: 1–26.
Chan, Clara Ho-yan (2011). The Use and Translation of Chinese Legal Terminology in the Property Laws of Mainland China and Hong Kong: Problems, Strategies and Future Development. *Terminology: International Journal of Theoretical and Applied Issues in Specialized Communication 17*(2): 249–273.
Chan, Clara Ho-yan (2018). Mistranslation of Legal Terminology Reconsidered. *Comparative Legilinguistics: International Journal for Legal Communication 32*: 7–36.
Dean, Owen H. (2001). *Handbook of South African Copyright Law*. Cape Town: Juta & Co.
Feinman, Jay M. (2003). *1001 Legal Words You Need to Know*. Beijing: Law Press.
Garner, Bryan A. (Ed.) (2009). *Black's Law Dictionary* (9th Ed.). St. Paul, MN: West.
Kant, Immanuel (1887). The Mode of Acquiring Anything External. In Kant, Immanuel (Ed.), *The Philosophy of Law: An Exposition of the Fundamental Principles of Jurisprudence as the Science of Right* (pp. 81–109). Translated from the German by Hastie, William, Edinburgh: T. & T. Clark. Reprinted 2002 by The Lawbook Exchange, Ltd.
Mostert, Frederick (1987). The Development of the Natural-Law Principle as One of the Principles Underlying the Recognition of Intellectual Property. *South African Law Journal 104*: 480–495.
Ohly, Ansgar (2010). Common Principles of European Intellectual Property Law? *Zeitschrift für Geistiges Eigentum* (*Intellectual Property Journal*) *2*(4): 365–384.
Perrins, Bryn (2000). *Understanding Land Law*. London: Routledge Cavendish.
Šarčević, Susan (1989). Conceptual Dictionaries for Translation in the Field of Law. *International Journal of Lexicography 2*(4): 277–293.
Šarčević, Susan (1997). *New Approach to Legal Translation*. The Hague: Kluwer Law International.
Sin, King-kui and Roebuck, Derek (1996). Language Engineering for Legal Transplantation: Conceptual Problems in Creating Common Law Chinese. *Language and Communication 16*(3): 235–254.
UNCTAD—ICTSD (2005). *Resource Book on TRIPS and Development*. Cambridge: Cambridge University Press.

Chinese references

Bilingual Dictionary Subdivision, Linguistics and Dictionary Division, Foreign Language Teaching and Research Press 外語教學與研究出版社語言學與辭書部雙語詞典編輯室 (Ed.) (2002). 《現代漢語詞典：漢英雙語》 (*The Contemporary Chinese Dictionary: Chinese/English Edition*) (Revised and Enlarged Ed.). Beijing: Foreign Language Teaching and Research Press.
Hsieh, Hsien-Jung 謝顯榮 (2011, April 26).〈亞信：兩岸智財權保護三要點〉(Three Main Elements in IPR Protection).《經濟日報》(*Economic Daily News*) A14.
Jiang, Xiangdong 江向東 (2005).《版權制度下到數字信息公共傳播》(*The Public Broadcast of Digital Messages Under Copyright System*). Beijing: Beijing Library Press.
Law Committee, Standing Committee of the National People's Congress of the PRC 全國人民代表大會常務委員會法制工作委員會 (Ed.) (2007).《物權法立法背景與觀點全集》(*Complete Background and Perspectives on Property Law*). Beijing: Law Press.

Law Dictionary Editorial Committee, the Institute of Law, China Academy of Social Sciences 中國社會科學院法學研究所法律辭典編委會 (2003). 《法律辭典》 (*Law Dictionary*). Beijing: Law Press.

Li, Kexing 李克興 and Zhang, Xinhong 張新紅 (2006). 《法律文本與法律翻譯》 (*Legal Texts and Legal Translation*). Beijing: China Translation and Publishing Corporation.

Lin, Choufu 林周富 (2010). 《智慧財產權法》 (*Intellectual Property Rights*) (4th Ed.). Taipei: Wu-Nan Book Publishing.

Liu, Chuntian 劉春田 (2003). 〈知識產權解析〉 (An Analysis of Intellectual Property Rights). 《中國社會科學》 (*Social Sciences in China*) 4: 109–121.

Lü, Shuqin 呂淑琴 (Ed.) (2006). 《知識產權法律小辭典》 (*Pocket Dictionary of Intellectual Property Law*). Shanghai: Shanghai Lexicographical Publishing House.

Lu, Zhiguo 魯志國 (2004). 〈知識產權與高技術產業發展〉 (Intellectual Property Rights and High Technology Industry Development). 《中國西部科技》 (*Science and Technology of Western China*) 2: 11–13.

Qu, Xinfeng 屈新峰 (2009). 〈著作權與版權的區別〉 (Differences Between Authorship and Copyright). 《知識產權律師》 (*Intellectual Property Lawyers*). Retrieved from: www.biplawyer.com/zzqzl/News/20098101714.html.

Trademark Registrations to Protect Small Businesses 〈保護小販商業權利　商業註冊局擬辦登記運動〉 (2005, December 20). 《光明日報》(馬來西亞) (*Guang Ming Daily*) (Malaysia).

Wang, Chenyan 王晨雁 (2005). 〈對智慧產權概念的質疑與反思〉 (Queries and Reflections on the Concept of Intellectual Property). 《福建論壇（人文社會科學版）》 (*Fujian Tribune (The Humanities & Social Sciences)*) 9: 118–121.

Wang, Liming 王利明 (2001, August 27). 〈物權立法：採納物權還是財產權〉 (Real Right Law: To Adopt Real Right or Property Right?) 《人民法院報》 (*People's Court Daily*) B1.

Wang, Qian 王遷 (2011). 《知識產權法教程》 (*Textbook on Intellectual Property Law*) (3rd Ed.). Beijing: China Renmin University Press.

World Intellectual Property Organization (Ed.) (2007). 《著作權與鄰接權法律術語匯編》(中英法對照) (*Glossary of Terms of the Law of Copyright and Neighboring Rights*). Translated by Liu, Bolin 劉波林. Beijing: Peking University Press.

Zhang, Liuqing 張柳青 (Ed.) (2007). 《物權法審判實務疑難精解》 (*Problems in the Judicial Practice of Property Law Explained*). Beijing: China Legal Publishing House.

Zhao, Lin 趙琳 (2011, May 17) 〈文交所數量激增 交易"藝術品"還是"產權"？〉 (Cultural Property Exchange Transaction on Shape Increase: Are They Trading 'Artwork' or 'Property Rights'?) 《中國新聞社》 (*China News Service*).

Zheng, Chengsi 鄭成思 (1997). 〈再論知識產權的概念〉 (Rethinking the Concept of Intellectual Property). 《知識產權》 (*Intellectual Property*) 1: 13–33.

4 Education in meeting challenges

4.1 Education and training: theory and practice

This chapter proposes a macro-level pedagogical approach that intends to broaden the horizons of students of two disciplines, translation and law, so that they can understand each other's basic concepts and principles. This is essential to their work on legal translation, whether as legal translators or as lawyers. This approach can also be applied to their continuing on-the-job training as part of their professional development.

The chapter starts with a broad approach to strengthening fundamental understanding by legal translation students beginning with their first lecture. The discussion will then illustrate learning activities to widen the horizons of students as well as practitioners of both law and translation. On one hand, it is suggested that translation students and legal translators should understand the legal systems and legal concepts of one or two fundamental legal subjects such as contract law or tort law. Such concepts can equip them to become more competent legal translators. Law students and legal professionals, on the other hand, are encouraged to enhance their language skills and understanding of concepts from the legal systems in other Chinese regions.

This approach offers a way forward through the dilemma of balancing accuracy and fluency by recognising the equal importance of 'law' and 'language' and taking both into account in the production of bilingual legal texts of various kinds. As law relies on language for representation, what is needed in the legal profession is to give more weight to 'language'. Therefore, great efforts should be made to achieve a proper mode for communication and appreciation. Lawyers, especially domestic lawyers who are bilingual, should learn to express law properly in both English and Chinese. Meanwhile, legal translators should make an effort to equip themselves with legal knowledge, so that they are not intimidated into blindly sticking to 'literalism' and sacrificing literary quality and flair.

The following will discuss a range of education and training methodologies for solving the language and legal problems raised in this book. They are broad, balanced and interdisciplinary approaches for both legal translators and members of the legal profession.

4.2 Broad and balanced approach: first lecture on legal translation

The differences between legal systems cause one of the main problems faced by legal translation, namely, a lack of conceptual and terminological correspondence. Therefore, it is important to impart knowledge of the two major legal systems into lectures on legal translation for both translation and law students. While doing so, focus should also placedon giving students a 'balanced view' by putting Chinese or Mainland law into perspective through a comparison of Chinese and Western legal cultures. Furthermore, a general picture of legal drafting styles of the two major legal systems should be given. This will particularly encourage students, especially Hong Kong students of the Anglo-Saxon legal system, to impartially consider the Chinese legal system in its own right and continue to learn concepts from Mainland China or civil law in general.

4.2.1 A broad approach: legal systems, legal traditions and legal language

The broad approach involves general introduction to and comparison of different legal systems and legal traditions and their corresponding legal language styles. In the very first legal translation lecture, the most important systematic comparison that needs to be made is that between the civil and the common law systems. Chinese law is widely considered to be based on the civil law system, which is in essence based on statutes. In contrast, common law is based on case law. Besides this systemic distinction, which is fundamental to the study of both Chinese and Western law, it should be noted that since Communist rule began in 1949, Chinese law can also be considered as having a basis in the Russian legal tradition. Despite sometimes being considered as opposed to the civil and common law systems of the West, the socialist legal system is seen in the eyes of many Western scholars as a development of the civil law system (Lo 1994: 6–7).

The legal traditions of China and the West are also worthy of a side-by-side comparison, since many legal concepts in China are still developing. This is best illustrated through concrete examples. Traditionally, Chinese society is based on 'rule by man' (*renzhi*) (人治) rather than 'rule of law' (*fazhi*) (法治) (Zhang 1994: 4). In Putonghua or Mandarin, 'rule of law' (*fazhi*) (法治) or *yifazhiguo* (依法治國) (governing according to law) and 'rule by law' (*fazhi*) (法制) or *yifazhiguo* (以法治國) (control by virtue of law), which are usually considered contrasting concepts, are both pronounced as *fazhi*. Moreover, *quanli* (權力) (power) and *quanli* (權利) (right) have the same pronunciation. In recent years, on the Tort Law (*Qinquan Zeren Fa* 《侵權責任法》) adopted by the PRC in 2009, some common-law lawyers in Hong Kong (Chen, Wang and Zimmerman 2010) have commented on how many tortious key concepts are still in the process of development in the PRC:

> The Tort Law lacks definitions of key terms used or alluded to throughout the Tort Law such as negligence, gross negligence, intentional acts, fraud,

misrepresentation, reasonable care, trespass to land, trespass to chattel (property), assault, battery, consent, informed consent, privilege, capacity and lack thereof, and causation. However, the lack of specificity is common in most PRC laws.

Even the term *qinquan* (侵權) itself may not be well defined. All in all, it is important to raise awareness of such conceptual issues among legal translators, so as to attain equivalence of legal terms in their work.

The different legal traditions result in different language styles, and these should also be dealt with in the education of legal translation students. Zhao (2000: 9) remarks on the stylistic variance between the legislative language of the common law and civil law legal systems:

> One of the main differences between civil law and common law legislation is the tendency for civil law drafters to rely more on context and inference, thus resulting in a looser texture that is not cluttered with detail. While civil law legislation is a broad statement of principles, common law legislation is an enumeration of instances. Believing that each section and subsection of a statute should be self-contained, common law lawyers intentionally repeat words and entire phrases.

Similarly, Tetley (2000: 703–704) distinguishes the two thus: 'Civil law codes and statutes are concise (*le style francais*), while common law statutes are precise (*le style anglais*). Indeed, civil law statutes provide no definitions, and state principles in broad, general phrases. Common law statutes, on the other hand, provide detailed definitions'. He attributes the distinction to the 'function of statutes', whereby civil statutes are 'not read restrictively', and common law statutes 'cover only the specific part of the law'.

Despite this, Driedger contends that many stylistic differences originate from 'differences in grammatical structure, differences in political institutions and their histories, and out of customs, habits and traditions', and are mostly 'cosmetic' without affecting the 'substance' (Šarčević 1997: 181–182). Concerning law drafting in China, the American scholar Keller (1994: 750) remarks, 'Chinese commentators on legislation normally describe the principles of generality, flexibility and the use of ordinary language as requirements for primary legislation. However, many would acknowledge that secondary and tertiary regulations are often drafted in the same broad, indeterminate language'. To Chinese officials and people, the law may derive a degree of 'predictability from its political and social context' (Keller 1994: 752).

It is advisable that students of legal translation learn both of these two styles when translating legislation from the two legal systems. Below are two examples taken from Hong Kong law and PRC law, respectively:

(1)
A person <u>exposing goods for supply</u> or <u>having goods in his possession for supply</u>
    shall be deemed to offer to supply them. (Section 7(2), Trade Descriptions Ordinance (Cap. 362))

Education in meeting challenges 77

任何人<u>為供應</u>而<u>展示貨品</u>或<u>為供應</u>而<u>管有貨品</u>，須當作要約供應該等貨品。(《商品說明條例》(第 362 章) 第7(2)條)

This short statute is a typical example of the strict style of common law drafting. For one thing, 'offer to supply' is detailed as consisting of two acts, that is, 'exposing goods for supply' and 'having goods for supply'. For another, the phrase 'for supply' is repeated for clarity in expression.

In contrast, the Tort Law of the PRC (2009) demonstrates the general and flexible style of PRC law:

(2)
因不可抗力造成他人損害的,不承擔責任。<u>法律另有規定的</u>,依照其規定。
　(《侵權責任法》第29條)
Where any harm to another person is caused by a force majeure, the tortfeasor shall not be liable, <u>except as otherwise</u> provided for by law.
(English translation, Article 29, Tort Law of the PRC)

The statute is ambiguous in that it does not specify which law is applicable.

4.2.2 A balanced approach: views on the Chinese legal system

In studying the Chinese legal system, the teacher is advised to adopt a neutral and balanced teaching approach and content. Western literature on Chinese law has two main criticisms of the modern Chinese legal system. The first is that the Chinese legal system 'lacks the rule of law'. Peerenboom (2002: 5) comments:

> Third, when claiming that China lacks rule of law, many Western commentators mean that China lacks the Liberal Democratic form found primarily in modern Western states with a well-developed market economy. Although some citizens, legal scholars and political scientists in China or living abroad have advocated a Liberal Democratic rule of law, there is little support for liberal democracy, and hence a Liberal democratic rule of law, among state leaders, legal scholars, intellectuals, or the general public.

Australian-Chinese researcher Cao (2004: 6) also notes such flaws in the legal system in China, which she asserts is known as 'communist/socialist, authoritarian or simply Chinese, is not a liberal democratic system based on the rule of law'.

The second criticism is that Chinese laws are poorly drafted. Peerenboom (2002: 13) criticises Chinese law as 'general and vague' and 'outdated'. He states that this is in part due to 'the lack of practical experience and the low level of competence of the drafters, especially at the local levels'. He also remarks that 'China's legislators simply cannot keep up with the pace of reforms. As a result, many laws are out-of-date, at odds with reality and current practices, and in need of amendment'.

To counterbalance such views from the West, it is suggested the teacher introduce a holistic and historical approach to understanding the development of Chinese law. Cao (2004: 5–6) argues that it is more sensible to 'understand such systems (Chinese legal and political systems) and bring about their transformation or demise', than simply to refer to Western law as the 'ultimate reference'. She also suggests that China's general drafting tradition is 'a highly flexible and contextualist approach to law', allowing statutes to be applied both at the national and the local levels (Cao 2004: 94). Hong Kong scholar Lo (1994: 11) emphasises that Deng Xiaoping took the initiative to build a 'socialist legal system with Chinese characteristics' after he resumed political power in 1978. He states that Deng encouraged the study of law, and that this motivated Chinese scholars and legal experts to find a new legal framework. Li (2000: 9) cites concrete examples to support the notion that statutes have been drafted more clearly in the 20 years after the 1978 reform. The amended Land Management Law, which consists of eight chapters with 86 articles, is 29 articles longer than the original version (seven chapters with 57 articles); and the amended Contract Law (27 chapters with 428 articles) is more than double the volume of the three laws it replaced, that is, the Law on Economic Contracts, the Law on Economic Contracts Concerning Foreign Interests and the Law on Technology Contracts.

In explaining the proper wording in English translation of Chinese law, Leung (2002: 258–259) cites an example that indicates Chinese law was incorporating the concepts from the common law system. Consider the following statute from the original Law on Sino-Foreign Equity Joint Ventures, with English translation provided by Leung:

(3a)
合營企業所需原材料、燃料、配套件等，應盡先在中國購買，也可由合營企業自籌外匯，直接在國際市場上購買。(《中外合資經營企業法》(1979) 第9條)

In its purchase of required raw and semi-processed materials, fuels, auxiliary equipment, etc., an equity joint venture shall give first priority to Chinese sources, but may also acquire them directly from the international market with its own foreign exchange funds.

(English translation, Article 9, Law on Sino-Foreign Equity Joint Ventures, 1979)

This statute was imprecise and ambiguous. The modal verb *shall* had imperative force, but the adverb *jinxian* (盡先) (as soon as possible) contradicted it, giving the equity joint venture the option to buy resources in China or the international market. The statute was then amended as follows:

(3b)
合營企業在批准的經營範圍內所需的原材料、燃料等物資，<u>按照公平合理的原則</u>，可以在國內市場或者在國際市場購買。(《中外合資經營企業法》(2001) 第10條)

For raw materials, fuels and other materials required within the permitted scope of its operation, an equity joint venture may, <u>based on the principles of fairness</u>

and reasonable practice, make the purchase on the domestic market or on the international market.

(English translation, Article 10, Law on Sino-Foreign Equity Joint Ventures, 2001)

The underlined part concerning 'fairness and reasonable practice' was the main amendment to the statute, possibly based on the common law standard of 'reasonable person'. The language of this second version of the statute thus made it more precise and objective.

4.3 Interdisciplinary approach: language and law

This section will first report on two pedagogical case studies that exemplify narrowing the split between 'language' and 'law' in undergraduate studies. This interdisciplinary approach combining language and law is based on the broad and balanced approach to introducing legal traditions, legal systems and drafting style to students discussed previously. The methodology can also be applied to courses at other levels, such as master's programmes, and in other regions. The last part of the section will elaborate on the language and law master's programmes in the three Chinese regions. Launched in Hong Kong in 1990, the Master of Arts in Language Studies (Language and Law) of the City University of Hong Kong was the first language and law programme in the three Chinese communities. Launched in 2004, this programme was already phased out starting 2016–2017 and now there are two master's programmes, namely the Master of Arts in Legal Translation offered by the Open University of Hong Kong launched in 2008, and the Master of Arts in Translation (Business and Legal) offered by the Hang Seng University of Management launched in 2015.

4.3.1 Case study: a legal knowledge-based translation course for Hong Kong translation students

4.3.1.1 Background and aims

In 2013–2014, the author designed and taught a course in legal translation, with the goal of adding the element of legal knowledge to translator training.[1] This course aimed to 'lay the foundation for, and to introduce students to the practice of legal translation' (http://lt.cityu.edu.hk/Programmes/Progs_ProgStruct_BATI.asp). It had three intended learning outcomes:

(i) Demonstrate a good grasp of the basic problems facing, and some of the common solutions available to, the translator and interpreter who must respond to, and manipulate the terminology, idiom and culture-bound language of legal discourse;
(ii) Manipulate the terminology, idiom and culture-bound language of legal discourse;
(iii) Translate with ease and skill common types of legal text.

80 *Education in meeting challenges*

4.3.1.2 Design and contents

To meet the second outcome of providing students with knowledge of legal terms, the course focused on the various concepts of contract law in class exercises and assessments. Contract law is a fundamental subject in legal studies and it is important for students without legal background to understand its terms. For example, many students may misunderstand or mistranslate 'action' (訴訟/法律行動), 'allegation' (聲稱/指稱) and 'damages' (損害賠償) as *xingdong* (行動) (a physical action), *zhikong* (指控) (accusation) and *sunhuai* (損壞) (damage). Of the 33 students in the course, 32 were translation majors, most from Hong Kong with a few from the Mainland, and one was a law student from Hong Kong. After an introduction to the systemic differences between the common law and civil law systems, the course furthered students' English-Chinese and Chinese-English legal translation skills and legal knowledge in four parts.

The first part consisted of a class exercise on a four-page bilingual tenancy agreement from Hong Kong, which was followed with a home assignment based on three major clauses of this agreement. Following is one of the English clauses with its existing Chinese translation. This practice, which required reading an English document and revising its Chinese translation, aimed to introduce students to the basics of legal language and English-Chinese legal translation.

(4)

7 The Tenant shall pay to the Landlord the Security Deposit set out in Schedule I for the due observance and performance of the terms and conditions herein contained and on his part to be observed and performed. Provided that there is no antecedent breach of any of the terms and conditions herein contained, the Landlord shall refund the Security Deposit to the Tenant without interest within 30 days from the date of delivery of vacant possession of the Premises to the Landlord or settlement of any outstanding payment owed by the Tenant to the Landlord, whichever is later. If the Rent and/or any charges payable by the Tenant hereunder or any part thereof shall be unpaid for seven (7) days after the same shall become payable (whether legally demanded or not) or if the Tenant shall commit a breach of any of the terms and conditions herein contained, it shall be lawful for the Landlord at any time thereafter to re-enter the Premises whereupon this Agreement shall absolutely determine and the Landlord may deduct any loss or damage suffered by the Landlord as a result of the Tenant's breach from the Security Deposit without prejudice to any other right of action or any remedy of the Landlord in respect of such breach of the Tenant.

7 租客須交予業主保證金(金額如附表一所列)作為保証租客遵守及履行此租約上租客所需遵守及履行的條款的按金。若租客在租期內並無干犯此合約內任何條款，則業主須於收回交吉的物業或一切租客欠款後(以較遲者作準)三十天內無息退還該保証金予租客。但若租客拖欠根據此合約需要支付的租金及/或其他款項超過七天(無論有否以法律行動追討) 或若租客違反此合約內任何條款，業主可合法收回該物業而此租約將立被終止；業主可從保証金內扣除因租客違約而令業主所受的損失，而此項權利將不會影響業主因租客違約而可採取的其他合法行動的權利。

The second part introduced the translation of judgment abstracts from contract law cases, each relating to a specific legal term. This exercise aimed to strengthen students' understanding of the common law tradition of *stare decisis* (the doctrine of binding precedents), to instil knowledge of legal terms and their underlying concepts and principles, and to develop the skills of translating judgments. The class of 33 students was divided into eight groups of 4–5 students, with each group responsible for one term from contract law. Each group conducted a 35-minute presentation, which consisted of two main tasks. The first task was to translate the abstract of one judgment relating to the assigned term, that covered the material facts and *ratio decidendi* (reason for deciding). The second task was to find authentic bilingual examples that use that particular term. The eight selected terms were 'offer', 'acceptance', 'intention', 'exemption clause', 'misrepresentation', 'mistake', 'duress' and 'damage', and the selected cases included *Entores Ltd v Miles Far East Corporation* [1955] 2 QB 327 (concerning the concept 'acceptance', *chengyue* 承約) and *Balfour v Balfour* [1919] 2 KB 571 (concerning the concept 'intention', *yixiang* 意向).

Before commencing, the students were given guidance on how to proceed with their presentations by examining the case abstract of *Pharmaceutical Society of Great Britain v Boots Cash Chemists (Southern) Ltd.* [1952] 2 QB 795, which was selected to illustrate to students the concept of 'invitation to treat' as opposed to the concept of 'offer'. They were shown translations of the first (material facts) and last paragraphs (*ratio decidendi*), and the second and third paragraphs (in grey) were given as a practice assignment. This laid the foundation for their preparation of the group presentations, that is, to translate the abstracts of judgments relating to contract law. Following is the abstract with keywords underlined and the teacher's proposed translation:

> ***Pharmaceutical Society of Great Britiain v Boots Cash Chemists (Southern) Ltd.* [1952] 2 QB 795**
>
> The <u>defendants</u>' branch shop, consisting of a single room, was adapted to the "<u>self-service" system</u>. The room contained <u>a chemist's department</u>, under the control of a registered pharmacist, in which various <u>drugs</u> and proprietary medicines included, or containing substances included, in Part I of the Poisons List compiled under section 17 (1) of the <u>Pharmacy and Poisons Act</u>, 1933, (but not in Sch. I to the Poisons Rules, 1949), were <u>displayed</u> on shelves in packages or other containers, with the price marked on each. A <u>customer,</u> on entering the shop, was provided with a wire basket, and having selected from the shelves the articles which he wished to buy, he put them in the basket and took them to the <u>cashier's desk</u> at one or other of the two exits, where the cashier stated the total price and received payment. That latter stage of every transaction involving the sale of a drug was <u>supervised by the pharmacist</u> in control of the department, who was authorized to prevent the removal of any drug from the premises.

82 *Education in meeting challenges*

> In an <u>action</u> brought by the <u>plaintiffs alleging</u> an <u>infringement</u> by the defendants of section 18(1) (a)(iii) <u>of the Pharmacy and Poisons Act</u>, 1933, which requires the sale of poisons included in Part I of the Poisons List to be effected by or under the supervision of a registered pharmacist: –

<u>Held</u>, that the self-service system did not amount to an <u>offer</u> by the defendants to sell, but merely to <u>an invitation to the customer to offer</u> to buy; that such an offer was <u>accepted</u> at the cashier's desk under the supervision of the registered pharmacist; and that there was therefore <u>no infringement</u> of the section.

Decision of Lord Goddard C.J. [1952] 2 Q.B. 795; [1952] 2 T.L.R. 340; [1952] 2 All E.R. 456 affirmed.

Reference translation:

　　被告之分店是單一房間，採用自助購買系統，設有藥劑部，由一名註冊藥劑師管理。藥劑部貨架上擺放各類藥物和成藥，皆有包裝或以容器貯存，全部標明價格。當中多種藥物和成藥，或其成份，列於《藥劑業及毒藥法》(1933年)第17(1)條內之〈毒藥表〉第1部分，唯不載於《毒藥規則》(1949年)附件1。
　　<u>...(This part is a home assignment)</u>
　　法院判決，自助購買系統並不構成被告之出售要約，只是邀請顧客提出購買要約；該購買要約於收銀處獲承約，過程由註冊藥劑師監察。因此，藥店並未違反有關條文。
　　法院維持首席法官葛達勳爵 在 [1952] 2 Q.B. 795; [1952] 2 T.L.R. 340; [1952] 2 All E.R. 456 等案件的判決。

This was followed by a home assignment on the factual part of the judgment abstract.

The third part developed students' skills by providing them with practice in reading and translating statutes through the contract-related provisions of Trade Descriptions Ordinance (Cap. 362) (*Shangpin Shuoming Tiaoli* 《商品說明條例》(第362章) from Hong Kong and Tourism Law of the PRC (*Zhonghua Renmin Gongheguo Lüyou Fa* 《中華人民共和國旅遊法》). This part was not linked to any home assignments, as all of the bilingual versions of the ordinances are available online. The following is Article 62, Tourism Law of the PRC, used for English-Chinese class practice:

(5)
訂立包價旅遊合同時，旅行社應當向旅遊者告知下列事項：
　　　　（一）旅遊者不適合參加旅遊活動的情形；
　　　　（二）旅遊活動中的安全注意事項；
　　　　（三）旅行社依法可以減免責任的資訊；

(四）遊者應當注意的旅遊目的地相關法律、法規和風俗習慣、宗教禁忌，依照中國 法律不宜參加的活動等；
(五）法律、法規規定的其他應當告知的事項。
在包價旅遊合同履行中，遇有前款規定事項的，旅行社也應當告知旅遊者。

(《中華人民共和國旅遊法》第62條)

When concluding an organized travel contract, a travel agency shall inform the tourists of the following issues:

(1) circumstances under which it is not appropriate for the tourists to participate in tourism activities;
(2) safety precautions during the tourism activities;
(3) information on circumstances under which the responsibility of the travel agency may be exempted or reduced in accordance with the law;
(4) the relevant laws, regulations, customs, and religious taboos of the tourism destinations to which tourists shall pay attention and the activities which are not appropriate for the tourists to participate in according to Chinese laws; and
(5) other matters that should be informed to the tourists in accordance with laws and regulations.

During the performance of an organized travel contract, in the case of any of the matters as prescribed in the preceding paragraph, the travel agency shall also inform the tourists.

(Article 62, Tourism Law of the PRC)

The fourth part focused on exemption clauses, which constitute a type of contractual text that is commonly encountered in daily life. An illustration of such clauses is the following 'disclaimer' taken from the Hongkong Post, The Government of the Hong Kong Administrative Region (www.hongkongpost.hk/en/imp_notices/index.html (English version); www.hongkongpost.hk/tc/imp_notices/index.html (Chinese version)).

(6)
Hongkong Post does not accept any responsibilities for any loss or damage whatsoever arising from any cause whatsoever in connection with this website. Hongkong Post is entitled to delete, suspend or edit all information on this site at any time at its absolute discretion without giving any reason. Users are responsible for making their own assessments of all information contained in or in connection with this site and are advised to verify such information by making reference to its original publication and obtain independent advice before acting on it.
對於與本網址有關連的任何因由所引致的任何損失或損害，香港郵政概不負責。香港郵政有絕對酌情權隨時刪除、暫時停載或編輯本網址上的各項資料而無須給予任何理由。使用者須負責自行評估本網址所載的各項資料或與本網址有關連的各項資料，並應在根據該等資料行事前，藉參照原本發佈的文本以核實該等資料，以及徵詢獨立意見。

84 Education in meeting challenges

The focus on contract law concepts provided students with a sense of achievement when finishing the course, that is, they learned some legal concepts in addition to translation skills that in turn laid a foundation for their competency in translating legal texts in general.

4.3.1.3 Feedback and reflections

Student feedback was generally good. In response to the questionnaire at the beginning of the semester, many demonstrated their interest in the course, although their impressions of legal translation included 'complicated'; 'long sentences'; 'repetition'; and the importance of being 'accurate'. At the end of semester, for the question 'To what extent did the presentation on contract law terminology help you acquire the translation skills for rendering judgments?', more than half of the students responded that it was 'very helpful' (Figure 4.1). It was also found that they had acquired a basic knowledge of legal terms for rendering legal texts, as well as interest in and motivation for studying legal translation.

Students were also asked to indicate how the course had helped them with the acquisition of legal translation skills. The results (Figure 4.2) show that almost all of the students thought the course was 'helpful', 'very helpful 'or 'extremely helpful' in acquiring the skills.

Reflecting on the course as a teacher, the author observes that legal terminology is still a relative weakness that students must overcome. In the assignment on translating the Hong Kong tenancy agreement into Chinese, students made many mistakes regarding the 'fixed translations' of some legal terminology. For instance, 'breach of contract' (違反合約) was translated as *ganfan* (干犯) (offend)

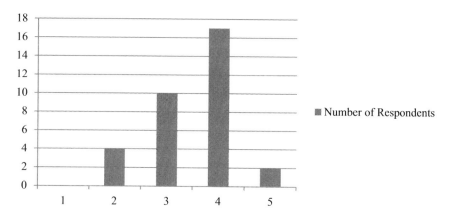

Figure 4.1 Students' responses to the question 'To what extent did the presentation on contract law terminology help you acquire the translation skills for rendering judgments?' at the end of the semester

Importance (5 is the highest and 1 is the lowest) (1 = no help; 2 = of little help; 3 = helpful; 4 = very helpful; 5 = extremely helpful)

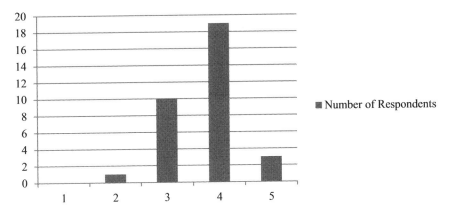

Figure 4.2 Students' responses to the question 'Speaking overall, to what extent did this course that centres on contract law terminology (translating contracts, ordinances relating to contract law concepts, etc.) help you acquire legal translation skills?' at the end of the semester

Importance (5 is the highest and 1 is the lowest) (1 = no help; 2 = of little help; 3 = helpful; 4 = very helpful; 5 = extremely helpful)

or *chufan* (觸犯) (offend) instead of *weifan* (違反) (breach), and the modal verb 'shall' was translated as *xu* (需) (need) instead of *xu* (須) (must). They also had difficulties in dealing with long sentences. Consider the following two examples from the student assignment:

(7)
The landlord shall refund the Security Deposit to the Tenant without interest within 30 days from the date of delivery of vacant possession of the Premises to the Landlord or settlement of any outstanding payment owed by the Tenant to the Landlord, whichever is later.
業主則須在租客交吉其所租之物業或結算其所欠之所有款項的三十天內向租客無息發還該筆保證金。

(8)
The Landlord shall keep and maintain the structural parts of the Premises including the main drains, pipes and cables in proper state of repair.
業主須保持該物業之結構部分（包括主要排污渠、喉管及電線）之妥善維修狀態。

These two Chinese clauses contain no punctuation and are both over 30 words in length.

Another relative weakness is inconsistency of register. According to Smith (1995: 181), aside from 'a basic knowledge of the legal systems' and 'familiarity with the relevant terminology', the legal translator must have 'competency in the TL-specific legal writing style'.

86 *Education in meeting challenges*

Generally speaking, students tend to use classical monosyllabic words together with the occasional modern disyllabic word. Consider the translations of Clauses 7 and 8 of the Hong Kong tenancy agreement by two students, the first from the Mainland and the second from Hong Kong:

(9)

7 The Tenant shall pay to the Landlord the Security Deposit set out in Schedule I for the due observance and performance of the terms and conditions herein contained and on his part to be observed and performed. Provided that there is no antecedent breach of any of the terms and conditions herein contained, the Landlord shall refund the Security Deposit to the Tenant without interest within 30 days from the date of delivery of vacant possession of the Premises to the Landlord or settlement of any outstanding payment owed by the Tenant to the Landlord, whichever is later. If the Rent and/or any charges payable by the Tenant hereunder or any part thereof shall be unpaid for seven (7) days after the same shall become payable (whether legally demanded or not) or if the Tenant shall commit a breach of any of the terms and conditions herein contained, it shall be lawful for the Landlord at any time thereafter to re-enter the Premises whereupon this Agreement shall absolutely determine and the Landlord may deduct any loss or damage suffered by the Landlord as a result of the Tenant's breach from the Security Deposit without prejudice to any other right of action or any remedy of the Landlord in respect of such breach of the Tenant.

租客<u>應</u>向業主支付附表一中規定的定金，<u>並</u>遵守及履行詳列於附表一單條款。**如果**租客<u>並未</u>違反任何條款條件，業主<u>應</u>在收回空置管有權<u>或</u>在租客還清所有款項後的30天之內，將定金無息退還至租客。在租客應付規定租金及其他雜費的七日之後（無論法律上是否要求），**如果**租客<u>仍未</u>能交付所有款項<u>或</u>違反<u>此</u>規定中的任何條款，<u>則</u>業主有權隨時進入房屋，<u>並</u>依據<u>此</u>協定，從租客的定金中扣除相應數額，以彌補因租客違反條款給業主造成的損失。<u>且此</u>項規定不妨礙業主因租客違約行使其他訴訟權<u>或</u>採取任何措施的權利。

(10)

8 Provided the Tenant shall have paid the Rent and other outgoings on the days and in the manner herein provided and observe and perform the terms and conditions herein contained and on the Tenant's part to be observed and performed, the Tenant shall peacefully hold and enjoy the Premises during the Term without any interruption by the Landlord.

<u>若</u>租客按時於租約期內繳清租金和有關雜費，**並且**<u>未</u>有違反<u>此</u>租約內列明<u>之</u>任何條款及條件，嚴謹遵守及履行租約內列明<u>之</u>任何條款及條件，業主<u>則</u>不得於租約期內干預租客享用<u>該</u>物業<u>之</u>權利。

In these two examples, the students have used a number of monosyllabic function words from Classical Chinese, including *ying* (應) (shall), *ruo* (若) (if), *bing* (並) (and) and *ze* (則) (however), which are all underlined. Nevertheless, disyllabic words including *ruoguo* (如果) (if) and *bingqie* (並且) (and) (both in bold) are also used. Such inconsistency may be an indication of 'instability' in the process of learning the formal register in legal writing. This is the feedback the author received from some functional linguists when presenting these student assignments in an international conference on 'Register in Context' in Shenzhen, China in 2018 (Chan 2018).

Overall, this course on contract law aimed to build a knowledge-based pedagogical framework for legal translation, in line with current trends in translation studies. It was designed to counter the shortcomings noted by Way (2016: 1022), that is, translation studies has 'tended to dwell on decision making for isolated translation problems (institutional names, metaphor, etc.) rather than on establishing an overarching framework'. Contract law was chosen because it permeates everyday life. Scholars observe that most legal translation students have had no grounding in the legal field, so legal texts are entirely foreign to their actual life experience. Due to this lack of familiarity, they have no confidence in translating legal texts (Prieto Ramos 2014; Way 2016). 'Few students have participated in a court case, bought a house, or signed a contract. These social practices are completely alien to them' (Way 2016: 1020).

To overcome this difficulty, the course curriculum started with contract law, which is part of one's daily life, and featured illustrations that they related to, such as purchasing various goods and services, renting an apartment, and entering a university to study translation and interpretation. All university students have these types of world experiences.

Rather than asking students to handle international trade agreements or judgments of commercial and criminal cases, the legal translation trainer should start with the basics, that is, the fundamental subjects of legal studies such as contract law, tort law and part of criminal law.[2] Students derive satisfaction from understanding the legal relations that form part of their daily activities. Kelly (2005: 32–33) proposes that translator competence at the macro level consists of a 'set of skills, knowledge and attitudes'. Only after building students' basic translating skills and legal knowledge can the teacher proceed to implant in legal translation students a right 'attitude' to learning, that is, a life-long openness to learning.

4.3.2 Case study: an English-Chinese glossary of terminology for Hong Kong law students

4.3.2.1 Background and aims

In Hong Kong, efforts have been underway to provide legal Chinese courses for law students who study law entirely in English. This section will report on the case study of a glossary compilation project that aimed to equip students with the skills and interest in exploring knowledge, in particular, knowledge of the close equivalents among the Chinese legal terms of Hong Kong, Mainland China and Taiwan. Before 2016, Bachelor of Laws (LLB) students of the City University of Hong Kong, one of the three Hong Kong universities that offer law programmes at different levels, were required to study a course named 'Legal Chinese'. The author taught this course twice between 2011–2013 and this case study describes a project undertaken by those law students to compile an English-Chinese glossary of legal terminology. This English-Chinese glossary of legal terms collected the terms used in two of the main first-year law subjects taught in Hong Kong, namely 'Hong Kong Legal System' and 'Contract Law'. Since Hong Kong law students study law entirely in English, the subject-based glossary was intended to enable them to learn the close Chinese equivalents from Hong Kong, Mainland China and Taiwan of English terms. The glossary also required students to undertake some analysis of the legal and linguistic differences of selected terms from the three Chinese communities.

This glossary compilation project set out to satisfy an important educational need of law and language students in Hong Kong who will be working in a bilingual legal system, and to provide a very useful and convenient reference tool for themselves, lawyers, and teachers of law, Chinese and translation. The project was intended to help law students to consolidate their legal knowledge and use Chinese effectively at work, especially during Hong Kong's increasingly more frequent trade contact with Mainland China and Taiwan. Equally important, it promoted the 'legal bilingualism' taking place in Hong Kong's legal system in both its legislative and judicial levels. Starting in 1997, a language policy was introduced to promote 'bi-literacy and tri-lingualism' (*liangwen sanyu* 兩文三語), where the former refers to the two written languages (English and Chinese) and the latter to the three spoken languages (English, Cantonese and Putonghua).[3] This is in line with Article 9 of the Basic Law, which stipulates the official status of both Chinese and English in Hong Kong. Articles 8 and 18 also stipulate the continuation of the previous common law system. To fulfill this goal, the Hong Kong Government had completed the translation of English common law into Chinese by the time of the handover to China and has also been increasingly using Chinese in court proceedings.

Despite these developments, legal education is conducted in English only, a practice the guarantees that the status quo will be maintained. Shortly after 1997, there was a proposal to implement a full-fledged bilingual legal education that could graduate lawyers competent in writing both legal Chinese and English (Li 1998: 201–203). However, the suggestion was not taken up for several reasons: many law professors are English-speaking expatriates; the curriculum has long been designed and taught in English; and those who are interested in the law programme may not be proficient in both languages. In order to prepare law students who are mostly native speakers of Chinese for these linguistic changes, the author has argued that 'one of the most effective and direct ways is the provision of legal Chinese courses' (Chan 2012: 138).

Since this legal Chinese terminology project involved collection of translated Chinese terms from a variety of sources, including legal dictionaries and bilingual legislation, it was expected that students would acquire valuable research skills for the discovery of new knowledge and develop an attitude of inquiry that would remain with them at university and at work. The collaborative nature of the work encouraged peer review and synergistically produced results with higher accuracy and reliability. Its primary purpose was to assist law students to use Chinese in their study and early careers. Law students are encouraged to use legal dictionaries to understand legal concepts during their studies (McBride 2010: 129–153). Local legal experts also believe that the law schools have a great responsibility to provide law students with Chinese training, especially in the area of legal terminology (Kwan 2011: 328–329).

4.3.2.2 Design and contents

Since legal terminology is the most prominent feature of legal language, it is recommended that law students taking legal Chinese first need to understand Chinese terms. The project involved 35 students of the 'Legal Chinese' course, mainly for second-year law students (32 LLB students, 2 Chinese translation students and 1 business student), who were divided into eight groups of 4–5 members. Each group was assigned four tasks as outlined next.

(i) First, students were required to find Chinese equivalents of 20 terms from the Hong Kong Legal System and make a glossary of these. This was to give students some practice in finding Chinese translations of English legal terms through the English-Chinese Glossary of Legal Terms provided by the Department of Justice Bilingual Laws Information System (www.legislation.gov.hk/eng/glossary/homeglos.htm). This system has now been redesigned and renamed Hong Kong e-Legislation (www.elegislation.gov.hk). Consider the glossary of one group of students in Table 4.1.
(ii) Second, students were required to find ten English terms from contract law and their Chinese equivalents from Hong Kong, Mainland China and Taiwan. A list of relevant statutes and up-to-date dictionaries/reference books from Hong Kong, the Mainland and Taiwan was given to students to use in working on the related terminology. They had to determine the terms' close Chinese equivalents from the three communities, first in their respective statutes and then in dictionaries, cases and scholarly works. To ensure the accuracy of their work, the sources of all terms found had to be detailed in the glossary. Examples are shown in Table 4.2.
(iii) Third, students undertook written analysis of the legal and linguistic differences between two contract terms across the three Chinese communities.
(iv) Fourth, an oral presentation of the findings was given in class at the end of semester.

In this project in which students were motivated to discover new knowledge based on what they had learnt, they encountered a number of difficulties and benefits. To prepare them for the project, a pre-project consultation session was conducted, where relevant concepts were explained and discussed so that they could tackle the difficulties. There were mainly four types. The first type was the nature of the project, which was essentially to conduct a comparative terminological analysis. To clarify that, the students were given the understanding that they were dealing

Table 4.1 Glossary of 20 terms from 'Hong Kong Legal System' course and their Chinese equivalents

English terms	Hong Kong translations
Appellant	上訴人
	《香港終審法院規則》第1條
Barrister	大律師
	《法律執業者條例》第2條
Bill	條例草案
	《法定語文條例》第4條
Bill of Rights	人權法案
	《香港人權法案條例》第2條
Case Law	案例法
	《香港英漢雙解法律詞典》第272頁
Chief Executive	行政長官
	《釋義及通則條例》第3條
Chief Justice	終審法院首席法官
	《釋義及通則條例》第3條
Court of Appeal	上訴法庭
	《高等法院條例》第3條
Court of Final Appeal	終審法院
	《釋義及通則條例》第3條
Court of First Instance	原訟法庭
	《高等法院條例》第3條
Labour Tribunal	勞資審裁處
	《勞資審裁處條例》第3(1)條
Lands Tribunal	土地審裁處
	《土地審裁處條例》第3條
Magistrates' Court	裁判法院
	《刑事案件訟費規則》第4(1)(i)條
Obiter (dicta)	附帶意見
	香港特別行政區訴信高亞洲有限公司 [2012] CHKEC 1056
Obscene Articles Tribunal	淫褻物品審裁處
	《淫褻及不雅物品管制條例》（第39章）第2條
Overrule	駁回
	《香港英漢雙解法律詞典》第1340頁
Plaintiff	原告人
	《高等法院規則》第1(1)(b)條規則
Prosecutor	檢控人
	《刑事案件訟費條例》（第492章）第2條
Ratio (decidendi)	判決理由
	張麗華及其他人士訴入境事務處處長 [1998] 2 HKC 382
	《香港英漢雙解法律詞典》第1566頁
Respondent	答辯人
	《高等法院規則》第6(3)條

with at least four circumstances: (i) similar or same terms with similar or same legal meanings; (ii) similar or same terms with different legal meanings; (iii) different terms with different legal meanings; and (iv) neither corresponding terms nor similar concepts. This framework made it easier to analyse and categorise the terms from the three Chinese communities.

Education in meeting challenges 91

Table 4.2 Glossary of ten terms from 'Contract Law' course and their Chinese equivalents from Hong Kong, Mainland China and Taiwan

English terms	Hong Kong translations	Mainland translations	Taiwan translations
Contract	合約 《貨物售賣條例》第3條	合同 《合同法》第2條	契約 《民法》第153條
Offer	要約 《管制免責條款條例》第3(1)(c)ii條	要約 《合同法》第13條	要約 《民法》第154條
Acceptance	承約 《管制免責條款條例》第3(2)(c)(ii)條	承諾 《合同法》第13條	承諾 《民法》第156條
Consideration	代價 《貨物售賣條例》第3(1)條	對價 《元照英美法詞典》第289頁	對價 《民法》第799條之一

The second type of difficulty reported by students was that the official English translations of Taiwan and Mainland statutes have no legal effects as the two jurisdictions are monolingual, that is, using Chinese only for both the drafting of law and official documents. They found that checking English translations was of little assistance in determining whether concepts were equivalents, as the official English translations of Mainland and Taiwan statutes may not be reliable.

The third type of difficulty was that sometimes they found more than one Chinese translation. This happened mostly in the Hong Kong texts, and they had to use their own judgment in selecting the best translation.

Last but not least, they had problems reading Chinese statutes from Hong Kong due to their complicated sentence structures and specialist terminology. On the other hand, they also found that it was not easy to read the classical style of Taiwan's codes.

4.3.2.3 Feedback and reflections

As to the benefits for students, two aspects were prominent. First, they gained knowledge of legal Chinese and techniques of translation. As shown in Figure 4.3, nearly 80% of students responded at the end of the course that the project was 'helpful', 'very helpful' or 'extremely helpful' in enhancing their legal Chinese and translation competency.

Here are some examples of written feedback from students in Chinese (with English translations by the author):

- '懂得如何在網上尋找相關字詞的翻譯' ('Know how to find translation of legal terms online');
- '知道中文翻譯不單只是一種，還有兩岸三地的不同' ('Know that there is not only one Chinese translation of legal terms, but there are differences among Hong Kong, Mainland and Taiwan'); and

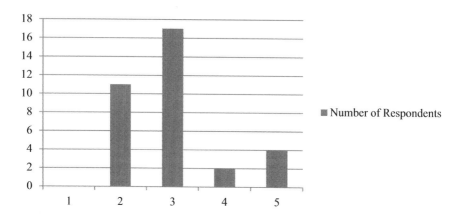

Figure 4.3 Students' responses to the question 'To what extent did you gain knowledge of legal Chinese and enhance translation competency?' at the end of the semester

Importance (5 is the highest and 1 is the lowest) (1 = no help; 2 = of little help; 3 = helpful; 4 = very helpful; 5 = extremely helpful)

- '學會了翻譯技巧，亦懂得很多法律專業術語的中英對照，日後工作可運用相關翻譯技巧' ('Learn not only translation techniques, but also various bilingual legal terms. Such techniques can be applied to future work').

The second aspect is knowledge of legal terms from the three jurisdictions. The following exemplifies the written feedback from students in Chinese (with English translations by the author):

- '認識到三地的不同法律術語' ('Know legal terms from three jurisdictions');
- '增加了對內地和臺灣法律的認識' ('Gain a better understanding of laws of the Mainland and Taiwan');
- '學會了很多不同類型的法律知識，如兩岸三地法律差異' ('Learn more about various kinds of legal knowledge such as the legal differences among Hong Kong, Mainland and Taiwan'); and
- '知道很多不同的法律條例' ('Know many different statutes').

Since both the course and the glossary focused on language training rather than legal training, it was expected that students would benefit more in terms of translation skills than in legal knowledge through the compilation of the glossary, but as these examples show, the students learned something about the legal systems as well.

On reflection as the teacher, this pedagogical project is only a beginning to providing more practical and interdisciplinary Chinese training for law students in the three law faculties in Hong Kong universities. Law students in the Chinese

University of Hong Kong are not provided with any training in legal Chinese, while those of the University of Hong Kong can study two elective courses titled 'Use of Chinese in Law'.[4] Besides providing basic Chinese training for legal purposes, universities should provide some optional advanced legal Chinese classes for law students who aspire to attain a high proficiency in legal Chinese, and they could also provide a legal translation course tailor-made to meet the demands of the legal profession. When lawyers have better skills in Chinese for translation from English law and co-drafting, they would not so readily sacrifice the communicative function and aesthetic value of language when addressing the complications and details of law. They would at least be equipped with some basic literary and rhetorical techniques such as the addition of appropriate punctuation marks and they might use incomprehensible coinages, over-repetition of words and unnecessary classical particles less frequently.

4.3.3 Master's programmes on language and law in three regions

Of the three Chinese communities, Hong Kong introduced the first programme combining language and law. Launched in 1990, the Master of Arts in Language Studies (Language and Law) of the City University of Hong Kong aims to provide students with an understanding of the nature of language and its interaction with society and culture in general. In specific terms, students learn how to apply linguistic and conceptual tools to tackle problems arising in legal writing, legal translation, bilingual legal drafting and so forth. They are also required to reflect critically on the transformation of Hong Kong from a unilingual to a bilingual legal system (www.cityu.edu.hk/catalogue/pg/201415/programme/MALS.htm). However, the programme was phased out starting 2016–2017, probably because of the lack of qualified teachers. In Hong Kong, there are fewer than ten academics who are specialists in legal translation studies, and only a few of them have legal training. Two other master programmes in legal translation remain, namely, Master of Arts in Legal Translation offered by the Open University of Hong Kong, launched in 2008, and the Master of Arts in Translation (Business and Legal) offered by the Hang Seng University of Management, launched in 2016.

These two programmes have different focuses: one concentrates on the Hong Kong legal system, and the other also includes business translation and translation in the other Chinese communities. According to their websites, the Open University programme, accredited by the Law Society of Hong Kong, is designed to meet the increasing demand for translators in the legal profession, with the aim to equip students with 'professional skills in legal writing, legal translation and bilingual drafting'. On completing the programme, students are expected to have an understanding of the common law system and areas of law such as constitution, contract and property, as well as techniques to translate different legal documents 'to meet the challenges arisen as a result of Hong Kong's transformation from a monolingual to a bilingual legal system' (www.ouhk.edu.hk/wcsprd/Satellite?pagename=OUHK/tcSingPage&c=C_ASS&cid=191110018000#Seminars0).

Launched eight years later, the Hang Seng University of Management programme aims to 'train students to master the theories and skills in writing, translating and interpreting in business and legal contexts, and to provide students with the essential knowledge of the translation industry in major Chinese communities' (https://stra.hsu.edu.hk/en/programme-objectives-master-in-translation-business-legal-matbl/). It is expected that graduates would be able to 'meet future challenges in the fast-growing language services industry with a particular focus on business and legal translation'.

The employment pathways include not only the general language professional jobs (project managers, technical writers, public relations/communication officers, language trainers/teachers), but also language jobs in the business and legal professions (financial/business/legal translators, law clerks/legal assistants and business executives).

Having served as an external reviewer of different modules in the Hang Seng programme since 2016, the author found that students were indeed trained to render complex business and legal texts, grasp the key underlying concepts and understand new developments in the translation industries in the major Chinese communities, including translation technology (https://stra.hsu.edu.hk/en/programme-objectives-master-in-translation-business-legal-matbl/). The expansion of the curriculum design in this master's programme reflects the need for cross-disciplinary graduates to cope with the converging development of law and business among the different Chinese communities.[5]

In comparison, in Mainland China, legal translation studies and forensic linguistics, as interdisciplines involving language and law, have been developing fast in the last two decades. Five universities are taking the lead in conducting master's degree programmes in language and law, namely, Guangdong University of Foreign Studies in Guangzhou, China University of Political Science and Law in Beijing, Southwest University of Political Science and Law in Chongqing, Northwest University of Politics and Law in Xi'an, and East China University of Political Science and Law in Shanghai. Most of these are located in affluent areas of China, which provide them with the necessary linguistic and legal support to develop the programmes. The most experienced institution is Guangdong University of Foreign Studies, where the Master Programme in Forensic Linguistics started in 1998 and the corresponding PhD Programme in 2002. The remaining four universities of political science and law, relying on their strong legal backgrounds, successively launched similar master's programmes in the 15 years following 1998.

In these forensic linguistics and legal translation programmes, students are given training in systematic theories of linguistics, applied linguistics and science of law, so that they are competent to tackle linguistics and translation problems in the field of law. For example, the Forensic Linguistics programme of Guangdong University of Foreign Studies aims to train professional language and law personnel with a strong foundation in legal theory and forensic linguistics, as well as related application skills. To achieve this goal, internship opportunities in legal and translation practice are offered (https://yjsdsfc.gdufs.edu.cn/info/1154/1461.

htm). Furthermore, in 2011, the East China University of Political Science and Law set up the Research Institute of Forensic Language and Translation as a support for their MA programme, which places special focus on combining language, legal knowledge and computer technology (http://llt.ecupl.edu.cn/show.asp?id=22). Three of the aforementioned programmes from China University of Political Science and Law, East China University of Political Science and Law and Southwest University of Political Science and Law are open to students from Hong Kong, Macau and Taiwan. Students are required to sit for examinations with varied content in testing centers in Guangzhou, Hong Kong, Macau and Beijing (http://yjsy.cupl.edu.cn/site/index_3.aspx?id=1022D45683B6558D; http://yjsy.swupl.edu.cn/zsgl/gatxszlxx/257235.html; http://yjsy.ecupl.edu.cn/2018/1129/c3801a95407/page.htm).

In Taiwan, seven universities offer a Master of Arts in Translation and Interpretation, including National Taiwan University, Fu Jen Catholic University, National Taiwan Normal University, National Changhua University of Education, National Kaohsiung First University of Science and Technology. While legal translation basically remains an elective course in most of these programmes, the Graduate Institution of Translation and Interpretation of Fu Jen Catholic University launched the first-ever Translation of Financial and Legal Texts Programme in 2009, in collaboration with the Department of Financial and Economic Law and College of Management. With financial support of NT$310,000 from the Ministry of Education, Taiwan to subsidise interdisciplinary education, this programme aims to foster interdisciplinary students with both language skills and understanding of financial services and law (www.cfl.fju.edu.tw/page.jsp?menuID=6&labelID=3).

4.4 Training for legal professionals and legal translators

As far back as the 1980s, an experienced Malaysian legal translator, Wong See Choon (Yin 1988: 84), commented on the special requirements for being a legal translator and the limitations of lawyers in working on legal translation:

> In countries and regions where laws are enacted in English, they all need to deal with the issues of translating law into Chinese. This is universal whether in Malaysia, Singapore, or Hong Kong, which is even more puzzled by this problem. Legal translation is the most challenging task in legal work, and a legal translator must possess some special qualities. While bilingual competency is the minimum requirement, legal sense and writing skills are indispensable. Due to the restraints, there are few people, or even no one, working in English-Chinese legal translation. . . . Except with translation training and experience, a bilingual lawyer is not necessarily a successful legal translator. It is simply because what he or she received is legal training, not translation training.
>
> (English translation by the author)

Wong's point is that lawyers lack the necessary specialised training in translation to perform the job well. Butt (2002: 173) describes law drafters as 'a remarkable

96 *Education in meeting challenges*

group of people' who are 'multi-skilled': 'They must be skilled in the law for their work has to fit into the framework of the existing law. They must be skilled in writing for their writing has to be precise and unambiguous. They must be clear thinkers for you cannot write clearly unless you can think clearly'. Therefore, law students and lawyers must undergo special language and translation training in order to be competent at the task.

Shortly after the 1997 handover, the lawyer Tang (1998: 21) commented that there was hesitation in using Chinese in the conservative legal profession:

> The Department of Justice has completed the compilation of bilingual statutes, yet most of the legal practitioners in Hong Kong continue to use English in drafting legal documents and in court. The use of Chinese is progressing slowly. The legal system is the cornerstone of social stability. Accordingly, we lawyers tend to be conservative and prefer to implement change slowly. We fear making mistakes and are unwilling to take the initiative required to use Chinese. A lack of training in Chinese compounds this fear, forming a vicious circle.

According to historical accounts of legal language policy, Sin and Chu (2000: 102–104) describe the resistance of the legal profession in regards to the possible damage of rule of law due to Chinese use. Some worried that the adoption of writing Chinese judgments would prevent Hong Kong from applying case law from other common law countries that is all written in English.

4.4.1 Government law drafters

A decade later, the Hong Kong Government initiated some changes. As mentioned in Chapter 2, amid strong criticism of the complex sentence structure and Europeanised style of the Chinese version of Hong Kong bilingual legislation, the Law Drafting Division (LDD) of the DOJ has been making efforts towards enhancing their language skills in drafting bilingual bills and subsidiary legislation. In February 2012, the DOJ published *Drafting Legislation in Hong Kong: A Guide to Styles and Practices* (named 'DOJ Drafting Guide' in the study), with the twin aims of helping law users understand how legislation is drafted and unifying drafting patterns across Hong Kong, including those of non-government entities. The Guide can be downloaded at the Hong Kong e-Legislation website of the DOJ (www.elegislation.gov.hk/b0000000004.attach). They also published a Chinese version, *Xianggang Falü Caoni Wenti ji Shiwu Zhiyin* 《香港法律草擬文體及實務指引》; it contains an additional Chapter 15A that details several special features of the Chinese parallel version, and will be referred to as 'Chinese version, DOJ Drafting Guide' in this book (www.doj.gov.hk/chi/public/pdf/2012/Drafting_booke.pdf). Chapter 9 of the Guide, 'Plain Language and Gender Neutral Drafting', *Qianbai Yuwen ji Wu Xingbie Secai Caoni Fangshi* 〈淺白語文及無性別色彩草擬方式〉, pp. 88–107), in which plain language drafting means 'writing easily understandable texts' (Law Drafting Division, Department of

Education in meeting challenges 97

Justice 2012: 88), outlines the following guidelines for writing 'understandable' texts' (Law Drafting Division, Department of Justice 2012: 88–89):

i   Organize legislative propositions simply and logically.
ii Present one topic per clause, one idea per subclause. (This applies to paragraphs and subparagraphs also.)
iii Generally, keep a clause to a maximum of 6 subclauses.
iv Use short sentences with a simple structure. (A division below paragraphs will make the structure complicated; a division below subparagraphs should not be used unless there is no possible alternative.)
v   Use well-constructed sentences, keeping related words as close together as possible.
vi Avoid double or triple negatives.
vii Avoid jargon and unfamiliar words.
viii Use short words.
ix Use the active voice instead of the passive voice.
x   Use the positive rather than the negative.
xi Avoid nominalization by using a base verb to show the action.

These suggested techniques were likely borrowed from Australia; they are almost identical to the plain language drafting techniques first proposed there. Consider the following 'Rules of Simple Writing' as 'The first Element' in plain language put forward by Ian M. L. Turnbull, the Australian Government's First Parliamentary Counsel (Turnbull 1990: 6):

- Using shorter, better constructed sentences.
- Avoiding jargon and unfamiliar words.
- Using shorter words.
- Avoiding double and triple negatives.
- Using the positive rather than the negative.
- Using the active voice instead of the passive voice.
- Keeping related words as close together as possible, e.g. not separating subject from verb, auxiliary verb from main verb, etc.
- Using parallel structures to express similar ideas in a similar form, e.g. not mixing conditions and exceptions, and not mixing 'if' and 'unless' clauses.

Turnbull (1990: 2) defines the nature of the Commonwealth's new approach of plain drafting as 'making laws easier to understand'. His view is that the widely held belief among law drafters since the 1960s that 'precision was all-important' led to 'an elaborate style of drafting which in some cases was unnecessarily complex'.[6]

According to the DOJ's Press Office, ordinances enacted in Hong Kong since the latter half of 2010 have used such plain language practices (Personal communication 12 March 2012). There are four main practices to be promoted. First, 'shall' is not to be used because it most commonly expresses a statement about

98 *Education in meeting challenges*

the future and not a mandatory statement. Instead, 'must' and 'must not' should be used to express obligations/prohibitions with sanction (Law Drafting Division, Department of Justice 2012: 90–99). Second, gender-neutral drafting should be the rule, using the techniques of repeating nouns, using 'the' instead of 'his', using both pronouns 'his' and 'her', and drafting in the plural and passive voice (Law Drafting Division, Department of Justice 2012: 100–105). Third, the use of some archaic language is stopped, for example, 'abovementioned', 'aforementioned', 'herein', 'hereby', 'hereof', 'whatsoever', 'thereby', 'therein', 'thereof', 'howsoever', 'save' and so on (Law Drafting Division, Department of Justice 2012: 109–113). Finally, there should be more careful use of determiners and legal expressions such as 'any', 'all', 'each', 'every', 'for the purposes of', 'if and only if', 'including but not limited to', 'in the case of', 'in the case where', 'notwithstanding', '*prima facie*', 'subject to this Ordinance' and so on (Law Drafting Division, Department of Justice 2012: 116–123).

In the middle of 2014, at the invitation of the DOJ, the author gave a talk to more than 30 Government Counsels of the LDD. Since most of them had studied law entirely in English without formal training in language-related disciplines, the author focused the talk on the fundamental concepts of linguistics and translation, the development and properties of Modern Standard Chinese since 1919, and the drafting methods of some sections of law. The participants actively discussed the examples and volunteered ideas and questions, with a strong willingness to learn. The author also had some departmental colleagues from the Chinese section who conducted Chinese writing workshops for the DLL law drafters about a decade ago. All has contributed to the ongoing language training of these officers, particularly with regard to the use of Chinese.

4.4.2 A mini-survey: use of Chinese by lawyers and legal translators

To understand translation and the use of Chinese in the legal profession, the author dispatched short questionnaires to three small groups of subjects in Hong Kong legal professions, a total of 30 subjects: 15 solicitors, 10 barristers and 5 legal translators. The three questionnaires were slightly different from one another but all concentrated on five issues, namely, (i) difficulties in legal translation/bilingual drafting, (ii) use of bilingual legal dictionaries, (iii) continuous learning, (iv) future demand for legal translation and (v) suggestions for enhancement of Chinese use and translation. For (ii) use of bilingual legal dictionaries, one varied question, for example, was the frequency of using bilingual dictionaries. As it is a general practice for translators to check in different dictionaries at work, this question was not posed to legal translators but to solicitors and barristers who acquired their specialised knowledge entirely in English.

With regard to the first issue, 28 out of 30 returned questionnaires identified 'texts (syntax, terminology, etc.)' as one of the difficulties in legal translation/bilingual drafting. One legal translator working in a law firm describes her experience:

> (1) Difficult to put a complex long sentence into another language while trying to keep it understandable and fluent. (2) Not sure about the exact meaning

of the original text due to lack of knowledge in a particular legal practice area, for example, the operation of 'Carried Interests' when dealing with fund agreements, so sometimes a lot of research is required to understand and come up with the right words to reflect the true meaning of the terms/ definitions.

Despite the difficulties in dealing with the texts, the field seems to have few resources to aid their actual work, which brings up the second issue of the availability of bilingual legal dictionaries/glossaries. For solicitors, only three out of 15 stated that they use bilingual legal dictionaries/glossaries 'always' or 'often'. The majority of solicitors, that is, nine of them, use them 'sometimes', with one using them 'rarely' and one 'never'. For barristers, only two responded with 'often', seven with 'sometimes' and one with 'rarely'. Four out of five legal translators think there are insufficient bilingual legal dictionaries/glossaries available.

In responding to the third issue, continuous learning, based on available choices in the questionnaires such as 'reading books/newspapers', 'attending workshops/ seminars' and 'studying courses', lawyers appear to have fewer opportunities to study Chinese terminology than legal translators do to study law. A total of seven out of 15 solicitors responded with 'reading books/newspapers', with two of them adding 'bilingual judgments' and 'Mainland agreements' as the reading materials, and one included 'attending workshops/seminars', 'studying courses' and 'others', specifically 'watching TV dramas and shows'. Three out of the 15 responded with 'others' only, specifying methods such as 'using legal glossary', 'Google Translate', 'getting feedback from boss' and 'no initiative outside work'. The remaining five responded with 'use English only'. For the ten barristers, one responded with 'reading books/newspapers', five responded with 'others' (including 'reading judgments', 'reading judgments and legal documents', 'Google Translate', 'learning on the job' and 'practice makes perfect'), and four with 'none'. In contrast, four out of the five legal translators, three who studied translation and two who studied linguistics in their undergraduate studies, have further taken law courses such as the Juris Doctor programme during their working life.

On the fourth issue of future demand for legal translation, solicitors are generally concerned about the growing ties with the Mainland. Of the 15 solicitors, 12 considered that there will be an increased demand, and six of them believe it will be due to increasing work from and cooperation with the Mainland. Three responded with 'remaining unchanged' and one predicted that it would decrease. Also, barristers generally thought that there will be an increase. Of the ten barristers, seven responded that it would increase and three that it would remain unchanged. Legal translators had more diverse opinions, with one out of the five responding that there will be an increase, three responding that the demand will remain unchanged, and one that it will decrease. The one who envisages an increase dismisses the use of AI translation tools in dealing with complex legal texts:

> Despite a significant improvement in the performance of various online translation tools, on most occasions they still fail to overcome the complexity of

the long sentences in legal documents, or fail to detect legal jargon in a legal context and instead put the words in a general sense. Legal translators thus remain essential for safeguarding the accuracy of the translation.

On the fifth issue, suggestions for the enhancement of Chinese use/translation, more than half of the 15 solicitors responded with a combination of actions: 'reading more bilingual documents/Mainland counsel's documents', 'more accredited courses on translation/Chinese', 'more online legal dictionaries/glossaries' and 'less haste at work'. Eight of the ten barristers responded with 'more legal resources in Chinese/reading more Chinese judgments/bilingual rulings and decisions to be published regularly/sharing of precedents', 'continuing professional education on Chinese in court proceedings/providing more training especially to junior members of the legal profession', 'introducing authoritative books on translation on use of terms', 'a good e-translation tool', 'Chinese language requirement for law programme applicants', and 'Chinese legal studies as part of the curriculum'. Four out of five legal translators responded with 'accreditation of legal translators by assessment', 'more legal translation programmes/workshops/seminars', 'an annual legal translation competition' and 'more practical training for students'.

Two important observations can be made from these findings. The first is that bilingual materials and practical training are in strong demand by legal professionals and legal translators to support their translation work. The second is that legal professionals tend to use the former, that is, bilingual materials, for self-enhancement, as there are not many legal Chinese language courses available, while legal translators tend to do the latter as they can study legal courses, and bilingual dictionaries and glossaries are insufficient for their practical needs.

4.5 Concluding remarks

Judging from this, there are different stages and objectives for training different legal translators and legal professionals. In designing the legal translation courses in Yaşar University, Selcen and Eryatmaz (2014: 74) make a good summary of the progression:

> undergraduate education should focus on gaining and instructing translation competence and student should graduate as translation specialists. Nevertheless, translator candidates should have the ability to develop his/her skills with time by using the tools he/she gains during undergraduate degree. Besides, translators who want to gain knowledge on a different field should join different programs and work on different fields. Field specialization requires huge resources and a change in current educational conditions.

They also emphase 'a lifelong learning and practicing process which requires a constant awareness of the ever-changing and developing nature of subject areas and the translation studies itself' (Selcen and Eryatmaz 2014: 69). These suggestions for the development of the path and attitude also should apply to the bilingual legal language education and training in Hong Kong.

Notes

1 By and large, this design has been used with modifications by the author in her delivery of an introductory legal translation course up to the present.
2 In the current three LLB programmes in Hong Kong, Contract Law, Tort Law and Criminal Law are first-year subjects in the curriculum.
3 Paragraph 84 of the Chief Executive's Policy Address 1997 states: 'Confidence and competence in the use of Chinese and English are essential if we are to maintain our competitive edge in the world. The Education Commission Report No.6 has already laid down a framework to achieve our goal for secondary school graduates to be proficient in writing English and Chinese and able to communicate confidently in Cantonese, English and Putonghua. Putonghua will become part of the curriculum in the next school year starting from Primary 1, Secondary 1 and Secondary 4, and a subject in the Hong Kong Certificate of Education Examinations by the year 2000'.
4 On various occasions the author has been made aware of the need for Chinese and translation courses at undergraduate law programmes. The most recent one was an invitation to a review exercise on all Chinese language courses for undergraduate programmes in a Hong Kong university. Among a number of graduates from different disciplines interviewed, one from the LLB programme suggested the university provide legal translation training in Chinese courses so that graduates can cope with the translation work in their current jobs.
5 Both of these two legal translation programmes admit relatively small numbers of students compared with a general translation and interpretation master's programme in Hong Kong. In Hong Kong and probably other parts of the world, a general translation and interpretation master's programme with its broad curriculum usually attracts the greatest number of applicants. The specialised translation programmes, such as those that focus on computer tools, usually attract fewer applicants.
6 Australia is one of the common law countries that proactively promotes plain legal language to target 'cost-effectiveness' and 'public access to justice'. In 1993, the Australian Parliament issued two reports that argued law should be made comprehensible to members of the public. One report recommended 46 ways of achieving this goal, most of which were accepted by the Government. In the past few decades, many federal and state laws have been written in simpler language (Asprey 2003: 4–5, 44–46).

English references

Asprey, Michele M. (2003). *Plain Language for Lawyers*. Sydney: Federation Press.
Butt, Peter (2002). The Assumptions Behind Plain Legal Language. *Hong Kong Law Journal 32*: 173–186.
Cao, Deborah (2004). *Chinese Law*. Aldershot, Hants: Ashgate.
Chan, Clara Ho-yan (2012). Bridging the Gap Between Language and Law: Translational Issues in Creating Legal Chinese in Hong Kong. *Babel: International Journal of Translation 58*(2): 127–144.
Chan, Clara Ho-yan (2018). *Teaching Formal Register in a Legal Translation Course*. Conference Presentation at Register in Context: New Questions and Possibilities. Shenzhen University, China, November 27–29.
Chen, Edison, Wang, Laura and Zimmerman, James M. (2010). China Adopts Tort Liability Law. *Lexology*, 3 February. Retrieved from: https://www.lexology.com/library/detail.aspx?g=ec4b826d-dc76-4a62-8883-2326b213c62f

Keller, Perry (1994). Sources of Order in Chinese Law. *The American Journal of Comparative Law 42*(4): 711–759.

Kelly, Dorothy (2005). *A Handbook for Translation Trainers: A Guide to Reflective Practice*. Manchester: St. Jerome.

Kwan, Susan (2011). The Dilemma of Conducting Civil Litigation in Chinese—Conversant Either in Chinese or the Law But Not in Both. *Hong Kong Law Journal 41*: 323–342.

Law Drafting Division, Department of Justice (2012). *Drafting Legislation in Hong Kong: A Guide to Styles and Practices*. Hong Kong: Department of Justice. Retrieved from: www.elegislation.gov.hk/b0000000004.attach.

McBride, Nicholas J. (2010). *Letters to a Law Student: A Guide to Studying Law at University* (2nd Ed.). Harlow: Longman.

Peerenboom, Randall P. (2002). *China's Long March Toward Rule of Law*. Cambridge: Cambridge University Press.

Prieto Ramos, Fernando (2014). Legal Translation Studies as Interdiscipline: Scope and Evolution. *Meta: Translators' Journal 59*(2): 260–277.

Šarčević, Susan (1997). *New Approach to Legal Translation*. The Hague: Kluwer Law International.

Selcen, Aslı and Eryatmaz, Selçuk (2014). An Interdisciplinary Approach for Academic Training in Translation: Legal Translation as a Specialized Translation. *Journal of Language and Literature Education 11*: 69–75.

Smith, Sylvia A. (1995). Cultural Clash: Anglo-American Case Law and German Civil Law in Translation. In Morris, Marshall (Ed.), *Translation and the Law* (pp. 179–200). Amsterdam: John Benjamins.

Tang, Herman W. C. (1998). Myths Mar Progress in Bilingualism. *Hong Kong Lawyer* January: 21.

Tetley, William (2000). Mixed Jurisdictions: Common Law vs. Civil Law (Codified and Uncodified). *Louisiana Law Review 60*: 677–738.

Turnbull, Ian M. L. (1990). Clear Legislative Drafting: New Approaches in Australia. *Statute Law Review 11*(3): 1–26.

Way, Catherine (2016). The Challenges and Opportunities of Legal Translation and Translator Training in the Twenty-first Century. *International Journal of Communication 10*: 1009–1029.

Zhao, Yuhong (2000). Drafting Policy on Bilingual Legislation: Comments on the Hong Kong Securities and Futures Bill. *The Legislative Council Library, Hong Kong Special Administrative Region of the People's Republic of China* 1–25. Retrieved from: http://sc.legco.gov.hk/sc/library.legco.gov.hk:1080/search*cht/X?SEARCH=m%3A%28draft ing+policy+on+bilingual+legislation%29&searchscope=10&l=&m=&Da=&Db=&SO RT=D.

Chinese references

Leung, Lo-yu 梁璐如 (2002). 〈英譯中國貿易政策法規〉(Translating Chinese Trade Policy Regulations into English). In Luk, Angelina Man-wai 陸文慧 (Ed.), 《法律翻譯：從實踐出發》(*Legal Translation in Practice*) (pp. 253–273). Hong Kong: Chung Hwa Book Co.

Li, Changdao 李昌道 (1998). 〈香港雙語法律的歷史發展和展望〉 (The Historical Development and Outlook of Hong Kong's Bilingual Law). In Leung, Priscilla Mei Fun 梁美芬 and Zhu, Guobin 朱國斌 (Eds.), *The Basic Law of The HKSAR: From Theory to Practice* (pp. 193–203). Hong Kong, Singapore and Malaysia: Butterworth Asia.

Li, Shishi 李適時 (2000). 〈我國立法的新特點〉(The New Features of Chinese Legislation). 《中國內地、香港法律制度與比較》 (*The Study and Comparison of Law Between Mainland China and Hong Kong*) (pp. 6–9). Beijing: Beijing University Press.

Lo, Wing-hung 盧永鴻 (1994). 《中國法律觀和法治的演進》 (*The Evolution of the Chinese Legal View and Rule of Law*). Hong Kong: Cosmos Books Limited.

Sin, Wai-man 冼偉文 and Chu Yiu-wai 朱耀偉 (2000). 《以法之名：後殖民香港法律文化研究》(*In the Name of Law: Legal Cultural Studies of Post-Colonial Hong Kong*). Taipei: Student Book.

Yin, Ming 言明 (1988). 〈馬來西亞法律翻譯專家 黃士春談法律中譯〉 (Malaysian Legal Translation Expert Huang Shichun Talks on Translating Law into Chinese). 《經濟與法律》(*Economics and Law*) *21*: 84–85.

Zhang, Xin 張鑫 (1994). 《中國法律：解說與實務》 (*The Chinese Legal System: Explanation and Practice*). Hong Kong: The Chinese University of Hong Kong.

5 Research in meeting challenges

As shown in Chapter 4, the solutions to the 'language' and 'legal' problems mentioned in previous chapters lie in two areas, namely, language training for law students and lawyers, and legal training for translation students and translators. With a view to long-term development, such educational efforts must be based on continuous research, because only research can provide direction and instructions as to where the field should go and the exact content to be taught to students and practitioners. Research can also provide evidence to change established mindsets and views through its appeal to the belief that we are 'reasonable persons' who trust scientific and empirical findings. Before introducing future possibilities for research, this chapter will review some books on legal translation and bilingual law drafting and legal dictionaries and glossaries in Hong Kong.

5.1 Major books and bilingual legal resources

There are two types of books dealing with these topics. The first type consists of research books that probe into the academic and practical issues of legal translation and bilingual law drafting. The second type consists of reference books such as bilingual legislation, translated judgments and bilingual legal dictionaries/ glossaries.

5.1.1 Research books

The following two Chinese edited books, published 17 years apart, are representative of discussions of the theory and practice of legal translation as a profession. *Falü Fanyi: Cong Shijian Chufa* (《法律翻譯：從實踐出發》, *Legal Translation in Practice*), edited by Angelina Luk Man-wai (Hong Kong: Chung Hwa Book, 2002), was the first edited Chinese book discussing various issues related to legal translation and bilingual law drafting in Hong Kong. Published five years after the 1997 handover, the book focuses on translation issues occurring during the early stage of the bilingual legal system. Comprising 15 articles written by prominent figures in the field including former law draftsman, judges, lawyers and legal translators, the volume is a comprehensive work, setting out the fundamental views of the concerned parties. The contributors all deal with practice-related issues such as introduction to legal translation, legal English structures, court interpretation, translation of legal documents for China's trade, prospects of the bilingual system, and so on. The second is *Xianggang Shuangyu Fazhi: Yuyan yu Fanyi* (《香港雙語法制:語言與翻譯》, *Bilingual Legal System in Hong Kong: Language and Translation*), edited by Edmund Cham Shu Kay and Elvis Lee Kim Hung (Hong Kong: University of Hong Kong Press, 2019). The book's contributors focus on translation and bilingual drafting issues in the bilingual legal system, mostly over the recent decade or so. This book is comprised of six long articles on the latest developments in Hong Kong's bilingual legal system, covering topics such as judgment translation, interpretation of bilingual legislation, court interpretation history, training of legal translators and bilingual lawyers, and raising questions in Chinese in courts.

For the training of legal translators in the 1970s, Yu Man-king wrote a book on legal translation, *Falü Fanyi de Lilun he Jishu* (《法律翻譯的理論和技術》, *Legal Translation: Theory and Techniques*) (Taipei: Lotus Publishing Company, 1976). It is likely the first book of its kind in Hong Kong. The book has three sections: Review on legal translation theory and techniques, Illustrations on translation of legal terms, and Samples of translated legal texts. Decades later, Wang Daogeng published *Falü Fanyi—Lilun yu Shijian* (《法律翻譯：理論與實踐》, *Legal Translation—Theory and Practice*) (Hong Kong: City University of Hong Kong, 2013, 2006) that focuses on legal translation as an academic subject. It is suitable for use both as a university course text and for self-study by translators, legal professionals and all interested readers. An experienced translator working in law firms, Wang systematically deals with both the theory and practice of legal translation including the features of terminology and syntax of legal texts, translators' competency, translation standards, methods and techniques, translation of long sentences, and so on. All examples are taken from authentic legal documents in Hong Kong.

5.1.2 Reference books

With regard to legal dictionaries and glossaries, as mentioned in Chapter 2, the DOJ has published three volumes of *English-Chinese Glossary of Legal Terms* (*Yinghan Falü Cihui*《英漢法律詞彙》(4th Ed.), 2004, with 32,000 entries) and *Chinese-English Glossary of Legal Terms* (*Hanying Falü Cihui*《漢英法律詞彙》, 1999, with 11,500 entries). The contents of these books are accessible on the Hong Kong e-Legislation《電子版香港法例》website of the DOJ (www.elegislation.gov.hk/glossary/chi (Chinese-English glossary); www.elegislation.gov.hk/glossary/en (English-Chinese glossary)). The DOJ has also published *English-Chinese Glossary of Civil and Commercial Law Terms* (*Yinghan Minshangshi Falü Cihui*《英漢民商事法律詞彙》, 4th Ed., 2015). However, none of these publications contains any definitions. Edited by Li Zonge, Ho Kwun-ki, Lui Tze-ying and Emily Poon Wai-yee, *English-Chinese Dictionary of Law* (*Yinghan Falü Da Cidian*《英漢法律大詞典》, Commercial Press (Revised version), 2015), together with its first edition in 1998, is the most comprehensive

English-Chinese legal dictionary in Hong Kong with Chinese definitions. Edited by Patrick Chan, Betty Ho, Margaret Ng, Michael Wilkinson, Vincent Liang, Sin King-kui and Tony Yen, *Hong Kong English–Chinese Legal Dictionary* (*Xianggang Yinghan Shuangjie Falü Cidian*《香港英漢雙解法律詞典》, LexisNexis, 2005) and *The Concise Hong Kong English-Chinese Legal Dictionary* (*Xianggang Jianming Yinghan Shuangjie Falü Cidian*《香港簡明英漢雙解法律詞典》, LexisNexis, 2005) also provide definitions, but no *ratio decidendi* (reasons for deciding).

Some references contain functionally equivalent terms from the three Chinese regions. In the *Yinghan Minshangshi Falü Cihui*《英漢民商事法律詞彙》(*English-Chinese Glossary of Civil and Commercial Laws*, 2nd Ed., 2004), published by the DOJ, there are 164 terms from civil law with translations or close equivalents from Hong Kong, the Mainland, Taiwan and Macao. There are also two glossaries of financial terminology. *An English-Chinese Glossary of Securities, Futures and Financial Terms* (4th Ed.) (edited by Securities and Futures Commission, 2006) has 15,000 entries, which are mostly close equivalents from Hong Kong and the Mainland. In the online *A Glossary of Securities and Financial Terms* (edited by Hong Kong Exchanges and Clearing Limited, 2019), some of the translated Chinese terms used in Hong Kong are provided with their Mainland counterparts marked by an asterisk (www.hkex.com.hk/eng/global/glossary.htm).

Between 2014–2017, the author published three monographs on Chinese legal terminology under the *Legal Translation Series* of the City University of Hong Kong Press, namely, *Falü Fanyi Xilie: Liang'an Sandi Heyue Fa Zhuyao Cihui* (《法律翻譯系列：兩岸三地合約法主要詞彙》, *Legal Translation Series: Key Terms in Contract Law of Hong Kong, Mainland China and Taiwan*, 2014), *Falü Fanyi Xilie: Liang'an Sandi Qinquan Fa Zhuyao Cihui* (《法律翻譯系列：兩岸三地侵權法主要詞彙》, *Legal Translation Series: Key Terms in Tort Law of Hong Kong, Mainland China and Taiwan*, 2015), and lastly, *Falü Fanyi Xilie: Liang'an Sandi Gongsi Fa Zhuyao Cihui* (《法律翻譯系列：兩岸三地公司法主要詞彙》, *Legal Translation Series: Key Terms in Company Law of Hong Kong, Mainland China and Taiwan*, 2017). Serving as a reference for legal professionals, legal translators, researchers and students in language and law, each of these three books compares and contrasts the Chinese legal terminology of Hong Kong, Mainland and Taiwan from the perspective of translational equivalence, together with an English-Chinese glossary based on statutes and legal dictionaries from all three regions. The books contain dozens of case summaries from the United Kingdom and Hong Kong. For example, in the first book on contract law, there is *Carlill v Carbolic Smoke Ball Co.* [1893] 1 QB 256 relating to 'unilateral offer', *Combe v Combe* [1951] 2 KB 215 relating to 'consideration', and *Krell v Henry* [1903] 2 KB 740 relating to 'frustration'.

For the translation of legislation, as soon as Hong Kong enacted the first bilingual legislation in 1989, the Mainland jurist Yu Zhenlong edited the book *Xianggang Fali Zhongyi Cankao* (《香港法例中譯參考》, *Chinese Translation of*

Hong Kong Legislation) (Shanghai: Shanghai Translation Publishing Co.). The book contains Chinese translations of five Hong Kong ordinances, including the Banking Ordinance (Cap. 155) and the Sale of Goods Ordinance (Cap. 26). In the preface, Yu emphasises that it is an enormously difficult task to translate English legislation into Chinese due to the complicated historical background. In view of the potential mutual borrowing between the legal systems of Hong Kong and the Mainland, he is of the opinion that the translation of Hong Kong legislation can facilitate not only the studies of comparative law but also judicial practice in the Mainland.

In 2003, *Shuangyu Putongfa: Xingshi Anli Zhailu* (《雙語普通法：刑事案例摘錄》, *Bilingual Common Law: Extracts from Criminal Cases*), edited by Angelina Luk and Eleanor Hui, was published as the inaugural volume of the *Bilingual Common Law Series* by Sweet & Maxwell Asia, Hong Kong in collaboration with the Judiciary of the the Hong Kong SAR Government. As a response to the increasing use of Chinese in Hong Kong courts, this volume features extracts from judicial decisions in Hong Kong and other common law jurisdictions and full translations of these extracts into Chinese. As described on the book cover, the translations are rendered 'in a lucid and highly readable style'. The second volume in this *Bilingual Common Law Series Shuangyu Putongfa: Tudi Anli Zhailu*《雙語普通法:土地案例摘錄》 (*Bilingual Common Law: Extracts from Land Cases*, 2005), appeared in 2005 and was compiled by Johnson Lam under editor-in-chief Edmund Cham. In 2009, law reporting in Chinese started with the launch of *Xianggang Zhongwen Pan'anshu yu Yingyiben Huibian* 《香港中文判案書與英譯本彙編》 (*Hong Kong Chinese Law Reports and Translations*, Hong Kong: Sweet & Maxwell/Thomson Reuters). The inaugural volume of this series contains 250 Chinese judgments delivered between 1995 and 2008, all selected on the basis of their jurisprudential value by bilingual judges and judicial officers. It is intended mainly for use by the judiciary and the legal profession.

5.2 Two potential research areas

Two research areas hold promise for supporting and strengthening the field of legal translation and bilingual law drafting in Hong Kong. The first area focuses on enhancing the linguistic quality of Hong Kong's bilingual legislation and judgments. Although it is based specifically on Hong Kong's law drafting policy, the methodology can be used in other multilingual countries, because it examines the world trend towards plain language drafting. The second area focuses on legal terminology, that is, the explanation of legal terminology and the compilation of a combined legal glossary for Hong Kong, the Mainland and Taiwan. One example of this is an ongoing project conducted by the author. As three related Chinese books in this potential area have already been completed, a summary of the first book's first chapter on the term 'contract' is given here, so that English readers can grasp an understanding of the key ideas of this series.

5.2.1 Enhancing language quality for bilingual legislation and judgments

In the face of fierce criticism of the Chinese ordinances in Hong Kong's bilingual legislation, a thorough investigation is needed to explore the key issues and problems exposed in a wider range of bilingual ordinances and put forward practical solutions. Previous studies have described the process of the governmental project to translate English common law before 1997, discussed contemporary translation theories to justify a communicative approach to rendering English laws into Chinese, and suggested revisions for one or two ordinances (Chan 2012, 2007; Sin 2000; Zhao 2000a, 2000b). Efforts have also been made to revise the English legislation drafting and Chinese translation of judgments (Poon 2006). The present discussion is divided into two parts, namely, legislation and judgments, and since they share common issues, they are not mutually exclusive. Each part will start with specific observations and suggestions, then explore likely future directions. In other words, both practical solutions and theoretical philosophies from scholars are needed to fill the gap in the field. All recommendations are made on the basis of the existing research and official guidelines.

5.2.1.1 Co-drafting of bilingual legislation: plain language drafting

Rimsky Yuen Kwok-keung (Yuen 2016), Senior Counsel and Secretary of Justice during 2012–2018, reiterated the significance of plain language drafting. In addressing the symposium 'Translation and the Profession' held in celebration of the Hong Kong Translation Society's 45th anniversary in November 2016, Yuen referred to Lord Bingham's statement in his 2010 book *The Rule of Law* that 'accessibility and intelligibility of law' is the first key principle in the rule of law, in that it enables people to understand it. Yuen also outlined the plain language initiatives in major common law countries, including the 'Plain English Manual' in Australia, 'Good Law' in Britain, 'Plain Writing Act' in America, and the mechanism to redraft laws in New Zealand. Locally, there was an increase in unrepresented litigants in the past five years. These international and local trends have paved the way for Hong Kong's adoption of plain language drafting in 2012.[1]

Against this background of 'reform' mainly in the English-speaking common law countries, research in Hong Kong should aim to help the public read and understand legislation to facilitate effective implementation of public policies. In the medium and long run, further study can reinforce legal transparency, the rule of law and the general bilingual policy of Hong Kong. It should have two directions: one is to investigate concrete methods of drafting more fluent and comprehensible legislation, and the other is to examine the meaning and implications of the 'plain language' principles. The goal in the first direction is to determine specific methods to create a parallel Chinese text in 'an elegant style in conformity with the Chinese grammar and clarity in semantic meanings' (Law Drafting Division, Department of Justice 2012b: 246; English translation by the author). These sound techniques are expected to be adopted to compile a detailed plain language guide for drafting Chinese legislation and training materials for law drafters.

Chan (2018) gives concrete suggestions on the drafting of Chinese legislation. In line with the plain language initiative in the DOJ Drafting Guide published in 2012, the three suggested techniques to create laws that communicate effectively while maintaining their legal meaning and legal effects. These three techniques are explained on the basis of English-Chinese contrastive grammar.

The first is to construct a definition-like short sentence for terms. For example, in the following statute, the Chinese version does not answer the underlined question, resulting in a lack of coherence with the preceding text.

(1a)
What is idling
For the purposes of this Ordinance, a motor vehicle is idling if any internal combustion engine forming part of, attached to or situated in or on the vehicle is operating while the vehicle is stationary. (Section 4, Motor Vehicle Idling (Fixed Penalty) Ordinance (Cap. 611))

(1b)
何謂引擎空轉
為施行本條例，當汽車停定時，任何屬該車輛一部分的、附於該車輛的、位於該車輛內的或在該車輛上的內燃引擎如在操作，該車輛即屬引擎空轉。(《汽車引擎空轉(定額罰款)條例》(第611章)第4條)

Thus, as illustrated in Example (1c), the Chinese version would be improved by copying the question-and-answer technique in the English text, that is, 'a motor vehicle is idling if . . .' transferred as '車輛引擎空轉，乃指 . . .', and placing the modifiers in a separate clause.

(1c)
何謂引擎空轉
在本條例，<u>車輛引擎空轉，乃指車輛停定時，其內燃引擎仍在操作</u>。內燃引擎可屬車輛一部分，或附置於車輛內外。(《汽車引擎空轉(定額罰款)條例》(第611章)第4條)

The second technique is to adopt 'zero anaphora', which is considered by linguists to be the anaphoric norm in Chinese (Chen 1991: 181–209; Li and Thompson 1979: 312–322; Xu 2003: 108), and classical pronouns as referential devices. The third technique is to convert legal terms from nouns to verbs. These suggested techniques aim to achieve the 'cohesion' (How do the clauses hold together?), 'coherence' (How do the propositions hold together?) and 'informativity' (What does it tell us?) requirements of a communicative text proposed by de Beaugrande and Dressler (1981) in their 'Seven Standards of Textuality'.

On the basis of this past study, future research should explore more examples relating to the use of zero anaphora and the classical pronoun *qi* (其), and words and terms that can be converted from nouns to verbs. The point of using zero anaphora and the classical pronoun *qi* (其) is to comply with the DOJ Drafting Guidelines as stated above: (iv) Use short sentences with a simple structure; (v) Use well-constructed sentences, keeping related words as close together as possible (Law Drafting Division, Department of Justice 2012a: 89). Consider the following examples:

(2a)
If <u>the owner</u> has undertaken to maintain any slope in relation to the development at that <u>owner</u>'s own cost, the sales brochure—... (Schedule 1, Section 27(2), Residential Properties (First-hand Sales) Ordinance (Cap. 621))
(2b)
如<u>擁有人</u>已承諾<u>擁有人(repetition)</u> 自費就發展項目維修任何斜坡，售樓說明書—...（《一手住宅物業銷售條例》（第621章）第27(2)條附表1)
(2c) Suggested Chinese version
如<u>擁有人</u>已承諾 <u>(zero anaphora)</u> 自費就發展項目維修任何斜坡，售樓說明書—...
（《一手住宅物業銷售條例》（第621章）第27(2)條附表1)

Example (2) demonstrates the use of zero anaphora in the Chinese version. Example (2b) shows the repetitive use of *yongyouren* (擁有人) (owner) that exactly follows the gender-neutral drafting technique of repeating nouns in the English version, while Example (2c) demonstrates the use of zero anaphora, that is, the omission of *yongyouren* (擁有人) (owner) in its second appearance.

(3a)
If it appears to <u>the Registrar</u> that the information contained in a document registered by <u>the Registrar (repetition)</u> in respect of a company is inconsistent with other information relating to the company on the Companies Register, <u>the Registrar (repetition)</u> may give notice to the company — ... (Section 39(1), Companies Ordinance (Cap. 622))
(3b)
如<u>處長</u>覺得<u>處長</u>就某公司登記的文件所載的資料，與公司登記冊內關乎該公司的其他資料相抵觸，<u>處長</u>可向該公司給予通知 — ...（《公司條例》（第622章）第39(1)條)
(3c)
如<u>處長</u>覺得其 <u>(classical pronoun qi)</u> 為某公司登記的文件所載資料，與公司登記冊內關乎該公司的其他資料相抵觸， <u>(zero anaphora)</u> 可向該公司給予通知 — ...（《公司條例》（第622章）第39(1)條)

Example (3) illustrates the use of the classical pronoun *qi* (其). Example (3b) contains repetitive use of *chuzhang* (處長) (registrar), which is an imitation of the gender-neutral drafting technique of repeating nouns, that is, replacing the masculine pronoun 'his' with 'the', in the English version, while Example (3c) is the use of the classical pronoun *qi* (其) and zero anaphora, that is, the omission of *chuzhang* (處長) (registrar), in its second and third appearances.

Research in meeting challenges 111

The purpose of converting words and terms from nouns to verbs is to satisfy DOJ Drafting Guidelines (vi) and (v) listed prior to Example (2), and (xi) Avoid nominalization by using a base verb to show the action (Law Drafting Division, Department of Justice 2012a: 89). Consider the following examples:

(4a)
After considering the representations, if any, made within the period referred to in section 10, the Commission may <u>make a decision</u> as to whether or not the agreement in question is excluded or exempt from the application of the first conduct rule or this Part. (Section 11(1), Competition Ordinance (Cap. 619))

(4b)
競委會在考慮於第10條提述的限期內作出的申述(如有的話)後，可<u>作出</u>有關協議是否被豁除於第一行為守則或本部的適用範圍之外或獲豁免而不受第一行為守則或本部規則的<u>決定 (noun)</u>。(《競爭條例》(第619章)第11(1)條)

(4c)
競委會在考慮於第10條提述的限期內作出的申述(如有的話)後，可<u>決定 (verb)</u>有關協議是否被豁除於第一行為守則或本部的適用範圍之外或獲豁免而不受第一行為守則或本部規限。(《競爭條例》(第619章)第11(1)條)

Chinese has no overt markers for parts-of-speech and a given form can enjoy categorical fluidity, for example, *fuwu* (服務) can be 'to serve' or 'service'. Example (4) shows this fluid use of *jueding* (決定) (decide/decision). Example (4b) shows the use of *jueding* (決定) (decision) as an abstract noun combined with the empty verb *zuochu* (作出) (make). As illustrated in Chapter 2, this kind of empty verb construction is a widespread feature of today's Europeanised Chinese. The use of *jueding* (決定) (decide) as a verb in Example (4c) has the added benefit of simplifying the sentence structure.

(5a)
Any person may, in accordance with guidelines issued under section 38, <u>lodge a complaint</u> with the Commission alleging that an undertaking has contravened, is contravening or is about to contravene a competition rule. (Section 37(1), Competition Ordinance (Cap. 619))

(5b)
任何人可按照根據第38條發出的指引，向競爭會<u>作出投訴(noun)</u>，指稱某業務實體已違反、正違反或即將違反某競爭守則。(《競爭條例》(第619章)第37(1)條)

(5c)
任何人可按照根據第38條發出的指引，向競爭會<u>投訴(verb)</u>，指稱某業務實體已違反、正違反或即將違反某競爭守則。(《競爭條例》(第619章)第37(1)條)

Similarly, Example (5) also illustrates the fluidity of *tousu* (投訴) (complain/complaint) in terms of speech. Example (5b) shows the use of *tousu* (投訴) (complaint) as an abstract noun following the empty verb *zuochu* (作出) (make). Example (5c) shows how the use of *tousu* (投訴) (complain) as a verb makes a more succinct sentence. Cham (2019: 107) suggests that if 'empty verbs' are used, there are more meaningful choices than *zuochu* (作出) (make). For example, *tichu* (提出) (put forward) can be used with *yaoqiu* (要求) (request) and *shenqing* (申請) (application), and *zhifu* (支付) (pay) can be used with *peichang* (賠償) (compensation).

With regard to the second direction of examining the 'plain language drafting' principle, the current practice is that law is higher than language, and as a result drafters are required to forgo conciseness in Chinese that is considered to lead to ambiguity (Law Drafting Division, Department of Justice 2012b: 246). This is opposite to the drafting experience of other bijural countries such as Canada, which adopts a bijural and bilingual legal system. Gémar (2014: 73) suggests that in Canada, which moved from translating to co-drafting laws in the second half of the twentieth century, the quest for equivalence is according to 'the spirit of the law, not the letter'. He further explains that 'Canada is a bilingual, bijural and multicultural state. This "natural-born translators' country" has evolved from the stage of a servile, heavy and awkward way of translating to co-drafting, a radical post-translational way of producing bilingual legislative texts'. Co-drafting is preferred for its ability to 'produce texts both idiomatic and readable and, at the same time, facilitate their interpretation' (Gémar 2014: 78). Why is there such a great difference between the goals of plain language in Hong Kong and Canada? It is mainly because Chinese grammar, unlike French, is very different from English due to its brevity. Since Hong Kong law drafters do not know how to balance legal precision with the inherent terseness of Chinese, it is easy to maintain and imitate the structure of the English version in the Chinese version. Therefore, awkward translationese-style Chinese prevails.

There is a view that Chinese is unsuited for use as a legal language because of the ambiguity that may result from its grammatical succinctness. In support of this view, Cao (2004: 95–117) cites examples that mainly relate to the economy rule and context dependency in Chinese. In particular, articles are non-existent, and subjects and grammatical markers such as conjunctions and modal verbs are optional. An example is *yiwai sunshi* (意外損失) (accident damage), where it is not clear whether it is 'accident and/or damage' or 'accidental damage'. The ambiguity extends to verbal tenses. She cites another example to illustrate how context renders lack of tense grammatical: *Xiaxingqi, jiayi shuangfang qianding hetong* (下星期，甲乙雙方簽訂合同) (Next week Party A and Party B will sign [a] contract), where the tense marker *jiang* (將) (will) is omissible without affecting the meaning. To assist law drafters to strike a balance between language and law, research must determine which specific rules of economy are appropriate to legal Chinese and which grammatical markers should be preserved. At this stage, it is understood that law is universal and legal English is mostly in the present tense, and modal verbs are optional in legal Chinese. In contrast, the use of and/or is critical, so the use of those terms in Chinese, *huo* (或)/*houzhe* (或者) (or) and *he* (和)/*ji* (及) (and), should not be optional.

5.2.1.2 Translation of judgments: Chinese proficiency and language style

Despite the legislative bilingualism commencing in the 1980s, the first Chinese judgment did not appear in Hong Kong until 1995. The translation of judgments closely concerns the language used in courts. As of 2017, the proportions of court proceedings conducted in Chinese in the High Court, District Courts and Magistrate's Courts were 36%, 64% and 90%, respectively, demonstrating a tendency for English to be used in higher courts and Chinese in lower courts. It is probable that this differentiation is due to the fact that lower courts mostly deal with cases involving parties who are Chinese-speaking, and the majority of judges and magistrates are proficient in both Chinese and English, while higher courts mostly deal with cases involving complicated laws and English documents, which are also likely presided over by expatriate judges and lawyers (Cham 2019: 89–91).

Discussion of the use of English and Chinese began early in the 1980s, and one proposal was precisely that English should be used in 'higher courts' and Chinese in 'lower courts'. Some of the arguments in support of this proposal were that 'most personnel of the legal profession are proficient in English and receive their legal training in English', 'courts of the higher level have to handle cases that involve complicated legal principles' and 'If Hong Kong is to maintain its position as an international commercial and financial centre as well as to attract foreign investment and technology, it is necessary that the international community has full confidence in its legal system' (Special Group on Law, Consultative Committee for the Basic Law of the Hong Kong Special Administrative Regions 1987: 6–7).

Against this linguistic background of the past 20-odd years, translations of two kinds of judgment are in progress in the Hong Kong Judiciary. These are (i) translation of English judgments of the Court of Final Appeal into Chinese (to date about 100 have been completed), and (ii) translation of Chinese judgments of lower courts into English (about 600 have been completed) (Cham 2019: 92). Starting in August 2008, according to the judiciary website, Chinese judgments of 'jurisprudential value' handed down since 1995 have been uploaded onto the website along with their English translations (www.judiciary.hk/en/legal_ref/judgments.htm).

There is limited past literature in this area and the following will examine the main contributions of the literature and explore future research possibilities in terms of translation methodology and principles.

In Chapter 2, the issue of Europeanisation of Chinese was touched upon. To the future proposed research directions, similar to that in the legislation, both the translation techniques and translation principles are worth investigating in translation of judgments. Three new proposals with regard to translation techniques have emerged in recent years. The first is related to language alone, and the second and third to the combination of language and law.

The first proposal is the creation of an elegant style that makes full use of the merits of Chinese. Cham (2019: 108) makes a strong appeal for this approach in his examination of translated judgments, arguing that the 'Europeanised style' can be remedied through greater emphasis on the 'paratactic structure' and 'natural collocation of words' in Chinese. Consider the following example:

(6a)
Dr. Wong opined that the deceased died of intracerebral haemorrhage, that the deceased's pre-existing heart disease did not directly cause her death, and that the haemorrhage was likely caused by heavy external blow on the deceased's head. Dr. Wong expressed no view as to whether the defendant's act of attacking the deceased with the hammer constituted such heavy blow.

(6b)
王醫生認為死者死于腦內出血，死者原有的心臟病並非直接死因，以及上述出血相當可能由死者頭部受到外物重擊所致。<u>王醫生沒有就被告人用錘子襲擊死者的行為是否構成該重擊的問題表達意見</u>。

While recognising the accuracy of this translation, Cham suggests revising the last sentence with the use of the conjunction *zhiyu* (至于) (as to). Now the sentence is broken down into two clauses in reverse word order from the original one. Through the restructuring, the embedded clause formed by the preposition *jiu* (就) taking a long object, that is, *jiu beigaoren yong chuizi xiji sizhe de xingwei shifou goucheng gai zhongji de wenti* (就被告人用錘子襲擊死者的行為是否構成該重擊的問題), is avoided (Cham 2019: 109).

(6c)
王醫生認為死者死于腦內出血，死者原有的心臟病並非直接死因，以及上述出血相當可能由死者頭部受到外物重擊所致。<u>至于被告人用錘子襲擊死者的行為是否構成該重擊，王醫生沒有表達意見</u>。

Given the paratactic property of the Chinese language, deletion of the conjunction *zhiyu* (至于) can further enhance the succinctness of the sentence. As to the elegance of judgment translation, Wong and Sin (2002: 196) had already advocated the use of Classical Chinese as a solution some seven years after the first Chinese judgment was written. They disapproved of the 'improper' mixture of old Chinese and vernacular Chinese in Chinese judgments, which are usually written in a higher register. For instance, *yiban eryan* (一般而言) (generally speaking), usually used in written language, sounds more appropriate than *yiban laishuo* (一般來說) (generally speaking), usually used in spoken language. Given that Modern Chinese retains classical elements as mentioned in Chapter 2, the promotion of old Chinese should not be restricted to the lexical realm, but extend to the syntactical and grammatical realms as well. Classical Chinese, with its terse and compact structure, appears to be the most effective method to refine translated Chinese judgments, since it naturally eliminates the adverse Europeanised impacts on Modern Chinese such as the overuse of pronouns, conjunctions and passive voice. Classical style can also naturally combat the persistent complications in legal English created by lawyers and jurists, such as the challenge of a long sentence as presented to translators in Example (6a). Among the three Chinese communities, Taiwan has retained the most classical element in the Modern Chinese, and Mainland China has retained the least. Hong Kong, where translators generally have good Classical Chinese training, should aim at exploiting this edge to combat the convoluted style of legal language.

The second new proposal is to provide both legally and linguistically informed translations for legal terms in judgments. Cham (2019: 94–98) cites examples from both civil law and criminal law, most of which do not regularly appear in legislation and as a result do not have standardised translations. In civil law, based on actual translation experience, 'settlement' is translated as *tingwai hejie* (庭外和解) (conciliation outside the court) in civil procedural law, and as *shouchan anpai* (授產安排) (arrangement of property entrustment) in trust law.

In criminal law, some terms have several translation candidates. For example, 'starting point' is translated both as *liangxing qidian* (量刑起點) (starting point of sentencing) and *liangxing jizhun* (量刑基準) (benchmark of sentencing). Since 'starting point' refers to the term of a sentence, which can be both increased and decreased, *jizhun* (基準) (benchmark) better reflects its meaning than *qidian* (起點) (starting point). A second example is 'totality principle', which refers to the principle that sentencing should be both just and proportionate. This term currently has three translations, namely, *zhengti liangxing* (整體量刑) (total sentencing), ((*kaolü*) *zong liangxing, yimian xingqi guozhong* ([考慮]總量刑，以免刑期過重), ((considering) sentencing in its totality to avoid over sentencing) and *zong xingqi de yuanze* (總刑期的原則) (the principle of total sentencing term). In order to balance legal meaning with linguistic economy, Cham recommends in this case *zong xingqi xu gongzheng he xiangchen yuanze* (總刑期需公正和相稱原則) (the principle of sentencing in justice and proportionality). For further refinement, two translations are suggested here. The first is *zong xingqi gongzheng xiangchen yuanze* (總刑期公正相稱原則), which deletes the words *xu* (需) and *he* (和) from Cham's recommended translation. The rationale for this is that *xu* (需) as a modal verb and *he* (和) as a conjunction are omissible in Chinese, and it appears that Cham has incorrectly used *xu* (需) (need) instead of *xu* (須) (must), which is habitually used in legal writings. The second is *zong xingqi yuanze* (總刑期原則) or *zong liangxing yuanze* (總量刑原則), which work on the basis that people presume sentencing to be just and proportional.

The third proposal is the 'demystification' of law to both lawyers and non-lawyers. Poon (2018: 459–460), in espousing the plain language approach to translating legislation and judgments, specifies the 'conversion' method as a means of making law accessible to all. She cites two examples in which there is use of passive voice in the English source text. Consider one of them in Example (7):

(7a)
Since it is not disputed that 'marriage' in art 37 refers to a union between a man and a woman, the dispute turns on the meaning of 'man' and 'woman' for the purpose of this article.

(7b)
因為此案中"婚姻"在37條中是指一男一女的結合，毋需爭議。爭論點在於"男"和"女"在這法例中的定義。

This Chinese translation by a student retains the passive structure 'it is not disputed'. In contrast, Poon suggests the use of active voice, the more natural word order in Chinese, by explicating the agents in the judicial procedure. Consider her improved version:

(7c)
由於控辯雙方對第37條"婚姻"一詞解釋為一男一女的結合，並無爭議，爭議在於為施行該條文時，"男"和"女"的定義。

She suggests rendering the formulaic 'it is not disputed' as *kongbian shuangfang dui . . . bingwu zhengyi* (控辯雙方對 . . . 並無爭議) (both the prosecution and the defence have no dispute that . . .).

Following the translation techniques suggested here, it is time to probe into the translation principles behind judgments, some views on which were mentioned in Chapter 2. A former judge of the Court of Final Appeal states a general guideline that judgments must be made easy to understand (Claytor 2016: 18):

> In this multilingual city, when a judgment is given in English, as most of them are in the higher courts, a duty falls on the court to speak in a manner that not only makes it easy to understand in English, but also easy to translate into Chinese. This, to me, is 'the guiding principle'.

Cham (2019: 93–94) makes a distinction between legislative texts and judicial texts, in that the strict requirement of faithfulness in the translation of the former can result in a form of 'extraordinary Chinese', while the latter's closeness to 'daily language' demands that the translator satisfy the requirements of fluency and elegance as well. In promoting the 'plain language approach', Poon (2006: 209) also contrasts legislative discourse with judicial discourse, by stating that the former has 'complicated or semi-complicated legal concepts and syntactic structure', while the latter is 'less formal and rigid'. Judgments have 'a certain format':

> The introduction introduces the nature of a case, the parties involved and their legal relationship, as well as the charge(s) the defendant(s) is/are facing or issues in dispute. The introduction is followed by the 'brief facts of the case', which may involve different topics and terminologies. The brief facts are followed by the arguments made by the involved parties from their perception of the legal points of view. Finally, the court's conclusion will be given with a detailed analysis of how it perceives the legal arguments presented by the parties.

Research in meeting challenges 117

In discussing the above components, Poon (2006: 210) believes that 'a judgment must be clear and precise so that it can be accessible to diverse readers'.

It is assumed that the general reader pays attention to the more accessible parts of a judgment, that is, the not-so-legal parts. Tung Chiao (2012: 85–86), a well-known Indonesian Chinese writer educated in Taiwan, highly praises the following translation of a judgment in English, in which the judge comforts the families of the deceased. It is believed that the translation was done by translators working in the judiciary who have undergone proper translation training. Consider the following:

(8)
To the families of the deceased I wish to say this. You have suffered a human tragedy that is beyond the comprehension of most people. Nothing can restore to you what you have lost. You have the deepest sympathy of all in Hong Kong. Because of the circumstances of the death of the members of your families your grief has become public. The inquest is now concluded. During the hearing you sought from me a means of leaving the court building so as to enable you to avoid the attention of the media. I am unable to offer this to you. There is no such facility available. You have the right now to be left in peace to grieve in private. I cannot do anything to give you the privacy to which you are entitled. I can only ask that you be treated with respect and dignity that persons who have suffered such tragedy ought to have.

對死者家屬，我有如下的話要說。你們所經歷的切膚之痛，實非多數人所能體會。你們蒙受的損失，天下無一物可以補償。對於你們的不幸，全港市民均寄予無限同情。由於你們的家人死於特殊環境，你們內心的哀痛不得不公開。死因聆訊現已完畢。聆訊期間你們曾要求我作出安排，讓你們在離開法院大樓時可以避開記者的注意。這裡缺乏有關設備，你們的要求我無法照辦。現在聆訊既已完畢，你們終於可以不受騷擾，在私底下哀念親人，這是你們應有的權利。我無法讓你們得到你們應有的私隱權利，但你們已橫遭慘變，實不應再受任何不敬及有損尊嚴的對待。這是我唯一的要求。

Tung comments that it is not difficult to achieve this 'touching' translation, as there are no legislative terms or provisions. Nevertheless, some of the translation techniques illustrated below are worth learning, especially by lawyers and judges in Hong Kong who mostly have not received translation and linguistic training. In the translated text, Chinese idioms and four-word expressions are underlined, for example, *qiefu zhi tong* (切膚之痛) (pain of cutting one's body), *wuxian tongqing* (無限同情) (immeasurable sympathy), and *hengzao canbian* (橫遭慘變) (meet a tragic accident). Also marked are classical monosyllabic words such as the functional words *dui* (對), *suo* (所), *shi* (實), *yi* (已) and *ji* (既), and the substantive words *tianxia* (天下) (under the sky) and *yiwu* (一物) (one object). Last but not least, the last final is rendered in the paratactic order of Chinese, that is, the main clause *zheshi wo weiyi de yaoqiu* (這是我唯一的要求) (I can only ask) is placed after the subordinate clause. These techniques echo the study's appeal to the use of Classical Chinese, and more good translation techniques for judgments should be studied and illustrated for legal professionals.

5.2.2 *Comparative study of legal terminology and legal glossary compilation*

5.2.2.1 Relations with comparative law and existing works

The ultimate solution to the challenges posed to legal translators by the transfer of terms from different jurisdictions lies in research. While translation scholars and legal linguists may produce law dictionaries and glossaries, the long-term development depends on comparative law and the collaboration between academics from the fields of law and language. 'Comparative law' is 'a highly complex and debatable notion in terms of its name, object, purpose and nature' (Jopek-Bosiacka 2013: 112; see also Brand 2009: 19; de Cruz 2007: 1–10; Glendon, Gordon and Osakwe 1985: 1–38). De Cruz (2007: 5) considers it a method for investigating the similarities and differences between different jurisdictions, such as those between civil-law and common-law countries. 'Traditional' comparative law is 'closely concerned with issues of translation' (Simonnæs 2013: 156). Thus, translation turns to comparative law and its comparisons and contrasts of various legal systems as a 'research tool' to identify issues and solutions in order to seek the 'common denominator' in various legal areas (de Cruz 2007: 26).

As briefly discussed in Chapter 1, China started the study of comparative law in the late Qing Dynasty. Under the pressure of foreign invasion, the Qing Empire established the law-drafting institution *Xiuding Falü Guan* (修訂法律館) (Law Revision Agency) to comprehensively study and imitate Western law. Shen Jia-ben, who was nominated as the principal of this institution, led large-scale research into comparative law. During the Republican Era, the Beiyang Government also conducted serious research in this area. In 1913, the first specialised institution— the Comparative Law Academy—was established, which represented the formation of China's comparative law community. Furthermore, Soochow University in 1922 launched *Faxue Zazhi* (《法學雜誌》) (*Law Review*), which was the first specialist comparative law journal. Formal comparative law courses were taught in law schools across China. For example, Soochow University started its common law and continental law comparative course at its establishment in 1915. In the north, Beiyang University, Peking University and Chaoyang University also offered comparative constitutional law and civil law courses (Pan 2001: 19; Zhou 2010: 51–52).

In recent decades, comparative law has been developing in all three Chinese regions. In the PRC, after 1978, the Chinese Academy of Social Sciences and other research institutions resumed comparative law studies. Many journals were launched with numerous papers published in the wake of the booming Chinese economy (Wen 2006: 54–57). Comparative law has remained active in Taiwan since 1949, with the German legal system serving as the main object of comparison. This is because Taiwanese law had its roots in continental legal theories. Courts in Taiwan have also adopted comparative study as an approach to legal interpretation that fills the gaps in statutes (Wang 2006: 7). Comparative law research in Hong Kong has been very pervasive due to the close ties between Hong Kong and other common law jurisdictions. Legal academics and practitioners there commonly adopt comparative law methodology to analyse UK law and reform Hong Kong law. So far, however, comparative law academics in the Chinese world have shown little interest in legal translation. Although there has been plenty of comparative law research, it seems that little of it is engaged directly with legal translation.[2]

Turning to the equivalence of legal terminology from Hong Kong, the Mainland and Taiwan, there is also little previous academic research in this area and related reference works on legal terms from the three communities are scarce. Therefore, lawyers and legal translators have few resources on which they can rely should they wish to check equivalence of terms from the three regions. Nevertheless, there are calls for the standardisation of Chinese legal terms across the different regions. In his analysis of the similarities and dissimilarities of the legal terminology in Mainland China, Taiwan, Hong Kong and Macau, Qu (2013: 267–275) predicts that the standardisation of terminology in Hong Kong and Macau will have an impact on the Mainland and Taiwan:

> Solely on the possible influence of the Hong Kong experience on the Mainland, some translated Chinese terms officially adopted in the Hong Kong legislation will possibly benefit the Mainland, for both its legal studies at present and legislative work in the future. The terms would bring us inspiration that should not be underestimated. For example, there are '辯論式/對辯式訴訟制度' (adversary system), '無合理懷疑點' (beyond reasonable doubt), '相對可能性的衡量' (balance of probabilities), '小額錢債審裁處' (small claims tribunal) and '入屋犯法' (burglary). A good translated legal term can serve the function of a navel belt, bonding the four jurisdictions effectively.
>
> (English translation by the author)

Furthermore, in criticising the mistranslation of 'mortgage' in the legal dictionaries of the Mainland where there is no close Chinese equivalent to the term, Qu (2013: 188) suggests the solution of borrowing the Hong Kong translation *anjie* (按揭), which is based on the Cantonese pronunciation of 'mortgage'.

Given the present circumstances, in order to explore the feasibility of such standardisation and the kinds of influence Hong Kong terminology might have on other Chinese regions, groundwork in terms of comparing law and legal terminology among the Chinese regions must be conducted. To this end, the author recently published a book explaining and comparing Chinese translated terms in contract law, which included a 100-term glossary listing the 'functionally' equivalent terms from the three Chinese communities (Chan 2014). This book was published under the *Legal Translation Series*, and two similar books were later published in the areas of tort law (Chan 2015) and company law (Chan 2017).

The following will provide a brief summary of the first chapter of the book on contract law published in 2014. In this book, each of the 16 translated terms is studied based first on the Hong Kong common law statutes and cases and second on the civil law of Mainland China and Taiwan, where the translated terms may be the same or different to those in Hong Kong. The 16 terms are organised in five chapters as follows:

Chapter 1: Introduction (Section 1: 'Contract')
Chapter 2: Formation of contract (Sections 2–5: 'Offer', 'Acceptance', 'Intention' and 'Capacity')
Chapter 3: Content of contract (Sections 6–7: 'Express and implied terms', 'Exemption clause')
Chapter 4: Vitiating actors and discharge of contract (Sections 8–14: 'Force majeure', 'Frustration', 'Misrepresentation', 'Mistake', 'Duress', 'Fraud' and 'Illegality')
Chapter 5: Remedies (Sections 15–16: 'Damages' and 'Specific performance')

The first chapter on 'Contract' provides a good representative sample of this book. The term has three different translations, namely *heyue* (合約) in Hong Kong, *hetong* (合同) in Mainland China and *qiyue* (契約) in Taiwan, which can all be traced back to ancient times. The chapter mainly explains the meanings of the ancient and modern meanings of the term and outlines its conceptual similarities and differences in the three Chinese regions that variously follow common law and civil law systems. Beginning with the original English meaning, according to *Black's Law Dictionary* (Garner 2009: 365), a contract is 'an agreement between two or more parties creating obligations that are enforceable or otherwise recognizable at law'. However, Chinese laws traditionally focused on the criminal area, and the use of contracts was not valued (Chen 2011: 18, 2003: 455). The current contract laws of Hong Kong, the Mainland and Taiwan therefore all originated in the West. Hong Kong adopted the English common law system, including its contract law theories, during British rule, and those in Mainland China and Taiwan originated from the Republican Era when China learnt from the Japanese laws modelled on the civil law systems of Germany and France. In its modern sense, a contract has four functions: (i) value of exchange, (ii) obligations and standard of performance of contractual parties, (iii) allocation of economic risks and (iv) solutions of conflicts and problems (Beatson, Burrows and Cartwright 2010: 3).

There are three major differences in the contract law of the three Chinese communities. First, in terms of the formation of contracts, while under the common law system, an agreement is recognised by the court with elements of consideration, intention, capacity, legality and compliance with formal legal requirements, the element of 'consideration' is unnecessary under the civil law system (Law and Martin 2009: 524). Second, in terms of the basis of liability, Hong Kong under the common law system uses the 'strict liability principle', by which the party in breach of contract shall bear the liability whether or not he or she makes subjective mistakes (Ren 2010: 16; Wang 2011: 428–432; Xue 2011: 271). Taiwan uses the 'fault liability principle', where the non-performing party shall bear the liability only if he or she makes a subjective mistake (Su 2011: 40). The Mainland uses both of these liability principles (Wang 2011: 436–449; Xue 2011: 271). Lastly, in terms of remedies for breach of contract, Hong Kong follows the common law system, where damages is the first and foremost remedial measure, whereas in both of the continental-based legal systems of the Mainland and Taiwan, specific performance is the main remedy (Poole 2010: 340; *Malik v BCCI* [1998] 1 AC 20, *Robinson v Harman* (1848) 1 Ex 850, *Surrey County Council v Bredero Homes Ltd* [1993] WLR 961). Although the terms *heyue* (合約), *hetong* (合同) and *qiyue* (契約) varied in meaning in ancient China and continue to do so in the modern contract laws of the Mainland, Hong Kong and Taiwan, the three terms are mutually intelligible and there are instances where the three terms are used interchangeably (e.g. the Mainland term *hetong* (合同) is used in the Arbitration Ordinance (Cap. 341) of Hong Kong).

5.2.2.2 Framework for comparison

The research endeavour can be a long process that takes time to produce results. The ideal goal is to build 'parametrized terminology banks' for the purpose of legal translation and other interlingual legal communication (Matulewska 2016: 65). Future success, though, depends on many factors, one of which is the ongoing collaborative efforts of language and law scholars. This will be discussed in the conclusion on the limitations and prospects for legal translation in Hong Kong.

The following three tables list Chinese terms according to the first four categories discussed in Chapter 3, mainly based on the glossaries in the author's three recent books on contract law, tort law and company law. Each of the three books contains a glossary of more than 100 terms in its subject area, with English source terms and their respective translations in Hong Kong, Mainland China and Taiwan sourced from statutes and legal dictionaries. Due to limited space, the three tables are designed to focus on the common translations of the three regions, meaning that many of the different, less common or unusual translations are not included. It should also be noted that the Hong Kong legal system uses terms from both common law (e.g. 'act of God' and 'winding up') and civil law (e.g. *force majeure* and 'liquidation') traditions, sometimes even interchangeably. While 'tort' is a common law term, it is used in the three tables. This is because the term has been widely used in civil law countries, for example, the PRC's *Qinquan Zeren Fa* 《侵權責任法》 (2009) have been translated as 'Tort Law' or 'Tort Liability Law' in many English translations (e.g. LawInfoChina, LexisNexis and Westlaw) (Chan 2017: 185–334, 2015: 187–297, 2014: 157–258).

By reference to these three tables, observations can be made regarding the similarities and dissimilarities of the translated Chinese legal terms in three Chinese regions. With regard to similarities, based on Table 5.1, there are three factors leading to the adoption of identical translations by all three regions, all relating to fundamental linguistic principles.

Table 5.1 One or more similar foreign source term(s) with same renditions of same/similar meaning in three Chinese regions

Category 1 (Near equivalents)	One or more similar foreign source term(s) with renditions of same/similar meaning in three Chinese regions
Civil law	'act of God' (天災、不可抗力) 'agent' (代理人) 'burden of proof' (舉證責任) 'cause of action' (訴因、訴訟理由) 'compensation' (補償、賠償) 'consent' (同意) 'damage' (損害) 'damages' (損害賠償) 'defence' (辯護) 'defendant' (被告) 'derivative action' (衍生訴訟) 'economic loss' (經濟損失) 'foreseeability/foreseeable/foresee' (預見) 'justification' (正當理由) 'legal person' (法人) 'liability' (法律責任、責任) 'limitation' (時效) 'malice' (惡意) 'minor' (未成年人) 'obligation' (責任、義務) 'omission' (不作為) 'party' (一方、當事人) 'plaintiff' (原告人、原告) 'right' (權利) 'trust' (信託) 'witness' (證人)
Contract law	'agreement' (協議) 'binding' (具約束力、有約束力) 'breach of contract' (違約) 'capacity' (行為能力) 'duress' (脅迫) 'exemption clause' (免責條款) *'force majeure'* (不可抗力) 'mistake' (錯誤) 'offer' (要約) 'performance' (履行) 'subject matter' (標的物) 'term' (條款) 'terminate' (終止) 'undue influence' (不當影響) 'void' (無效)
Tort law	'battery' (毆打) 'defamation' (誹謗) 'freedom of speech' (言論自由) 'manufacturer' (製造商) 'personal injury' (人身傷害、人身損害) 'product liability' (產品責任) 'self-defence' (自衛、正當防衛) 'sexual harassment' (性騷擾) 'tort' (侵權) 'trespass' (侵入、侵犯)

Category 1 (Near equivalents)	One or more similar foreign source term(s) with renditions of same/similar meaning in three Chinese regions
Company law	'accountant' (會計師) 'acquisition/acquire' (收購) 'bankruptcy' (破產) 'beneficiary' (受益人) 'bond' (債券) 'book debts' (賬面債項) 'capital' (資本) 'company" (公司) 'conflict of interests' (利益衝突) 'debt' (債務) 'deed' (契據) 'director' (董事) 'disclosure/disclose' (披露) 'endorsement' (背書) 'financial statement' (財務報表) 'financial year/fiscal year' (財政年度、會計年度) 'insolvency/insolvent' (無力償債、無力清償債務) 'insurance/insure' (保險) 'investment' (投資) 'issuer' (發行人) 'lien' (留置權) 'limited company' (有限公司) 'listing' (上市) 'loan' (借貸、貸款) 'merger' (合併) 'minutes' (會議記錄) 'misfeasance' (不當行爲) 'notary public/notary' (公證人) 'option' (選擇權) 'partnership' (合夥) 'preference share' (優先股) 'premium' (溢價) 'price' (價格) 'profit' (利潤) 'promoter' (發起人) 'prospectus' (招股章程) 'purchase' (購買) 'quorum' (法定人數) 'ratification/ratify' (追認) 'receivership/receive' (接管) 'redemption' (贖回) 'register/registry' (登記), 'resolution' (決議) 'securities' (證券) 'security' (保證) 'share' (股份) 'share capital' (股本) 'shareholder' (股東) 'sole proprietorship/proprietorship' (獨資經營) 'solvency' (償付能力)

(Continued)

Table 5.1 (Continued)

Category 1 (Near equivalents)	One or more similar foreign source term(s) with renditions of same/similar meaning in three Chinese regions
	'stock' (股票) 'surety' (擔保) 'takeover' (收購) 'transfer' (轉讓) 'trust' (信托) 'unlimited company' (無限公司) 'unsecured loan' (無擔保貸款) 'veto' (否決) 'vote' (表決) 'yield' (收益率)

The first factor is ordinary word usage, for example, *tongyi* (同意) for 'consent', *cuowu* (錯誤) for 'mistake', *sunhai* (損害) for 'damage' and *zeren* (責任) for 'liability'. These words are often used in daily life without legal meanings. As law is made for the development of human society in which legal language deals with everyday matters, it is easy to understand how ordinary language becomes embedded in the technical language of the law. Furthermore, ordinary words are also flexibly used to refer to different English terms, for example, *zeren* (責任) (responsibility/liability) is used in *juzheng zeren* (舉證責任) for 'burden of proof' and sometimes for 'obligation'.

The second factor is the fixed translation, for example, *faren* (法人) for 'legal person', *xing saorao* (性騷擾) for 'sexual harassment', *chanpin zeren* (產品責任) for 'product liability' and *jingji sunshi* (經濟損失) for 'economic loss'. This factor, which is often found in compound legal terms in Chinese, is essentially facilitated by the first factor. In other words, *xing* (性) (sex), *sairao* (騷擾) (harassment), *chanpin* (產品) (product), *zeren* (責任) (responsibility/liability), *jingji* (經濟) (economy) and *sunshi* (損失) (loss) are all ordinary words, so however they are combined, they retain the meanings of the individual parts.

The third factor is transparency to readers, especially for important legal terms where specialised translation techniques have been adopted to reflect legal meanings. Examples include *sunhai peichang* (損害賠償) for 'damages', *shixiao* (時效) for 'limitation', *yuangao* (原告) for 'plaintiff' and *beigao* (被告) for 'defendant' in civil law in general, *tiaokuan* (條款) for 'term' in contract law', and *qinquan* (侵權) for 'tort' in tort law. The compression techniques of blending and compounding used in such terms as *sunhai peichang* (損害賠償) for 'damages' succinctly convey the legal concept of 'damages' by combining *sunhai* (損害) (damage) and *peichang* (賠償) (compensation). 'Damages' in English refers to 'Money claimed by, or ordered to be paid to, a person as compensation for loss or injury' (Garner 2009: 445). Sager (1990: 108) remarks: 'The concentration of complex relationships into short expression forms increases our cognitive capacity'. Likewise, the rendering of 'plaintiff' as *yuangao* (原告) (original suer) and 'defendant' as *beigao* (被告) (being sued) in Chinese are self-explanatory. In addition to the compression techniques, the imagery technique traditionally used in the formation of the Chinese lexicon can vividly help the reader understand the meaning of a term. The combination of *tiao* (條) (strip/article) and *kuan* (款) (paragraph) gives a clear picture of the image of 'terms' in a written contract. A 'term' in English is 'a contract stipulation' (Garner 2009: 1608). These three linguistic factors of ordinary word use, fixed translation and specialised 'transparent' techniques can explain the large number of common translations across the three regions in 'company law' (60 terms listed in Table 5.1). According to a study in the 1990s, many business terms customarily used in Hong Kong such as *gongsi* (公司) (company), *youxian gongsi* (有限公司) (limited company), *dongshi* (董事) (director), *gudong* (股東) (shareholder) and *jingli* (經理) (manager) had 'migrated' to Mainland China before the 1997 handover (Tian 1996). Certainly, the relatively minor legal difference in the business terms used across the regions is also a cause for the standardised use across the regions.

Some possible factors for the dissimilarities of terms can be gleaned from Table 5.2. The factors are mostly legal ones. The first one is that the Mainland and Taiwan use the same terms borrowed from Japanese during the Qing Dynasty. For instance, while *dongchan* (動產) and *shanyi* (善意) are used in the Mainland and Taiwan, *shichan* (實產) and *zhencheng* (真誠) are the official translations of 'chattel' and 'good faith' in Hong Kong. The different linguistic representations suggest significant underlying legal differences. In another study on property law terminology, the author traces the source of the term *shanyi* (善意) as *bona fides* in civil law, while that of *zhencheng* (真誠) is 'good faith' in common law. *Bona fides*, which may cover negligence, confidential relationships and minimal standards of commercial conduct, is a broader civil law term than its common law counterpart 'good faith' (Chan 2011: 253–254).

To complicate matters, Hong Kong has created a number of new compound terms to represent legal concepts. Whereas the Hong Kong law drafters has combined the morphemes *ya* (押) with *ji* (記) in the coinage *yaji* (押記) for 'charge', the Mainland and Taiwan use the general translation *diya* (抵押) used in daily life.

The second factor for dissimilarity is the borrowing of translated legal terms that has been taking place between the three regions. Table 5.3 contains examples of translated terms that are basically 'empty' because the concepts to which they refer belong to another legal system. For example, 'reasonable person' and 'consideration' are common law concepts and their Chinese translations in Mainland China and Taiwan have no legal effects in their legal systems. Yet, that does not mean that Hong Kong should be content with the Chinese translations it has already adopted for such common law terms that have legal effect in that legal system. The two existing translations may not be satisfactory: *Daijia* (代價) is misleading as it means 'cost' in ordinary language. *Yueyin* (約因) (contract reason), which means *heyue yuanyin* (合約原因) (the reason for a contract), is semantically opaque to understand.

Table 5.2 One or more similar foreign source term(s) with different renditions of same/similar meaning in three Chinese regions

Category 2 (Near equivalents)	One or more similar foreign source term(s) with different renditions of same/similar meaning in three Chinese regions
Civil law	'chattel' (HK：實產、動產/MC: 動產/TW: 動產), 'claim' (HK: 申索、索償/MC: 索賠、主張/TW: 求償權、主張) 'claimant' (HK: 申索人、索償人/MC: 請求權人/TW: 請求權人) 'fault' (HK: 過失、過錯/MC: 過錯/TW: 過失) 'fraud' (HK: 欺詐/MC: 欺詐/TW: 詐欺) 'infringement' (HK: 侵犯/MC: 侵害/TW: 侵害) 'injunction' (HK: 強制令、禁制令/MC: 禁制令/TW: 強制令、禁止令) 'mental incapacity/mental disability' (HK: 心智上無行為能力/MC: 智力不全/TW: 心智缺陷) 'premises' (HK: 處所、房產/MC: 場所、房屋/TW: 場址、房屋) 'principle' (HK: 主事人、委托人、本人/MC: 被代理人、委托人、本人/TW: 被代理人、委托人、本人) 'remedy' (HK: 補救/MC: 救濟/TW: 救濟) 'stay' (HK: 擱置、暫緩/MC: 中止/TW: 停止) 'third party' (HK: 第三者、第三方/MC: 第三人、第三方/TW: 第三人)
Contract law	'acceptance' (HK: 承約/MC: 承諾/TW: 承諾) 'contract' (HK: 合約/MC: 合同/TW: 契約) *consensus ad idem* (HK: 一致合意、同意、合意/MC: 合意/TW: 雙方就同一事物達成協議、意見一致)
Tort law	'defective product/defective goods' (HK: 欠妥的貨品/MC: 缺欠產品、瑕疵產品/TW: 有缺欠的產品、有瑕疵的產品) 'fair comment' (HK: 公允評論/MC: 公正評論/TW: 公正評論) 'false imprisonment' (HK: 非法禁錮/MC: 非法拘禁/TW: 非法拘禁) 'privacy' (HK: 私隱/MC: 隱私/TW: 隱私) 'tortfeasor' (HK: 侵權人/MC: 侵權行為人/TW: 侵權行為人)
Company law	'annual general meeting' (HK: 周年大會、股東周年大會/MC: 股東年會、年度股東大會/TW: 年度大會、年度股東大會) 'article of association' (HK: 公司組織細則、公司章程細則、公司章程/MC: 公司章程/TW: 公司章程) 'audit' (HK: 核數師、審計師/MC: 審計師/TW: 審計師) 'board of directors' (HK: 董事局、董事會/MC: 董事會/TW: 董事會) 'chairperson/chairman' (HK: 主席/MC: 主席、董事長/TW: 主席、董事長) 'corporate governance' (HK: 企業管治、公司管治/MC: 公司治理/TW: 公司治理) 'equity financing' (HK: 股本融資/MC: 增加註冊資本、股權融資/TW: 增資) 'insider dealing' (HK: 內幕交易/MC: 內幕交易/TW: 內線交易) 'liquidation' (HK: 清盤/MC: 清算/TW: 清算) 'winding up' (HK: 清盤/MC: 清算/TW: 清算)

Note: HK: Hong Kong; MC: Mainland China; TW: Taiwan

Table 5.3 One or more different foreign source term(s) with different renditions of different meanings in three Chinese regions

Categories 3 and 4 (Partial or non-equivalents)	One or different foreign source term(s) with different renditions of different meanings
Civil law	'good faith' (HK: 真誠/MC: 善意/TW: 善意)
	'reasonable person/man' (HK: 合理的人/MC: 理性人/TW: 有理性的人)
Contract law	'consideration' (HK: 代價、約因/MC: 對價/TW: 對價)
	'frustration' (HK: 受挫失效/MC: 合同落空/TW: 受挫失效、挫折)
	'misrepresentation' (HK: 失實陳述/MC: 虛假陳述/TW: 虛偽陳述、不實陳述)
Tort law	'contributory negligence' (HK: 共分疏忽、共同疏忽/MC: 混合過失、與有過失/TW: 與有過失)
	'duty of care' (HK: 謹慎責任/MC: 注意義務/TW: 必要之注意)
	'negligence' (HK: 疏忽/MC: 過失/TW: 過失)
	'occupiers' liability' (HK: 佔用人法律責任/MC: 佔用人責任/TW: 住戶的責任)
	'strict liability' (HK: 嚴格法律責任/MC: 嚴格責任、無過錯責任/TW: 無過錯責任、危險責任)
	'vicarious liability' (HK: 轉承責任/MC: 替代責任/TW: 替代責任)
Company law	'charge' (HK: 押記/MC: 抵押/TW: 抵押)
	'mortgage' (HK: 按揭/MC: 抵押/TW: 抵押)

Note: HK: Hong Kong; MC: Mainland China; TW: Taiwan

It is hoped that the tables and the preliminary analysis here will encourage and facilitate future endeavours to compare the legal terms across the three regions. Chapter 6 will conclude with more examples and methods based on this research framework.

Notes

1 Yuen delivered his keynote speech on 'Language and Rule of Law' in Cantonese. When commenting the plain language movement, the limitation of language is put forward by linguists and lawyers, in that plain language cannot simplify the complexity of law itself. Given the limitation, legislation drafted in plain language also create some danger of being too plain. Australian legislation has received such criticism (Assy 2011; Barnes 2010; Galdia 2014: 245–247).
2 The observations of strong interest in comparative law but weak interest in legal translation among Hong Kong legal academics is made based on a general check of the profiles of three law faculties in Hong Kong (www.law.hku.hk/faculty/acadstaff.php; www.law.cuhk.edu.hk/en/people/staff-list.php?staff=2&filter=char&value=A; www.cityu.edu.hk/slw/people/fulltime.html).

English references

Assy, Rabeea (2011). Can the Law Speak Directly to Its Subjects? The Limitation of Plain Language. *Journal of Law and Society 38*(3): 376–404.

Barnes, Jeffrey (2010). When Plain Language Legislation Is Ambiguous—Sources of Doubt and Lessons for the Plain Language Movement. *Melbourne University Law Review 34*: 671–707.

Beatson, Jackson, Burrows, Andrew and Cartwright, John (2010). *Ansons' Law of Contract*. New York: Oxford University Press.

Beaugrande, Robert D. and Dressler, Wolfgang U. (1981). *Introduction to Text Linguistics*. London: Longman.

Brand, Oliver (2009). Language as a Barrier to Comparative Law. In Olsen, Frances, Lorz, Alexander and Stein, Dieter (Eds.), *Translation Issues in Language and Law* (pp. 18–34). London: Palgrave Macmillan.

Cao, Deborah (2004). *Chinese Law*. Aldershot, Hants: Ashgate.

Chan, Clara Ho-yan (2007). Translated Chinese as a Legal Language in Hong Kong Legislation. *Journal of Specialized Translation 7*: 25–41.

Chan, Clara Ho-yan (2011). The Use and Translation of Chinese Legal Terminology in the Property Laws of Mainland China and Hong Kong: Problems, Strategies and Future Development. *Terminology: International Journal of Theoretical and Applied Issues in Specialized Communication 17*(2): 249–273.

Chan, Clara Ho-yan (2012). Bridging the Gap Between Language and Law: Translational Issues in Creating Legal Chinese in Hong Kong. *Babel: International Journal of Translation 58*(2): 127–144.

Chan, Clara Ho-yan (2018). Hong Kong Bilingual Legislation and Plain Language Drafting: A Communicative Approach. *Multilingua: Journal of Cross-Cultural and Interlanguage Communication 37*(6): 681–700.

Chen, Hung-yee Albert (2011). *An Introduction to the Legal System of the People's Republic of China* (4th Ed.). Hong Kong: LexisNexis.

Chen, Zhiwu (2003). Capital Markets and Legal Development: The China Case. *China Economic Review 14*: 451–472.

Claytor, Cynthia G. (2016). Hon. Henry Litton GBM CBM JP—Face to Face with Former Permanent Judge of the Court of Final Appeal. *Hong Kong Lawyer* February: 16–21. Retrieved from: www.hk-lawyer.org/sites/default/files/field/journal/201602_hk_lawyers-rev2_0.pdf.

de Cruz, Peter (2007). *Comparative Law in a Changing World* (3rd Ed.). London and New York: Routledge-Cavendish.

Galdia, Marcus (2014). *Legal Discourses*. Frankfurt: Peter Lang.

Garner, Bryan A. (Ed.) (2009). *Black's Law Dictionary* (9th Ed.). St. Paul, MN: West.

Gémar, Jean-Claude (2014). Catching the Spirit of the Law: From Translation to Co-Drafting. In Glanert, Simone (Ed.), *Comparative Law—Engaging Translation* (pp. 67–84). Abingdon, Oxon and New York: Routledge.

Glendon, Mary Ann, Gordon, Michael W. and Osakwe, Christopher (1985). *Comparative Legal Traditions: Text, Materials and Cases on the Civil Law, Common Law and Socialist Law Traditions with Special Reference to French, West German, English and Soviet Law*. St. Paul, MN: West Publishing.

Hong Kong Exchanges and Clearing Limited (2019). *A Glossary of Securities and Financial Terms*. Retrieved from: www.hkex.com.hk/eng/global/glossary.htm.

Jopek-Bosiacka, Anna (2013). Comparative Law and Equivalence Assessment of System-Bound Terms in EU Legal Translation. *Linguistica Antverpiensia (Special Issue: Research Models and Methods in Legal Translation) 12*: 110–146.

Law, Jonathan and Martin, Elizabeth A. (2009). *Oxford Dictionary of Law* (7th Ed.). New York: Oxford University Press.

Law Drafting Division, Department of Justice (2012a). *Drafting Legislation in Hong Kong: A Guide to Styles and Practices*. Hong Kong: Department of Justice. Retrieved from: www.elegislation.gov.hk/b0000000004.attach.

Li, Charles N. and Thompson, Sandra A. (1979). Third-Person Pronouns and Zero-Anaphora in Chinese Discourse. In Givon, Talmy (Ed.), *Syntax and Semantics: Discourse and Syntax* (Vol. 12) (pp. 311–335). New York: Academic Press.

Matulewska, Aleksandra (2016). Walking on Thin Ice of Translation of Terminology in Legal Settings. *International Journal of Legal Discourse 1*(1): 65–85.

Poole, Jill (2010). *Textbook on Contract Law* (10th Ed.). New York: Oxford University Press.

Poon, Emily Wai-yee (2006). *The Effectiveness of Plain Language in the Translation of Statutes and Judgments*. Doctoral Dissertation, The HKU Scholar Hub, The University of Hong Kong, Pokfulam, Hong Kong. Retrieved from: http://dx.doi.org/10.5353/th_b4501564.

Poon, Emily Wai Yee (2018). Sex and Gender in Legal Translation. In Shei, Chris and Gao, Zhao-Ming (Eds.), *The Routledge Handbook of Chinese Translation* (pp. 449–465). London and New York: Routledge.

Sager, Juan C. (1990). *A Practical Course in Terminology Processing*. Philadelphia: John Benjamins Publishing Company.

Securities and Futures Commission (2006). *An English-Chinese Glossary of Securities, Futures and Financial Terms* (4th Ed.). Retrieved from: www.sfc.hk/web/doc/EN/inutilbar/glossary/2006/full_list.pdf.

Simonnæs, Ingrid (2013). Legal Translation and 'Traditional' Comparative Law—Similarities and Differences *Linguistica Antverpiensia, New Series—Themes in Translation Studies 12*: 147–160.

Sin, King-kui (2000). The Missing Link Between Language and Law: Problems of Legislative Translation in Hong Kong. In Herberts, Kjell and Turi, Joseph G. (Eds.), *Multilingual Cities and Language Policies* (pp. 195–210). Vaasa: Abo Akademi University.

Special Group on Law, Consultative Committee for the Basic Law of the Hong Kong Special Administrative Regions (1987). *Final Report on Language of the Law* 1–9.

Zhao, Yuhong (2000a). Drafting Policy on Bilingual Legislation: Comments on the Hong Kong Securities and Futures Bill. *The Legislative Council Library, Hong Kong Special Administrative Region of the People's Republic of China* 1–25. Retrieved from: http://sc.legco.gov.hk/sc/library.legco.gov.hk:1080/search*cht/X?SEARCH=m%3A%28drafting+policy+on+bilingual+legislation%29&searchscope=10&l=&m=&Da=&Db=&SORT=D.

Zhao, Yuhong (2000b). Legal Legislation in the Legislative Genre. *Journal of Translation Studies 4*: 19–41.

Chinese references

Cham, Edmund Shu Kay 湛樹基 (2019). 〈談翻譯判案書的技巧與方法〉(On Techniques and Methods of Judgment Translation). In Cham Shu Kay, Edmund 湛樹基 and Lee Kim Hung, Elvis 李劍雄 (Eds.), 《香港雙語法制:語言與翻譯》 (*Bilingual Legal*

System in Hong Kong: Language and Translation) (pp. 89–110). Hong Kong: Hong Kong University Press.

Chan, Clara Ho-yan 陳可欣 (2014). 《法律翻譯系列：兩岸三地合約法主要詞彙》 (*Legal Translation Series: Key Terms in Contract Law of Hong Kong, Mainland China and Taiwan*). Hong Kong: City University of Hong Kong Press.

Chan, Clara Ho-yan 陳可欣 (2015). 《法律翻譯系列：兩岸三地侵權法主要詞彙》 (*Legal Translation Series: Key Terms in Tort Law of Hong Kong, Mainland China and Taiwan*). Hong Kong: City University of Hong Kong Press.

Chan, Clara Ho-yan 陳可欣 (2017). 《法律翻譯系列：兩岸三地公司法主要詞彙》 (*Legal Translation Series: Key Terms in Company Law of Hong Kong, Mainland China and Taiwan*). Hong Kong: City University of Hong Kong Press.

Chen, Ping 陳平 (1991). 《現代語言學研究：理論，方法與事實》 (*Studies in Modern Linguistics: Theory, Methodology and Fact*). Chongqing: Chongqing Press.

Law Drafting Division, Department of Justice 律政司法律草擬科 (2012b). 《香港法律草擬文體及實務指引》 (*Drafting Legislation in Hong Kong: A Guide to Styles and Practices*). Hong Kong: Department of Justice. Retrieved from: www.doj.gov.hk/chi/public/pdf/2012/Drafting_booke.pdf.

Pan, Handian 潘汉典 (2001). 〈比較法在中國：回顧與展望〉 (Comparative Law in China: Review and Outlook). In Jiang, Ping 江平, Liu, Zhaoxing 劉兆興 and Qian, Hongdao 錢弘道 (Eds.), 《比較法在中國》 (*Comparative Law in China*) (pp. 7–29). Beijing: Law Press.

Qu, Wensheng 屈文生 (2013). 《從詞典出發：法律術語譯名統一與規範化的翻譯史研究》 (*Lexicography: A Study of Unification and Standardisation of Translated Legal Terms*). Shanghai: Shanghai Renmin Press.

Ren, Mingqi 任明琦 (2010). 〈兩大法系違約責任歸責原則的比較〉 (Comparison of the Liability Principles of the Two Major Legal Systems). 《法制與社會》 (*Legal Systems and Society*) 35: 16–17.

Su, Nan 蘇南 (2011). 〈公共工程契約損害賠償責任之成立──以臺灣地區「民法」及大陸《合同法》作比較〉 (The Establishment of the Liability of the Contract of Public Construction—Comparison of Civil Law of Taiwan and Contract Law of Mainland China). 《廈門大學法律評論》 (*Xiamen University Law Review*) 1: 36–63.

Tian, Xiaolin 田小琳 (1996). 〈中國內地和香港地區詞彙之比較〉 (A Comparison of the Lexicons of Mainland China and Hong Kong). 華語橋 (*Bridge of Chinese*). Retrieved from: www.huayuqiao.org/articles/tianxiaolin/txl01.htm.

Tung, Chiao 董橋 (2012) 〈把法治精神譯成中文〉 (Translating Rule of Law Spirit into Chinese). In Tung, Chiao (Ed.), 董橋《英華浮沉錄》(五) (*Swimming in the Seas of English and Chinese*) (pp. 85–86). Oxford: Oxford University Press.

Wang, Liming 王利明 (2011). 《合同法研究》（第二卷） (*Research of Contract Law*) (Vol. 2). Beijing: China Renmin University Press Co.

Wang, Tse-Chien 王澤鑑 (2006). 〈德國民法的繼受與臺灣民法的發展〉 (The Adoption of Germany's Civil Law and Developments in Taiwan's Civil Law). 《比較法研究》 (*Journal of Comparative Law*) 6: 1–19.

Wen, Qi 文琦 (2006). 〈中國崛起與比較法學的發展〉 (The Rise of China and Development of Comparative Law). In Liu, Zhaoxing 劉兆興 and Zhang, Shaoyu 張少瑜 (Eds.), 《比較法在中國》 (*Comparative Law in China*) (pp. 54–58). Beijing: Social Sciences Academy Press (China).

Wong, Pui-kwong 王培光 and Sin, King-kui 冼景炬 (2002). 〈香港中文判決書的語言問題〉 (Language Problems in Chinese Judgments of Hong Kong). In Zhou Qingsheng 周慶生, Wang Jie 王潔 and Su Jinzhi 蘇金智 (Eds.), 《語言與法律研究的新視野──語言

與法律首屆學術研討會論文集》 (*New Perspectives in Studies of Language and Law: Proceedings of the First Conference on Language and Law*) (pp. 193–201). Beijing: Law Press.

Xu, Jiujiu 徐赳赳 (2003). 《現代漢語篇章回指研究》 (*Anaphora in Chinese Texts*). Beijing: China Social Sciences Press.

Xue, Nan 薛楠 (2011). 〈論中國合同法的違約責任歸責原則〉 (Fault Liability Principles of China's Contract Law). 《法制與社會》 (*Legal System and Society*) 4: 271.

Yuen, Rimsky Kwok-keung 袁國強 (2016). 〈語言與法治〉 (Language and Rule of Law). Keynote Speech at 'Translation and the Profession' Symposium—Celebrating 45th Years of the Hong Kong Translation Society and 20 Years of the Translation Quarterly, November 12. Retrieved from: www.doj.gov.hk/chi/public/pdf/2016/sj20161112c2.pdf.

Zhou, Shizhong 周世中 (2010). 《比較法學》 (*Comparative Law*). Beijing: China Renmin University Press.

6 Conclusion

Trends and prospects

Based on the analysis of the previous chapters, the field of legal translation and bilingual law drafting in Hong Kong, particularly in the direction of English to Chinese, can be enhanced and enriched by the integration of language and law through endeavours in education and research. With education, the main goal is to solve long-standing language issues, in particular the style of translationese prominent in English-Chinese transfer. The training of 'cross-disciplinary' abilities is critical to such a development. With research, the main goal is to make a conceptual comparison of Chinese legal terms that originate from two different legal systems and vary with the Chinese language styles of the three regions concerned. The results of research can be expected to clarify legal meanings and establish equivalence of terms across all three regions. The two goals are interrelated in the Chinese world, in that when there is more frequent legal exchange among the three regions, the terms, as well as legal phrases and sentence structures, will influence each other.

The following is an evaluation of the prospects of the two endeavours, supported by the observations from the mini-survey conducted in Chapter 4. As far as education is concerned, while Hong Kong took the lead in establishing programmes that combine language and law, Mainland China has been developing more programmes to meet the rising demand for legal translators. Cross-disciplinary training also concerns the status of legal translation as an academic subject in Hong Kong. With regard to research, it is important for legal translation to combine with comparative law in comparing Chinese legal terms.

We may well find that the best methods of translating Chinese terms seem to be those that have stood the test of time, that is, long-use terms across the three regions. Lastly, some recommendations are made for the field after a summary of its development over the past 30 years.

6.1 Training practitioners with language and law skills: status of legal translation

Mattila (2013: 22) remarks that 'legal translation will remain an essentially human activity, at least in the near future'. Therefore, the specialised training of personnel who have competency in both language and law remains a central task in legal translation and law drafting. Galdia (2013: 92) concludes that to equip oneself for today's complex professional settings with the rise of many translation tools, 'expanding one's knowledge of the relevant legal languages and the reflection upon specialized language use remain basic tasks for the professional training that never stops'. On the basis of the overall development of such undertakings in the three Chinese regions as elaborated in Chapter 4, the following will explore the status of legal translation, which also includes some consideration of the status of the Chinese language in Hong Kong.

While the educational world endeavours to train language and law practitioners, the success of their efforts depends on the current status of legal translation as an academic subject. The status of translation in bilingual Hong Kong, like that in other parts of the world that are bilingual, is generally low. The field of legal translation is in the same situation. While legal translation is a relatively popular subject in the translation programmes of Hong Kong, students are not required to study translation in the law programmes of Hong Kong.[1] Other parts of the world are generally facing a similar situation, that is, it is difficult to add regular courses of language or translation to a law programme, as language is always seen only as a 'component'. Lambert (2009: 77) remarks:

> To the extent that 'language' is—until now, the academic canonical traditions—supposed to be (just?) a component of legislation and legal traditions, it is not surprising at all that 'translation' tends to be treated as—just—an interesting but marginal component in the various programmes devoted to law.

Nevertheless, in a bilingual and bijural legal system such as Canada, the requirements of lawyers and law drafters are high from the very outset; they are expected to acquire 'a firm grasp of the formal, conceptual, stylistic and organizational (apprehension of the world, genius of the language) differences between the two languages and between the two legal systems' (Beaudoin 2009: 136). Hong Kong should emulate this elevated linguistic requirement, especially given that most lawyers are native Chinese speakers, who already have the necessary base to receive more advanced written Chinese training.

The status quo is that in the Hong Kong legal profession, legal translation may be viewed as 'not very difficult'. Most lawyers are native Cantonese speakers who are usually verbally quite eloquent in their native language. Yet only a small number of lawyers were enrolled in the 'language and law' programmes.[2] The mini-survey of 15 lawyers and ten barristers in Chapter 4 also shows that only one has studied a course to improve his Chinese competency. The reason may simply be that they are too busy, or that they think they know how to translate since they know Chinese and English. In contrast, it must be recognised that good translation requires training. In his analysis of a bilingual conveyancing contract from a lawyer student in his master's translation class in Hong Kong, Li (2018: 241) describes this student as 'undoubtedly an expert in conveyancing, but is still a student receiving training in mastery of language (to accurately comprehend a text and analyse super long sentences), and translation competency (to express sophisticated thoughts)'. Li's various revisions to this bilingual agreement, including both its source and target texts, demonstrate the training required to achieve the communicative function of writing and translation.

In Hong Kong, the status of translation is highly influenced by the status of the Chinese language, which may still be perceived as 'not as important as English'. Before 1997, only competency in English was emphasised in the public service. The status of Chinese has risen significantly since 1997, but those who received their primary and secondary education before 1997, including all the law graduates, do not necessarily possesses a good foundation in Chinese. Hong Kong universities do not consider Chinese as a critical subject for a student to be admitted into the LLB programme; that is, usually students only need to have a passing grade in the Chinese subject to qualify for admission. Until Chinese acquires equal status to English in the governmental, business and legal sectors, true bilingualism will remain a dream. However, it is anticipated that attitudes toward Chinese will gradually change as more Chinese is used in Hong Kong, including Putonghua as a spoken language.

In 1997, the Hong Kong Government introduced the language policy of promoting bi-literacy and tri-lingualism, where the former involves two written languages (English and Chinese) and the latter three spoken languages (English, Cantonese and Putonghua). Putonghua, the 'common' language intensively promoted in Mainland China since the 1950s and widely known as Mandarin, has been greatly promoted in recent years in Hong Kong's schools as well as society at large. Such promotion is actually part of the national language policy to promote Putonghua stipulated in the Law of the PRC on the Standard Spoken and Written Chinese Language 2000. Although it is understood that frequent use of a language does not guarantee its high quality, the demand that it generates will likely prompt people's interests to study it for practical reasons: better communications and easier work. We can anticipate that a growing interest will change the perception of a language.

The status of Chinese is influenced by the status of English. In the legal profession, English is still the dominant language due to its long and exclusive and it is considered that using Chinese only may even affect the social status of legal professionals. In his sociolinguistic analysis of the language phenomenon of code-mixing in Hong Kong court proceedings, Lee (2019: 67) comments as follows:

> Some sociolinguists point out that code-mixing such as adding English words into spoken Chinese can represent a great number of symbolic meanings, such as wealth, power, social status and educational background . . . if Chinese is the only language in a certain legal context, the social status of legal professionals may not be as before. This has more or less explained why legal professionals are not passionate about dealing with legal work in Chinese. The development of legal Chinese does not look like it will be a smooth path.
>
> (English translation by the author)

This view regarding the status of spoken Chinese in court applies also to written judgments as the choice of language for these depends on the language that is spoken in court.

6.2 Research work on terminology comparison: 'universal' translation methods

Chapter 5 discussed the strong foundation of comparative law research that has been laid, starting in the Imperial Qing Dynasty and extending up to present day Hong Kong. It is believed that if the groundwork already undertaken in comparative law were to be built on with a conceptual comparison of Chinese legal terms, there would be more exchange and mixed use of legal terms among the Chinese communities, and some standardisation might become possible. It is too early to advocate for standardisation of Chinese legal terms across the Chinese communities before the completion of such hard work. Without a good legal understanding of the terminology, any linguistic moves would have little chance of success. Law must form the basis of its language development and in doing so, will naturally bring influence to bear on its terminology. For instance, although Šarčević (2017: 11) maintains that legal translation is a culture-bound activity, she acknowledges that, in a globalised world with many established transnational laws such as trade law, financial law and human rights law, 'national legal languages are slowly converging as national laws are increasingly harmonized and international standards and norms are recognized worldwide'. The linguistic process is a gradual and natural reflection of changing reality. While standardisation of terminology is yet an 'unattainable' ideal, as will be shown in the discussion to follow, the immediate task is to make use of the findings of the term comparison to explore the ideal translation methods for Chinese terms that have been long used in the three communities. In Chapter 5, some analysis of the similarities and differences among civil law terms from the three regions was undertaken. The following will summarise this research direction with more concrete findings.

There are theoretical explanations for the current use of Chinese legal terms. It is known that translation can change the target language, and that the Chinese language has been impacted in this way by translations from Western languages. However, such change is limited by the nature of language itself. For decades, linguists have contended on one hand, that linguistic borrowing must be conducted between languages of similar structures, and on the other hand, that social factors can break all the internal constraints to make language change possible (Harris and Campbell 1995: 123). Thomason and Kaufman (1988: 57) also place structural and non-structural factors in language change on an equal footing, and remark, 'A language accepts foreign structural elements only when they correspond to its own tendencies of development' (Thomason and Kaufman 1988: 17). Similarly, Wang (1984: 435, 487–488) argues that Chinese grammar is a counterbalance to Europeanisation, and that external factors arise out of internal ones in language change. In contrast to coinages such as 'possession' (*guanyou*) (管有),

'conveyance' (*zhuanyi*) (轉易), 'condition' (*yaojian*) (要件) and 'satisfy' (*xinna*) (信納) that are intended to be precise but are not particularly compatible with Chinese grammar, many translated Chinese legal terms that are more transparent, such as 'damages' (*sunhai peichang*) (損害賠償), 'limitation' (*shixiao*) (時效) and 'term' (*tiaokuan*) (條款), have been well-received in all three Chinese regions. The successful adoption of these legal terms can naturally reveal some qualities that make a good term in general and in Chinese in particular.

Generally, there are three criteria whereby to assess a term in a professional field. Sager (1990: 105–106) proposes that 'economy', 'precision' and 'appropriateness' assist in the evaluation of the effectiveness of 'special communication terms' and 'standardised terms'. Cabré (1999: 47) lists the same standards: 'in specialised texts, concision, precision and suitability are the relevant criteria'. For *sunhai peichang* (損害賠償) as the translation of 'damages', the four-word term is economical and precise, which means that it is linguistically adequate and transparent in meaning by using the ordinary words, *sunhai* (損害) (harm) and *peichang* (賠償) (compensation).

What is more critical for the success of the term is its 'appropriateness', which refers to 'a proper appreciation of the cognitive effort required of the recipient' (Sager 1990: 111). It is a common knowledge that, a harm would attract compensation in a civilised society, so the coordinating four-word structure is also logical and understandable. This implies that an arbitrary contraction of a four-word structure into a two-word structure requires more mental effort to understand. *Shixiao* (時效) as the translation of 'limitation', the period during which actions can be brought, is also economical and precise. The two-word compound term made up of two plain words *shi* (時) (time) and *xiao* (效) (effect) can be easily expanded to the daily phrase *youxiao shijian* (有效時間) (effective time). *Tiaokuan* (條款) as the translation of 'term' has also satisfied the three criteria as a coordinating compound, a common method to create words in Chinese, by combining two similar words *tiao* (條) (clause) and *kuan* (款) (paragraph). The combination can vividly describe the image of a contract that has the format of clauses and paragraphs.

So from these examples, what makes a good legal term in Chinese? Apparently, logical coordination, ordinary phrases and image projection are some key elements in the creation of compound words to express new legal concepts in the three Chinese regions. Hong Kong has created some good terms based on these techniques, together with its inclination to use Classical Chinese. Examples of the latter include two four-word compounds. One is *burong fanhui* (不容反悔) (no allowance for going back on a promise) as the translation of 'estoppel' in contract law, in which *burong* (不容) is customarily used in written language meaning 'disallow' and *fahui* (反悔) is an everyday word meaning 'regret'. Similarly, there is *gongfen shuhu* (共分疏忽) (commonly shared negligence) as the translation of 'contributory negligence' in tort law. The term *gongfen* (共分) can be easily understood as originating in *gongtong fendan* (共同分擔) as a daily phrase, and *shuhu* (疏忽) is also frequently used by ordinary people when describing careless acts in everyday life.

In line with the above linguistic properties in the established Chinese terms, the DOJ (Law Drafting Division, Department of Justice 1996: 40) already acknowledges the limitations of their new compound coinages: 'What should be noted is the fact that when a Chinese term is used to express a common law concept, the full meaning behind the term cannot be grasped by merely taking the literal meaning of the term or deciphering its morphemic elements in the Chinese language'. Hence, law drafters need not be too aggressive in pushing the limits of language. Lessons can be learnt from the examples of 'possession' (*guanyou*) (管有), 'conveyance' (*zhuanyi*) (轉易), 'condition' (*yaojian*) (要件), 'satisfy' (*xinna*) (信納) and 'convenant' (*qinuo*) (契諾) that it is difficult to gain public and professional support by expressing the legal meaning through the 'random' combination of morphemes. Perhaps one or two of these new creations may take root in the Chinese language after long years of use, but the high cost of further attempts in this direction advise against this approach. In sum, a successful translated term must be communicative owing to its submission to the internal linguistic rules, not its alteration of the rules. It is advised that the future creation of terms should not change language for the sake of law as some scholars have advocated (Li 1998; Qu 2013; Sin 2018).

6.3 Epilogue: a new era with new visions

With the development of courses and programmes in legal translation and related disciplines to equip translators and legal professionals, and preliminary comparative research on Chinese terms, it is evident that the integration of language and law necessary for building the field of legal translation is underway in Hong Kong. These efforts are highly beneficial to a bilingual city whose combination of colonial history and predominantly Chinese population demand good legal translation. The following is a summary of the past 30 years and a forecast for the future.

6.3.1 Past experience

In the past 30-odd years, the field of legal translation in Hong Kong has undergone important changes due to its natural course of development and changing social and cultural situations. First, in drafting legislation, translation was gradually replaced by bilingual co-drafting during the ten years before the government translation project finished in 1997. The linguistic effects of the English language remain prevalent in the bilingual laws drafted since its introduction in the late 1980s, largely because the Chinese version is drafted after the English version, and so bilingual drafting proper is not yet in place. Most newly coined Chinese legal terms have not taken root in Hong Kong society, let alone other Chinese societies as some academics once hoped. The main cause is that the methods used to coin these terms did not take into consideration their acceptability to users, so both lawyers and non-lawyers find many of them too novel and artificial.

Second, in the judiciary, there is ongoing translation of judgments from English to Chinese and vice versa. The same Europeanised influence is found in translated judgments, but since many parts of these, including judges' opinions, are close to ordinary language with terms that are less technical, it has been easier to achieve good translation. The involvement of lawyers in the translation of judgments has provided a good demonstration of the benefits of integrating language and law.

At this point, what have we learnt from these three decades of development? And what is the next step in legal translation and bilingual law drafting? Over the past three decades, law professionals and translators have earnestly pursued concordance between English and Chinese texts, with the result that drafters were not able to express English concepts in Chinese effectively. If the goal is to elevate the standard of bilingual law drafting and translation of judgments, it is wise to base achievement of that goal on hard-earned experience. The past witnessed the first-ever translation into Chinese of the entire set of common law legislation, in which the source English legislation was drafted in a convoluted style with core legal terms and phrases, and this was followed by a preliminary form of co-drafting.

Those early efforts have created a sound basis for future development. First, the pioneers, with their adventurous spirit, laid a solid foundation for the building of a bilingual legal system in Hong Kong. Only with bilingual legislation and core legal terminology in place can the bilingual legal system kick-start and operate on a daily basis. The Chinese legislation and legal terminology, mainly as the product of translation with a strong Europeanised style, is basically understandable and justifiable by the translators working behind the job. Second, this bold undertaking has undergone trials and errors, many of which were necessary and should be learnt from in the next stage. For example, legal terms used at the judicial levels can be created by different methods, so as to avoid the translation methods that have tended to attract criticism in the translation of old legislation.

It is time to find sensible and practical ways to take legal translation and bilingual law drafting forward. The limitations include the long use of English language in legal education and legal profession, lack of training in Chinese language and translation of legal professionals, and enormous grammatical differences between English and Chinese. Under these constraints, some calls for legal translation and bilingual law drafting appear unrealistic. Wang's (2018) exhortation that Chinese serve as a 'primary' official and legal language is simply impossible to achieve in the foreseeable future. A study by the sociologist Ng (2011) demonstrates that English is still not only dominant in the Hong Kong higher courts, it is still similarly dominant in many other postcolonial common law systems in the world such as India. Leung (2014) challenges translators to render the legal intent of law by growing use of the purposive and contextual interpretation methods. This obviously requires a great deal of translators and lawyers. If one is barely able to do literal but comprehensible translation based on 'seeable' source texts, how can one do free or liberal translation based on interpretations that can be both 'foreseeable' and 'unforeseeable'? This is the case whether it is a legal term or a statute being translated. Given that the primary readership of legislation and judgments is the general public, complicated legal issues should be put aside and attention first focused on the linguistic issues. The following section will focus on two practical suggestions for the advancement of legal translation and bilingual law drafting in Hong Kong.

6.3.2 Development for the future

Two main recommendations can be made for the future bilingual legal system of Hong Kong. The first is to shift the focus to writing and translating judgments. Having gained experience in translating the 'special' style of legislation, legal translation in Hong Kong should return to its 'less special' parts, that is, judgments. Unlike the bilingual legislation based on English-Chinese transfer and co-drafting, in which priority is given to English, the translation of judgments has developed on a local and native basis and with much greater success.[3] As mentioned in Chapter 2, the first Chinese judgments in 1995 and those appearing in the years immediately following are not translations, but works written in Chinese. Chapter 5 notes that around 600 Chinese translations of judgments have been delivered, prompting the initiative of Chinese law reporting in 2009.

In the Hong Kong context, in which English as a legal language is dominant over Chinese, this wealth of judgments written originally in Chinese by lower court judges may have two functions: First, they provide a trial ground for judges to practice writing in Chinese, using a wide lexicon ranging from material facts dealing with local customs and culture to decisions which involve legal terms and phrases. As Chinese is the original language, more attention should be paid to its improvement, including the standardisation of terms and simplification of sentences. Second, with the progression of time, they also serve as a model for the higher courts in their Chinese translation of English judgments by supplying more standardised Chinese terms and phrases and eliminating the awkwardness that can arise when translated Chinese imitates the original English.

While legal Chinese remains a translated language, it will remain secondary, and an authentic Chinese legal language will not take shape. In the long run, this 'bilateral' development of judgment translation is more healthy and should face less difficulties than legislation that is essentially an English-Chinese transfer.

This next stage in the development of the Hong Kong bilingual legal system has attracted strong support from the legal profession itself. In a recent interview with two academics from the Law Faculty of the University of Hong Kong, Alice Lee argues that, apart from the Court of Final Appeal, which seats foreign judges and handles multinational commercial cases with English documents, the proceedings of local courts can be conducted entirely in Chinese. In keeping with the increasing maturity of Chinese use in courts, Edmund Cham agrees; he advocates the 'development of a set of Chinese judgments that will help develop the common law using the Chinese language' (Chan 2017). He further argues that the two-stage development of the Hong Kong common law system that has been producing judgments to expound legal principles in the Chinese language is a unique phenomenon in the world: 'First, Hong Kong has "imported" the English common law from the UK by applying appropriate or relevant cases. Second, our local, "home-grown" common law, expressed in Chinese, is developing' (Personal communication 27 October 2019). Commenting on the local Chinese media interest aroused by Chinese use in court, Carlye Chu Fun-ling (2012: 5), Justice of Appeal of the Court of Appeal of the High Court, suggests that availability of judgments in Chinese has also increased the legal knowledge of the general public:

> The media reports on court cases can be described as 'overwhelming' and 'full of detail', not only promoting their sales and audience size, but also having a great impact on the public. On the one hand, the reports have satisfied the curiosity of people to peer into others' private lives, giving them topics for discussion in their leisure. On the other, those who are not so interested have also passively absorbed knowledge of these court cases and legal procedures. Law has unconsciously seeped into people's daily lives.
> (English translation by the author)

Furthermore, Chu (2012: 5) expects that as the Chinese legal language matures, Hong Kong citizens will gain 'a deep and accurate understanding of a society based on the rule of law and the role of the court and judicial independence in a society based on rule of law'. Poon (2010: 89) explains that this 'legal awakening' is due to the social and political changes that have occurred since the handover, in which the people of Hong Kong are more motivated to safeguard their interests through knowledge of law. As judgments make greater impact on readers, the translators should be more cognisant of enhancing their techniques and methods in order to achieve the intended communicative goal. Reader response can constantly serve as a guide for all the decisions around translation of judgments.

The process of enhancing the writing and translating of Chinese judgments can commence with legal education at university, with the provision of legal translation courses focusing on the drafting and translating of two types of texts: judgments and correspondence. These two text types can certainly help aspiring solicitors and barristers, while receiving a legal education conducted entirely in English, to acquire some basic and essential techniques for translating to and from Chinese. The same approach—focusing on judgments and correspondence—can be applied to the design of a legal translation course for translation majors; to deal with judgments means also including their abstracts as illustrated in the first pedagogical case study in Chapter 4, and other less technical texts first.

Besides, the dominance of English in Hong Kong higher courts implies that English-Chinese translation would still play an important role in the Hong Kong bilingual system, and it can remain a norm in translation training in all of the Chinese regions that English-Chinese translation be practiced before Chinese-English. From the perspective of developing a bilingual legal system, it is reasonable to translate the legislation first. In contrast, from the perspective of developing a bilingual person, it is reasonable to translate legal texts such as judgments written in ordinary language first. While legal language is always regarded as a professional register, its discursive nature should not be forgotten, as mentioned in

Chapter 1. Everything should start with the basics, and only from this foundation can specialisation proceed. This approach to developing understanding of equivalence and basic translation techniques is also intended to overcome the pervasive belief that there is always a gap between the Chinese and English versions, and that use of Chinese undermines the Hong Kong legal system.

In addition to these proposed courses, perhaps the three law faculties in Hong Kong should consider making written Chinese proficiency such as measured by the results of the Chinese Language in the Hong Kong Diploma of Secondary Education examination, an admission criterion.[4] Only when one is able to deal with ordinary language can he or she proceed to deal with specialised language with interest, confidence and linguistic sense.

The second recommendation for Hong Kong is that it could take the lead in providing a translated Chinese legal lexicon for the entire Chinese world. Therefore, it must balance all of the linguistic and legal factors in the creation of Chinese legal terms, so that the terms can be used in the other communities when functionally equivalent concepts are encountered. As mentioned in Chapter 2, Hong Kong written Chinese has retained the classical style to an extent that falls somewhere between the two sides of the Taiwan Strait. This forms a good linguistic environment to create a lexicon that is acceptable to a great number of target readers. More importantly, of the three Chinese communities, Hong Kong has the longest history of interaction with the West and experience of translation in all fields, both English-to-Chinese and Chinese-to-English directions. The city is usually the first to contact and translate materials in the English language because of its bilingual legal system, and it has continued this direct relationship with the world under the 'one country, two systems' stipulation in the Basic Law. As illustrated in Chapter 3, the Hong Kong legal system is readily able to absorb terms and their meanings from international treaties through its bilingual law.

As a result, in the Layout-design (Topography) of Integrated Circuits Ordinance (Cap. 445), the Hong Kong translation *butu sheji* (布圖設計(拓撲圖)) has almost exactly the same definition as that of 'layout-design' in TRIPS. The role of borrowing new terms can also be exemplified by the term 'adoption'. To the ordinary Hong Kong people, 'adoption' translated as *lingyang* (領養) (obtain to foster) in Hong Kong legislation has acquired the meaning of taking legal procedures to adopt a child or an animal, while the everyday word *shouyang* (收養) (receive to foster) refers to adopting a child or an animal with or without legal procedures. In contrast, in the legislation of the Mainland, Taiwan and Macao, the more general term *shouyang* (收養) (receive to foster) is used instead of the specialised term *lingyang* (領養) (obtain to foster) (Qu 2013: 271).

To assume the leading position in creating Chinese legal terms, Hong Kong should adopt the standardised use of Modern Written Chinese so that the translated terms can be used in other Chinese regions. For instance, *ruwu fanfazui* (入屋犯法/入屋犯法罪) (breaking-in violation of law) as the translation of 'burglary' is not suitable for use in the Mainland and Taiwan, as in Putonghua or Mandarin, *ruhu* (入戶) (enter a household) and *rushi* (入室) (enter a room) are customarily used instead of *ruwu* (入屋) (enter a house). However, these three words are mutually intelligible to Chinese-speakers mostly due to the common basis of Modern Written Chinese in Classical Chinese.

At present, there are some terms created in Hong Kong that satisfy both the linguistic and legal requirements of good drafting. For example, the explanatory translations of 'slander' as *duanzan xingshi feibang* (短暫形式誹謗) (temporary form defamation) and 'libel' as *yongjiu xingshi feibang* (永久形式誹謗) (permanent form defamation) strike a balance between succinctness and precision. The ordinary language translations of *koutou feibang* (口頭誹謗) (oral defamation) and *shumian feibang* (書面誹謗) (written defamation) found in the legal dictionaries of the Mainland and Taiwan may be easier to understand, but not as accommodating in the modern technological world where defamation may occur using communicative means other than speaking and writing.

As discussed, a good Chinese legal lexicon should balance language and law in its translation of English terms, meaning that, as much as possible, the coinage of words should observe the rules of logical coordination, use of ordinary phrases and image projection. Above all, terms created through literal translation and the appending of new legal meanings to ordinary words and phrases appear to be most acceptable to users. While learning from this experience and creating the most receptive Chinese translations, Hong Kong could gradually become a centre for absorbing Western legal terms.

The need for legal translation in Hong Kong arose internally from its colonial history and predominantly Chinese population. The main obstacle to its development in the past has been the relatively low status of legal translation, which has resulted partially from the low status of Chinese language, legal professionals' lack of time and formal Chinese language study opportunities, and the lack of research interest from legal academics. Notwithstanding the internal constraints, the external environment now plays a more important role, and in the past two decades it has been more favourable to the development of legal translation in Hong Kong, its neighbouring Chinese regions and the international world. Although Hong Kong launched the first language and law programme, more such programmes are now on offer on the Mainland than in Hong Kong.

All these programmes can benefit from the experience of the fast developing legal translation programmes in Western countries, especially in Europe. The three regions now have more economic, trade and personnel contact than ever before.[5] Following the growing ties after Hong Kong's return to China in 1997 and the PRC's implementation of 'three direct links' across the Taiwan Strait in 2008, language borrowing has intensified. In the process, more practical legal work such as the signing of contracts has been done across the regions. And while Hong Kong has been learning from the Chinese laws from the Mainland and Taiwan, both of them may in turn have been learning from both the Chinese- and English-language laws and legal documents of Hong Kong. History has shown that economic openness brings forth language contact and language change. As practical issues inevitably arise from the increasing legal contact, it is hoped that legal academics will become more interested in investigating them from linguistic and other perspectives, and conduct collaborative and cross-disciplinary work with linguists. The legal translation and legal linguistics boom in Europe is well grounded in practical work in the multilingual context.

Set against the increasing globalisation of the twenty-first century, this book has identified the hurdles and problems prevalent in legal translation in Hong Kong, explored some existing practices and strategies, and opened new opportunities and paths to move forward. If Hong Kong aspires to eliminate inelegant drafting, it is time for it to set its sights higher and embrace the globally accepted goal of 'the spirit of the law, not the letter'. The world is welcome to analyse the unique Hong Kong experience as it discovers its way forward. Some proposals in this book could be universal. In the near future, it is hoped that this book will invite further research into this interdisciplinary area of growing importance, especially Chinese terminology in other legal areas and translation of Chinese terminology and legislation into English, as legal globalisation is vital to all other areas of development and exchange in and among the regions.

Notes

1 Eight universities in Hong Kong provide BA and MA in Translation programmes, and three universities in Hong Kong provide LLB, JD and LLM programmes.
2 Based on the author's years of teaching and reviewing experience in the language and law master's programmes in Hong Kong, the majority of students have no or little legal background, and there was only a small number of practising lawyers enrolled as students. The situation is generally the same in the legal translation course at the bachelor's level. The author taught two legal translation undergraduate courses over a few years, in which only one law school student was enrolled.
3 Ng Kwai Hang (2009: 6) makes this distinction: 'Barristers who use both languages describe English and Cantonese trials as trials that take place in two different worlds. English trials are, in their words, solemn, respectful, and dignified. Cantonese trials, again their words, are noisy, mundane, and belittling'. The flip side of this picture is that the use of Cantonese makes the Hong Kong bilingual system more accessible to the native population, contributing to development of the rule of law in the jurisdiction. Given that Cantonese is primarily a spoken language, the judge can still produce the Chinese judgments primarily in Modern Written Chinese, with the use of Cantonese lexical items that are key to the case.
4 The Hong Kong Diploma of Secondary Education Examination (HKDSE) is administered by the Hong Kong Examinations and Assessment Authority. Most candidates sit for four core subjects (Chinese Language, English Language, Mathematics and Liberal Studies) and two or three elective subjects. HKDSE started in 2012, replacing the previous Hong Kong Certificate of Education Examination (for Secondary Form five leavers) and Hong Kong Advanced Level Examination (for Secondary Form seven leavers).
5 Hong Kong has long been open to the cultures of both the Mainland and Taiwan through various channels including the sale and library collections of Chinese publications. The books and journals published in Mainland China are in simplified characters, and those published in Taiwan and Hong Kong are in traditional characters. Since Hong Kong has been exposed to books from all Chinese regions and overseas Chinese people, most educated Hong Kong people are able to read simplified characters and a small proportion write them, some even proficiently, as along with the traditional characters taught at school and used in daily life. It is believed that traditional character users find it easier to learn simplified characters than vice versa.

English references

Beaudoin, Lowis (2009). Legal Translation in Canada: The Genius of Legal Language(s). In Olsen, Frances, Lorz, Alexander and Stein, Dieter (Eds.), *Translation Issues in Language and Law* (pp. 136–144). London: Palgrave Macmillan.

Cabré, Teresa M. (1999). *Terminology: Theory, Methods and Applications*. Philadelphia: John Benjamins.

Galdia, Marcus (2013). Strategies and Tools for Legal Translation. *Comparative Legilinguistics: International Journal for Legal Communication 16*: 77–94.

Harris, Alice C. and Campbell, Lyle (1995). *Historical Syntax in Cross-linguistic Perspective*. Cambridge: Cambridge University Press.

Lambert, José (2009). The Status and Position of Legal Translation: A Chapter in the Discursive Construction of Societies. In Olsen, Frances, Lorz, Alexander and Stein, Dieter (Eds.), *Translation Issues in Language and Law* (pp. 76–95). London: Palgrave Macmillan.

Leung, Janny H. C. (2014). The Object of Fidelity in Translating Multilingual Legislation. *Semiotica 201*: 223–238.

Mattila, Heikki E. S. (2013). *Comparative Legal Linguistics. Language of Law, Latin and Modern Lingua Francas* (2nd Ed.). Aldershot, Hants: Ashgate.

Ng, Kwai Hang (2009). *The Common Law in Two Voices: Language, Law, and the Postcolonial Dilemma in Hong Kong*. Stanford: Stanford University Press.

Ng, Kwai Hang (2011). Is There Chinese Common Law? an Empirical Study of the Bilingual Common-Law System of Hong Kong. *Journal of Empirical Legal Studies 8*(1): 118–146.

Poon, Emily Wai-yee (2010). Strategies for Creating a Bilingual Legal Dictionary. *International Journal of Lexicography 23*(1): 83–103.

Sager, Juan C. (1990). *A Practical Course in Terminology Processing*. Philadelphia: John Benjamins Publishing Company.

Šarčević, Susan (2017). Challenges to Legal Translators in Institutional Settings. In Prieto Ramos, Fernando (Eds.), *Institutional Translation for International Governance: Enhancing Quality in Multilingual Legal Communication* (pp. 9–24). London: Bloomsbury Methuen Drama.

Thomason, Sarah G. and Kaufman, Terrence (1988). *Language Contact, Creolization, and Genetic Linguistics*. Berkeley: University of California Press.

Chinese references

Chan, Man-wai 陳雯慧 (2017, June 20). 〈法庭全英世界不再 新晉律師也要學曉"煲冬瓜"〉 (No More Exclusive-English Environment in Court: New Lawyers Must Also Study Putonghua) 《香港01》 (*Hong Kong 01*). Retrieved from: www.hk01.com/社會新聞/95158/回歸20載-法庭全英世界不再-新晉律師也要學曉-煲冬瓜.

Chu, Carlye Fun-ling 朱芬齡 (2012). 〈法庭使用中文的深層影響〉 (*The Deep Impact of Using Chinese in Court*). Speech at a Talk Series Organised by Faculty of Law and Alumni Association, the University of Hong Kong, November 29. Retrieved from: www.law.hku.hk/alumni/files/Activities/29112012.pdf.

Law Drafting Division, Department of Justice (1999). The Common Law and the Chinese Language. *Hong Kong Lawyer*, February: 39–42.

Lee, Elvis Kim Hung 李劍雄 (2019). 〈香港雙語法制下法律人員在法庭以中文發言的問題〉 (Use of Chinese by Legal Professionals in Court under the Bilingual Legal

System). In Cham, Edmund Shu Kay 湛樹基 and Lee, Elvis Kim Hung 李劍雄 (Eds.), 《香港雙語法制: 語言與翻譯》 (*Bilingual Legal System in Hong Kong: Language and Translation*) (pp. 49–71). Hong Kong: Hong Kong University Press.

Li, Changdao 李昌道 (1998). 〈香港雙語法律的歷史發展和展望〉 (The Historical Development and Prospects of Hong Kong's Bilingual Law). In Leung Mei Fun, Priscilla 梁美芬 and Guobin, Zhu 朱國斌 (Eds.), *The Basic Law of The HKSAR: From Theory to Practice* (pp. 193–203). Hong Kong, Singapore and Malaysia: Butterworth Asia.

Li, Kexing 李克興 (2018). 〈對一份房地產買賣協議的譯、評、注〉 (Translating, Criticising and Annotating an Agreement for Sale and Purchase). In Qu, Wensheng 屈文生 (Ed.), 《法律翻譯研究》 (*Legal Translation Studies*) (pp. 240–297). Shanghai: Shanghai Renmin Press.

Qu, Wensheng 屈文生 (2013). 《從詞典出發：法律術語譯名統一與規範化的翻譯史研究》 (*Lexicography: A Study of the Unification and Standardisation of Translated Legal Terms*). Shanghai: Shanghai Renmin Press.

Sin, King-kui 冼景炬 (2018). 〈從佛經翻譯到雙語法制的建立：香港法例翻譯的啓示〉 (From the Translation of Buddhist Scriptures to the Establishment of the Bilingual Legal System: Inspirations from the Translation of Hong Kong Legislation). In Qu, Wensheng 屈文生 (Ed.), 《法律翻譯研究》 (*Legal Translation Studies*) (pp. 316–394). Shanghai: Shanghai Renmin Press.

Wang, Li 王力 (1984). 《王力文集》 (*Collected Essays of Wang Li*) (Vol. 1). Shandong: Shandong Education Press.

Wang, Xuanwei 王玄瑋 (2018). 〈香港雙語法制：現有問題及其解決〉 (Hong Kong Legal System: Existing Problems and their Solutions). 《"一國兩制"研究》 (*Studies of 'One Country, Two Systems'*) 2: 97–106.

Index

accurate/accurately/accuracy 29, 46, 74, 84, 88–89, 100, 114, 133
Administrative Procedure Law 8
Agreement on Trade-Related Aspects of Intellectual Property Rights (TRIPS) 9, 55, 60–69, 71, 141
America 108
American 60, 76
Arbitration Ordinance (Cap. 341) 121
Australia 97, 101, 108
Australian 97, 101, 127

Bachelor of Laws (LLB) 87, 89, 101, 134; see also law courses; law programme
baihua 10, 23; see also *wenyan*
Banking Ordinance (Cap. 155) 107
barrister 19, 32, 44, 98–100, 133, 140; see also counsel; lawyer; solicitor
Basic Law of the Hong Kong Special Administrative Region/Basic Law of Hong Kong 5–6, 18, 88, 141
Beiyang Government 118
Beiyang University 118
Berne and Paris Conventions 9
bilingual 3, 6–7, 17, 19, 29, 33, 40, 45, 47, 51, 65, 69, 71, 74, 80–82, 88, 93, 96, 98–101, 104–105, 108, 112, 133–134, 137, 140, 143
bilingual city 137
bilingual intellectuals 17
bilingualism 15, 17, 134; legal 44, 88; legislative 113
bilingual judges and judicial officers 107
bilingual judgments 99
bilingual jurisdiction 3
bilingual law 18–19, 51, 64, 137, 141–142
bilingual law drafting 5, 7, 15–16, 18, 104, 107, 138–139
Bilingual Laws Advisory Committee 6

bilingual lawyers 71, 105
bilingual legal system 3, 5–6, 17, 88, 93, 104–105, 112, 138–141
bilingual legislation 4, 6–7, 16–17, 29, 33, 44, 47, 88, 96, 104–108, 132, 138–139
bilingual legislative drafting 7
bilingual materials 100
bilingual person 140
bi-literacy and tri-lingualism 88, 134
Black's Law Dictionary 12, 58–59, 120
borrowing 1, 5, 25, 29–31, 54, 63, 119, 125, 141; language 142; linguistic 54, 135; mutual 107
British colony 2
British rule 3, 120

Canada 3, 112, 133
Cantonese 19, 39, 88, 101, 119, 127, 133–134, 143
case law 12, 44, 75, 96; see also statute law
Chaoyang University 118
China University of Political Science and Law 94–95
Chinese Academy of Social Sciences 118
Chinese communities 4–5, 10–12, 16, 19, 24, 54, 79, 88–90, 93–94, 115, 119–120, 135, 141; see also Chinese regions
Chinese language 4–6, 10, 16, 23–25, 29, 32, 37, 39–40, 54, 56, 100–101, 114, 132–135, 137–139, 141–142
Chinese law 17–18, 45–46, 60, 75, 77–78, 83, 120, 139
Chinese linguistics 12; see also Chinese linguists
Chinese linguists 26; see also Chinese linguists

Index

Chinese regions 4–5, 13, 18–19, 34, 53, 55, 71, 74, 79, 106, 118–122, 126, 133, 136, 140–143; *see also* Chinese communities
Chinese training 89, 92–93, 115, 133
Chinese University of Hong Kong, The 93
Chinese University of Hong Kong Ordinance, The (Cap. 1109) 19
Chinese world 4, 17, 53, 58, 119, 132, 141
City University of Hong Kong 79, 84, 93, 106
Civil Code of Taiwan (Taiwan *Minfa*《臺灣民法》) 55–57, 59
civil law 2, 4–5, 12, 15, 17, 53–55, 59, 63, 75–76, 80, 106, 115, 118, 120–121, 124–125, 135; *see also* common law; criminal law
Classical Chinese 24, 86, 114–115, 118, 136, 142; *see also* Modern Chinese
co-drafting 5, 7, 17, 45, 93, 108, 112, 137–139; *see also* parallel drafting
coinage 11, 30–33, 93, 125, 135, 137, 142
common law 3–6, 9–12, 15–16, 30–33, 51–53, 55, 58–59, 75–81, 88, 93, 96, 101, 107–108, 118–121, 125, 137–140; *see also* civil law
communicative 7, 45, 60, 137, 140, 142
communicative approach 45, 108
communicative function 15, 46, 71, 93, 134
communicative purposes 52
communicative text 47, 109
communicative value 47
Companies Ordinance (Cap. 622) 30–31, 110
Company Law/company law 8, 17, 119, 121, 125
comparative law 14, 107, 118–119, 127, 132, 135
Comparative Law Academy 118
competency 84, 105, 132, 134; Chinese 133; cross-disciplinary 16; professional 71; translation 91–92, 134
Competition Ordinance (Cap. 619) 111
compound 24, 30, 32, 56, 59, 124–125, 136–137
comprehensible/comprehension 32, 35, 38, 45, 101, 104–105, 108, 138
connotation 59
constitution 1–2, 5, 8, 12, 93
constitutional law 118
Constitution of the PRC 8, 19
Contemporary Chinese Dictionary, The 56
continental law 2, 9, 118; *see also* civil law
Contract Law/contract law 16–17, 32, 74, 78, 80–81, 84–85, 87–89, 91, 101, 106, 119–122, 124, 136
Conveyancing and Property Ordinance (Cap. 219) 54–55, 57, 59
convoluted structures 28, 44
convoluted style 115, 138
Copyright Act of Taiwan (Taiwan *Zhuzuoquan Fa*《臺灣著作權法》) 55, 63
Copyright Law of the PRC (*Zhonghua Renmin Gongheguo Zhuzuoquan Fa*《中華人民共和國著作權法》)/ Copyright Law 8, 9, 18, 54, 58
Copyright Ordinance (Cap. 83) 37, 54, 57
counsel 97–98, 100, 108; *see also* barrister; lawyer; solicitor
court 3, 8, 14, 19, 40, 52, 105, 107, 113, 115, 119–120, 135, 138–140
Court of Final Appeal 113, 116, 139
court proceeding 3, 46, 88, 100, 113, 134
criminal law 2, 17, 32, 87, 101, 115; *see also* civil law
Criminal Law of the PRC 52
cross-disciplinary 143
cross-disciplinary abilities 132
cross-disciplinary competency 16
cross-disciplinary training 132
curriculum 87–88, 94, 101

De l'esprit des lois (*The Spirit of Laws*) (*Tianyan Lun*《天演論》) 1
Deng, Xiaoping 78
Department of Justice (DOJ) 7, 31, 33–34, 45, 47, 89, 96–98, 105–106, 109–111, 137
Department of Justice Bilingual Laws Information System/Bilingual Legislation Information System 47, 89; *see also* Hong Kong e-Legislation
dialect 10, 19, 24
dialectal variation 25
discourse 79, 116
District Court 113
domestic codes 64
domestic law 5, 8–9, 62–63, 74; *see also* international law
Drafting Legislation in Hong Kong: A Guide to Styles and Practices 96
drafting technique 45, 47, 97, 110

East China University of Political Science and Law 94–95
elegant/elegance 108, 114, 116, 143

148 Index

Elements of International Laws: With a Sketch of the History of the Science (*Wanguo Gongfa*《萬國公法》) 1
English-Chinese Glossary of Securities, Futures and Financial Terms, An 106
Environment Protection Law 8
equivalence 4–5, 7, 10–11, 13, 16, 19, 51, 53–54, 64–65, 67, 69–70, 76, 112, 119, 132, 141; functional 53, 64; near 5; non- 5, 70; partial 5, 67, 70; semantic 33; terminological 10–11, 14–15, 71; total 12; translational 106
equivalent 11, 13, 32, 37, 54, 58, 61, 141; absolute 52; functional 64; near 71; non- 66, 70
Europe 12, 142–143
Europeanisation 3, 23–26, 29, 43, 113, 135
Europeanised Chinese 15, 44, 111
Europeanised feature 4, 34, 37, 42
European languages 24
expatriate 88, 113

faithful 29, 57, 70–71
faithful approach 4, 34
faithfulness 116
Falü Fanyi: Cong Shijian Chufa (*Legal Translation in Practice*《法律翻譯：從實踐出發》) 104
Falü Fanyi de Lilun he Jishu (*Legal Translation: Theory and Techniques*《法律翻譯的理論和技術》) 105
Falü Fanyi Xilie: Liang'an Sandi Gongsie Fa Zhuyao Cihui (*Legal Translation Series: Key Terms in Company Law of Hong Kong, Mainland China and Taiwan*《法律翻譯系列：兩岸三地公司法主要詞彙》) 106
Falü Fanyi Xilie: Liang'an Sandi Heyue Fa Zhuyao Cihui (*Legal Translation Series: Key Terms in Contract Law of Hong Kong, Mainland China and Taiwan*《法律翻譯系列：兩岸三地合約法主要詞彙》) 106
Falü Fanyi Xilie: Liang'an Sandi Qinquan Fa Zhuyao Cihui (*Legal Translation Series: Key Terms in Tort Law of Hong Kong, Mainland China and Taiwan*《法律翻譯系列：兩岸三地侵權法主要詞彙》) 106
Faxue Zazhi (*Law Review*《法學雜誌》) 118
First Sino-Japanese War 1
First World War 23

fluent/fluency 108, 116
Food and Safety Bill 45
foreign languages 10, 24
foreign law 1, 4, 8, 15–16
foreign term 54–55, 57
forensic linguistics 94
France 120
French 24, 57, 59, 112
French and German civil codes 8
Fu Jen Catholic University 95

gender neutral drafting 96, 98, 110
German 8, 24, 59, 118
German civil law 59
Germany 57, 120
glossary 16, 34, 87–89, 90–92, 99, 105–107, 118–121
grammar 10, 19, 24–26, 29, 45–46, 109, 112, 135–136
grammatical 10–12, 15–16, 23, 25, 37, 39, 42, 112, 114, 138
Guangdong University of Foreign Studies 94
Guarantee Law of the PRC (*Zhonghua Renmin Gongheguo Danbao Fa*《中華人民共和國擔保法》) 55, 59

Hang Seng University of Management 79, 93–94
Hanying Falü Cihui (*Chinese-English Glossary of Legal Terms*《漢英法律詞彙》) 33, 105
High Court 113, 140
Hong Kong Bar Association 45; *see also* Law Society of Hong Kong, The
Hong Kong Bill of Rights Ordinance (Cap. 383) 44
Hong Kong e-Legislation 34, 47, 89, 96, 105; *see also* Department of Justice Bilingual Laws Information System/Bilingual Legislation Information System
Hong Kong Government 3, 6, 88, 96, 134
Hong Kong Judiciary 113
Hong Kong law 12, 29, 45, 52, 65, 69, 76, 119; *see also* Laws of Hong Kong
Hong Kong Post, the Government of Hong Kong Special Administrative Region 83
Hong Kong Translation Society 108
Hong Kong universities 87, 92, 134
Hong Kong University of Science and Technology, The 47

idiomatic Chinese 46
idiomatic expression 33
idioms 26, 117
incomprehensible 93
Indo-European languages 25
inelegant drafting 143
Insolvency Law 8
Integrated Circuit Layout Protection Act (*Jiti Dianlu Dianlu Buju Baohu Fa*《積體電路電路布局保護法》) 64, 68, 71
Intellectual Property Department, the Government of the Hong Kong Administrative Region 71
intellectual property law/IP law 5, 9, 16–17, 51, 54
Intellectual Property Office (IPO), Ministry of Economic Office, Taiwan 71
interdisciplinary 92, 95, 143
interdisciplinary approach 74, 79
interdisciplinary education 95
interdisciplinary study 4, 14
interdiscipline 94
international agreement 4, 51, 60, 63–64, 71; *see also* international convention
international convention 58, 62; *see also* international agreement
internationalisation 8–9
international law 2, 5, 8–9, 15, 58, 63; *see also* domestic law
international treaties 8–10, 15, 141
international world 2, 142
Interpretation and General Clauses Ordinance (Cap. 1) 6

Japan 2, 9
Japanese 1–2, 9, 24–25, 63, 120, 125
judge 3, 19, 53, 104, 107, 113, 116–117, 138–139, 143
judgment 3, 5, 15–17, 27 36–37, 39–40, 42, 44, 46, 81–82, 84, 87, 91, 96, 99–100, 104–105, 107–108, 113–118, 135, 137–140, 143
judicial texts 14, 116; *see also* legislative texts
jurisdiction 2–4, 11, 52–53, 91–92, 107, 118–119, 143
jurist 44, 106, 115

Land Management Law 78
language and law 2–4, 6, 16, 79, 93–94, 106, 112–113, 121, 132–133, 137–138, 142–143
language change 135, 142
language policy 88, 96, 134
language professional 94
language skills 74, 95–96
language style 75–76, 113, 132
language training 92, 98, 104
Law and Regulations Database, Ministry of Justice, Taiwan 18
law courses 99, 118; *see also* Bachelor of Laws (LLB); law programme
law drafters 7, 16, 46, 56, 95–98, 109, 112, 125, 133, 137
Law Drafting Division (LDD) of the Department of Justice (DOJ)/LDD 7, 29, 96, 98
law draftsman 6, 104
law faculty 139; *see also* law school
LawInfoChina, Peking University/LawInfoChina 18, 60, 121
Law of Nations, The (*Geguo Lüli*《各國律例》 & *Haiguo Tuzhi*《海國圖志》) 1
Law on Economic Contracts Concerning Foreign Interests 78
Law on Prevention and Treatment of Infectious Diseases 9
Law on Sino-Foreign Equity Joint Ventures 78–79
Law on Technology Contracts 78
law professor 2, 45, 88
law programme 79, 87–88, 100–101, 133, 142; *see also* Bachelor of Laws (LLB); law courses
law school 89, 118, 143; *see also* law faculty
Law Society of Hong Kong, The 93; *see also* Hong Kong Bar Association
Laws of Hong Kong 19, 120; *see also* Hong Kong law
lawyer 12, 16–17, 29, 44, 47, 53, 71, 74–75, 88, 93, 95–96, 98–99, 104–105, 113, 115, 117, 119, 127, 133, 137–138, 143; *see also* barrister; counsel; solicitor
Layout-design (Topography) of Integrated Circuits Ordinance (Cap. 445) 64, 69, 71, 141
learning 8, 74, 79, 87, 98–99, 117, 142; *see also* teaching
legal Chinese 4, 5, 10–11, 15, 23, 29, 45, 87–89, 91–93, 100, 112, 139
legal codes 9
legal concept 5, 9–10, 16, 30–32, 58, 60, 74–75, 84, 89, 124–125, 136

Index

legal dictionary(ies) 33, 88–89, 98–100, 104–106, 119, 121, 142
legal documents 16, 29, 40, 93, 99–100, 105, 142
legal education 88, 138, 140; *see also* legal training
legal effect 10, 29, 52, 66, 91, 125; *see also* legal force
legal force 6, 18, 29; *see also* legal effect
legal genre 35
legal globalisation 5, 7–9, 15, 17, 143
legal glossary 16, 99, 107, 118
legal knowledge 16, 32–33, 60, 62, 71, 74, 79–80, 87–88, 92, 95, 140
legal language 6, 10–11, 14, 23, 46, 53, 75, 80, 89, 96, 101, 112, 115, 124, 139, 140
legal linguistics 143
legal linguists 118
legal meaning 29–33, 54, 58–59, 70–71, 90, 109, 115, 124, 132, 137, 142
legal profession 16, 45, 74, 93–94, 96, 98, 100, 107, 113, 133–134, 138–139
legal professionals 11, 14, 53, 74, 95, 100, 105–106, 118, 134, 137–138, 142
legal system 1–2, 4–6, 8–10, 12, 15–17, 19, 53, 74–77, 79, 88–90, 92–93, 104–105, 107, 112, 118, 121, 125, 132–133, 138–141
legal term 4, 11–14, 16, 30, 33, 51, 53, 60, 62, 76, 80–81, 84, 87–89, 92, 105, 109, 115, 119, 121, 124–125, 127, 132, 135–139, 141–142
legal terminology 4, 5, 10–11, 13, 15–16, 29, 33, 51, 53–54, 84, 88–89, 106–107, 118–119, 138
legal texts 14–15, 31, 40, 44–45, 74, 79, 84, 87, 94–95, 99, 105, 140
legal tradition 9, 13, 57, 75–76, 79
legal training 92–93, 104, 113; *see also* legal education
legal translation 1–5, 7, 10–11, 13–18, 23–29, 30–39, 40–49, 50–59, 60–69, 70–76, 79–80, 84–85, 87, 93–95, 98–101, 104–105, 107, 119, 121, 127, 132–133, 135, 137–140, 142–143
legal translator 13–14, 16–17, 47, 53, 59, 71, 74, 76, 85, 94–95, 98–100, 104–106, 118–119, 132
legal writing 87, 93, 115
legislation 2–11, 15–19, 29, 33–34, 44–45, 47, 56, 60, 63–64, 71, 76, 88, 96, 104–109, 113, 115, 127, 132, 137–143

legislative texts 116; *see also* judicial texts
lexical items 25, 143; *see also* lexicon
lexicon 16, 19, 29, 39, 125, 139–142; *see also* lexical items
Lin, Zexu 1
literal 138
literal approaches 17
literal meaning 17, 58
literal translation 13, 29–31, 34, 40, 68, 71, 142
Liufa Quanshu (*The Six Laws*《六法全書》) 2, 8
Lunyu (*The Analects*《論語》) 30
Magistrate's Court 113
Mandarin 10, 17, 19, 24, 75, 134, 141; Northern 10, 19, 25
MA programme 95
marker 25–26, 28, 39, 42–44, 111–112
Martin, W. A. P. 1
Master of Arts in Translation 79, 93, 95
master's programme 79, 93–94, 101, 143
May Fourth Movement 16, 23
Meiji period 2, 9
Ministry of Education, Taiwan 95
mistranslation 5, 60–62, 71, 119
Modern Chinese 19, 24, 46, 77, 114–115; *see also* Classical Chinese
Modern Standard Chinese 23–25, 98
Modern Written Chinese 10, 12, 15, 19, 24, 37, 141, 143
monolingual 91, 93
monolingual jurisdiction 11
morpheme 26, 30, 32, 56, 125
Motor Vehicle Idling (Fixed Penalty) Ordinance (Cap. 611) 109
multilingual context 143
multilingual countries 107
multilingual law 19
multilingual legal systems 19
multilingual texts of law 19

National Changhua University of Education 95
National Intellectual Property Administration (CNIPA), PRC 71
National Kaohsiung First University of Science and Technology 95
National Taiwan Normal University 95
National Taiwan University 95
New Culture Movement 23
New Territories Land Exchange Entitlements (Redemption) Ordinance (Cap. 495) 31

New Zealand 108
non-Northern Mandarin dialects 10, 24
Northwest University of Politics and Law 94

official language 3, 6
Official Languages Ordinance (Cap. 5) 6
'one country, two systems' 6, 13, 141
Open University of Hong Kong, The 79, 93
Opium War 24

parallel Chinese text 108
parallel drafting 46; *see also* co-drafting
parallel texts 45
Patent Law of the PRC (*Zhonghua Renmin Gongheguo Zhuanli Fa*《中華人民共和國專利法》)/Patent Law 9, 64, 66, 67
pattern 25, 34, 40, 96
pedagogical approach 74
pedagogical case study(ies) 79, 140
pedagogical framework 87
Peking University 18, 118
Pharmacy and Poisons Act 81–82
plain language 45–46, 96–97, 108, 112, 127
plain language approach 115–116
plain language drafting 96–97, 107–108, 112
plain language guide 4, 109
plain language movement 127
plain language practices 97
plain language principle 40, 108
plain language use 39
Poisons Rules 81
practitioners 16, 74, 104, 119, 132–133
Prevention of Copyright Piracy Ordinance (Cap. 544) 54, 63
property law 17, 54–55, 125
Putonghua 19, 75, 88, 101, 134, 141

Qing Dynasty 1, 8, 15, 17, 63, 118, 125, 135

readable/readability 12, 26, 31, 41, 46
reader 37, 46, 62, 70, 105, 107, 117, 124–125, 140–141
Real Right Law of the PRC (*Zhonghua Renmin Gongheguo Wuquan Fa*《中華人民共和國物權法》)/Real Right Law 54–57, 59–60
Reform and Opening Up Policy 5, 8

Regulations on Protection of Integrated Circuit Layout Design (*Jicheng Dianlu Sheji Baohu Tiaoli*《集成電路布圖設計保護條例》) 66
Regulation on the Urgent Handling of Public Health Emergencies 9
renditions 55, 57, 59, 122, 126–127
Republican Era 2, 118, 120
Residential Properties (First-hand Sales) Ordinance (Cap. 621) 110
Roman law 12
rule of law 45, 75, 96, 108, 127, 143
Rule of Law, The 108

Sale of Goods Ordinance (Cap. 26) 18, 34, 107
Second World War 8–9
Securities and Futures Bill 45
Securities and Futures Commission Ordinance (Cap. 24) 6, 19
Self-strengthening Movement 1
sentence structure 25, 27, 34, 38, 40, 45–46, 91, 96, 111, 132; *see also* syntactic structure; syntax
Shen, Jiaben 1, 118
Shuangyu Putongfa: Tudi Anli Zhailu (*Bilingual Common Law: Extracts from Land Cases*《雙語普通法：土地案例摘錄》) 107
Shuangyu Putongfa: Xingshi Anli Zhailu (*Bilingual Common Law: Extracts from Criminal Cases*《雙語普通法：刑事案例摘錄》) 107
Sino-British Joint Declaration 6
Sino-British War 1
solicitor 3, 98–100, 140; *see also* barrister; counsel; lawyer
Soochow University 118
source language 34; *see also* target language; translated language
source term 51, 54–55, 57, 59, 63, 66, 68, 121–122, 126–127; *see also* translated term
source text 13, 42, 115, 138; *see also* target text; translated text
Southwest University of Political Science and Law 94–95
sovereignty 2, 4, 5
spoken language 19, 25, 88, 114, 134, 143; *see also* written language
standardisation 12, 119, 135, 139

statute 12, 64, 75–79, 82, 89, 91, 106, 109, 119, 121, 138; civil law 76; common law 76, 120; legal 34
statute law 33; *see also* case law
Supreme People's Court of the PRC 52
syntactic structure 47; *see also* sentence structure; syntax
syntax 3, 29, 34, 45–46, 98, 105; *see also* sentence structure; syntactic structure

Taiwanese law 119
target language 7, 34, 40, 135; *see also* source language; translated language
target readers/target Chinese readers 62, 70, 141
target text 134; *see also* source text; translated text
teacher 77, 81, 84, 87–88, 92–94; *see also* trainer
teaching 4, 34, 41, 47, 77, 143; *see also* learning
terminological correspondence 5, 75
Theft Ordinance (Cap. 210) 51–52
theory 51; functional 51; legal 94
theory and practice 74, 104–105
theory and techniques 105
Tianjing Treaty 3
Tort Law of the PRC (*Qinquan Zeren Fa*《侵權責任法》)/Tort Law/Tort Liability Law 74–75, 77, 87, 101, 119, 121, 124, 136
Tourism Law of the PRC (*Zhonghua Renmin Gongheguo Lüyou Fa*《中華人民共和國旅遊法》) 82–83
Trade Descriptions Ordinance (Cap. 362) 82
Trademark Law of the PRC (*Zhonghua Renmin Gongheguo Shangbiao Fa*《中華人民共和國商標法》)/Trademark Law 8, 9, 54, 62
trainer 87, 94; *see also* teacher
translated language 23, 139; *see also* source language; target language
translated term 4, 33, 61, 119–120, 125, 137, 141; *see also* source term
translated text 18, 29, 117; *see also* source text; target text
translationese 11, 29, 112, 132
translation industry 94
translation issues 7, 14, 104
translation method 12, 25, 53, 70–71, 135, 138
translation methodology 113
translation problems 87, 94

translation standard 105
translation student 74, 76, 79, 87, 89, 104
translation studies 1, 14, 87, 93–94
translation techniques 41, 113, 116–118, 124, 141
translation theories 45, 108
translation tool 99–100, 133
translation training/translator training 16, 79, 96, 101, 117, 140
Treaty of Shimonoseki 9

University of Hong Kong, The 93, 139

vernacular Chinese 10, 114
vernacular style 24
vocabulary 10, 24

Washington Treaty on Intellectual Property in Respect of Integrated Circuits/Washington Treaty 65–67
wenyan 23–24; *see also baihua*
Westernisation 2, 23
Western languages 27–28, 135
Western law 1, 5, 8–9, 17, 75, 78, 118
Western world 53
Wheaton, Henry 1
WIPO Copyright Treaty 9
World Health Organization 9
World Intellectual Property Organization (WIPO) 9, 57
World Trade Organization (WTO) 5, 9, 60, 64
written language 23, 88, 114, 134, 136; *see also* spoken language

Xianggang Fali Zhongyi Cankao (*Chinese Translation of Hong Kong Legislation*《香港法例中譯參考》) 106
Xianggang Jianming Yinghan Shuangjie Falü Cidian (*The Concise Hong Kong English-Chinese Legal Dictionary*《香港簡明英漢雙解法律詞典》) 106
Xianggang Shuangyu Fazhi: Yuyan yu Fanyi (*Bilingual Legal System in Hong Kong: Language and Translation*《香港雙語法制：語言與翻譯》) 105
Xianggang Yinghan Shuangjie Falü Cidian (*Hong Kong English-Chinese Legal Dictionary*《香港英漢雙解法律詞典》) 106
Xiuding Falü Guan (修訂法律舘) (Law Revision Agency) 1, 118

Yan, Fu 1
Yaşar University 100
Yinghan Falü Cihui (*English-Chinese Glossary of Legal Terms* 《英漢法律詞彙》) 33, 105
Yinghan Falü Da Cidian (*English-Chinese Dictionary of Law* 《英漢法律大詞典》) 105

Yinghan Minshangshi Falü Cihui (*English-Chinese Glossary of Civil and Commercial Laws*《英漢民商事法律詞彙》) 106

zero anaphora 109–110
Zhou, Zuoren 23

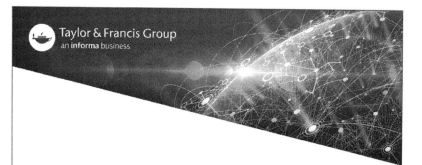

Taylor & Francis eBooks

www.taylorfrancis.com

A single destination for eBooks from Taylor & Francis with increased functionality and an improved user experience to meet the needs of our customers.

90,000+ eBooks of award-winning academic content in Humanities, Social Science, Science, Technology, Engineering, and Medical written by a global network of editors and authors.

TAYLOR & FRANCIS EBOOKS OFFERS:

- A streamlined experience for our library customers
- A single point of discovery for all of our eBook content
- Improved search and discovery of content at both book and chapter level

REQUEST A FREE TRIAL
support@taylorfrancis.com